T0265609

BEFORE THE GILDED AGE

BEFORE THE GILDED AGE

W. W. CORCORAN AND THE RISE OF AMERICAN CAPITAL AND CULTURE

MARK L. GOLDSTEIN

GEORGETOWN UNIVERSITY PRESS | *Washington, DC*

The publisher is not responsible for third-party websites or their
content. URL links were active at time of publication.

Library of Congress Cataloging-in-Publication Data

Names: Goldstein, Mark L., author.
Title: Before the gilded age : W. W. Corcoran and the rise of
american capital and culture / Mark L. Goldstein.
Description: Washington, DC : Georgetown University Press, 2023. |
Includes bibliographical references and index.
Identifiers: LCCN 2022037042 (print) | LCCN 2022037043 (ebook) |
ISBN 9781647123611 (hardcover) | ISBN 9781647123628 (ebook)
Subjects: LCSH: Corcoran, W. W. (William Wilson), 1798-1888. |
Bankers—United States—Biography. | Capitalists and financiers—
United States—Biography. | Philanthropists—United States—
Biography. | Finance—United States—History—19th century. |
LCGFT: Biographies.
Classification: LCC HG2463.C65 G65 2023 (print) | LCC HG2463.C65
(ebook) | DDC 332.092 [B]—dc23/eng/20220923
LC record available at https://lccn.loc.gov/2022037042
LC ebook record available at https://lccn.loc.gov/2022037043

♾ This paper meets the requirements of ANSI/NISO Z39.48-1992
(Permanence of Paper).

24 23   9 8 7 6 5 4 3 2 First printing

Printed in the United States of America

Cover design by Faceout Studio, Spencer Fuller

Interior design by Classic City Composition

For Michael and Zachary

CONTENTS

ACKNOWLEDGMENTS

I have accrued many debts in researching and writing this book that can hardly be repaid. To everyone who supported this project, I gratefully offer a sincere thank you for your encouragement and guidance. Nevertheless, I must mention several people whose assistance was instrumental in the development of my manuscript and without whom my efforts may never have succeeded.

First and foremost is David B. Sicilia, an associate professor of history at the University of Maryland at College Park. David was my PhD faculty adviser, and he politely, but persistently, encouraged me to publish William Wilson Corcoran's biography. David also introduced me to Hilary Claggett, a senior editor at Georgetown University Press, who has enthusiastically supported the Corcoran project from the beginning. Archivists, curators, and experts from a variety of institutions were incredibly helpful in finding resources and conveying their context, a particular art form practiced when libraries were generally closed during the Covid pandemic. Specialists from the Library of Congress, the George Washington University, the former Corcoran Gallery of Art, the Smithsonian Institution, and the National Gallery of Art, among other institutions, were generous in giving of their time and expertise over the years of my research. I am especially grateful for the professional support and personal enthusiasm expressed by Marisa Bourgoin, formerly the archivist of the Corcoran Gallery of Art and now the chief of reference services at the Archives of American Art, Smithsonian Institution; and Sarah Cash, the former curator at the Corcoran Gallery of Art and now an associate curator at the National Gallery of Art.

Friends and family have gently prodded me toward publication, asking when the project would be finished. My mother, Carole Goldstein, was particularly concerned that continued delay on my part would prevent her from kvelling about the book while she still had time! Martin Murray, Jerry Zremski, John McClenahen, and Pieter Roos probably got tired of hearing about Corcoran and antebellum America. Truly, any delay in completing the manuscript can be blamed on an exuberant black Pomsky named Leader.

Most important, I thank Michael Lacey and Zachary Lacey for allowing me the freedom and time away from our family life to complete this book. Their love and support—and patience—were beyond measure. To the extent the book is not boring, I thank Zachary for warning me against the danger.

Finally, I thank William Wilson Corcoran for allowing me to live in four centuries.

BEFORE THE GILDED AGE

INTRODUCTION

On a warm, sunny day in early October 1862, an elegant, portly man settled into a first-class cabin on the RMS *Scotia* in New York harbor. The ship, bound for Liverpool, England, and constructed by the Cunard Line, was just five months past its maiden voyage and was the last oceangoing paddle steamer ever built. New propeller technology was emerging quickly, but the *Scotia* would still beat most transatlantic sailing records for the next decade. This Atlantic voyage was no pleasure cruise for the passenger William Wilson Corcoran, who was transporting himself and much of his wealth—reputedly $34 million in gold stashed in the ship's hold—out of the United States and harm's way. At sixty-three years old, Corcoran had ample reason to leave America: It was the middle of the Civil War, and newspaper reports had associated his name with treasonous plots. Additionally, Corcoran's only child, a daughter named Louise, was married to a Confederate diplomat; the couple and their young children lived in France.

Corcoran was one of the wealthiest and most successful men in mid-nineteenth-century America. Like the growing country itself, Corcoran was a man of possibilities and contradictions: He started life in Georgetown with the advantages born of White Southern privilege, thanks to his ambitious and well-connected father, and was raised in a world of slavery that touched his family and community. Corcoran once enslaved several people himself, including a woman named Mary and her children. As the struggle over abolition intensified, he freed Mary and her children seventeen years before emancipation in the District of Columbia required it.

Corcoran freed several other slaves and bought the freedom of a woman captured by bounty hunters.

There were other conflicts in his character, too. As a bachelor approaching forty years old, he had scandalously eloped with a beautiful sixteen-year-old girl of significant pedigree—only to see her die of tuberculosis at twenty-one. He lived across the street from the White House in Washington, DC, for nearly fifty years and was a confidant of nearly all sixteen presidents from Andrew Jackson to Grover Cleveland regardless of region or political party. Nevertheless, Corcoran never hid his Southern lineage or leanings; he was clearly comfortable around slaveholders, associated with politicians who espoused secession, and interacted daily without obvious objection in a society that permitted subjugation. However, he also counted Northerners among his close friends and associates, including abolitionists and politicians who sought the eradication of White supremacy. Like many people, both North and South, Corcoran hoped the country could find a solution to the "irrepressible conflict" and avoid a bloody war. Then there was his generosity: His elite pedigree and accumulation of wealth and finery notwithstanding, Corcoran gave away most of his money. Whether privately supporting people in need or publicly contributing to the arts, education, and the refinement of the capital city itself, Corcoran's munificence made a difference in the world around him years before Gilded Age industrialists embraced the philanthropic impulse.

Corcoran has been largely forgotten in the sweep of history. Students of finance may recall his contributions to early banking and the nascent securities business. People familiar with the history of Washington, DC, may recognize his indelible mark on the capital's unique urban landscape. If he is remembered by the general public, it is likely for his association with the Corcoran Gallery of Art, the first art museum in America built for that singular purpose, an iconic cultural repository that lasted as an independent institution for nearly 150 years.[1] His obscurity is a striking historical omission. Corcoran is absent from most studies of mid-nineteenth-century America despite his significance to the country's commerce and culture, as well as its capital city. Corcoran has become so forgotten by time that almost no one has chronicled his role in American life. Historical research on Corcoran comprises a few articles on art and a monograph on some financial transactions published in the early 1970s. An admirer's antiquarian book of praise and a partial collection of his letters—

including Corcoran's own curated selection—make up the remainder. His papers in the Library of Congress have been largely undisturbed since they were donated a century ago.

Yet, Corcoran warrants careful attention. His reputation as a power-broker and early rainmaker in banking, lobbying, and politics, and his admirable ability to transcend time, place, and faction make him an intriguing figure. So, too, does the perseverance through a long lifetime with which he influenced the economic, cultural, and urban landscapes around him. *Before the Gilded Age: W. W. Corcoran and the Rise of American Capital and Culture* explores the fascinating and multifaceted life of one of the nation's earliest and most successful political insiders, financiers, art collectors, philanthropists, and shapers of the emerging cultural elite. Corcoran helped establish and normalize many important components of modern American society we take for granted today. Indeed, he did it so adroitly that his character at times seems almost chameleon in nature; Corcoran maneuvered in the early Southern slave society as smoothly as he did in the Northern Gilded Age fifty years later. This book traces those developments and attempts to establish them in the historical context of an evolving nation on the edge of the modern age. It simultaneously reveals the complexities of success and failure entwined in the American experience, the privilege and wealth of one's man life against the backdrop of contemporary hardship and oppression, and the influence of race, values, and patriotism contesting and coexisting in an emergent national capital.

A Unique Context

A variety of factors, including strong family connections and financial wherewithal, helped make Corcoran successful in mid-nineteenth-century America, but certain questions remain: Why did some individuals, such as Corcoran, have outsize influence on the world around them? Did the erosion of paternalism and the rise of market capitalism during the antebellum period create a temporary space that allowed for more equality and mobility in a previously rigid, hierarchical society? Was America suddenly less burdened by the old strictures of the eighteenth century while yet unencumbered by the constraints looming at the end of the nineteenth century? Did the advantages Corcoran gained by virtue of his race, gender, and class merely reinforce the hegemony he reflected, or did they help contribute to something larger or more equitable?

Before the Gilded Age—a biographical inquiry into one man's relatively unexplored, complex, and, yes, privileged life—can help reveal the contours of mid-nineteenth-century America, fostering a better understanding of the capital city, the antebellum era, the changing nature of capitalism, and their collective contribution to the nation's development. Given the scope of its subject, this book does not illuminate the social structure much beyond the world of White privileged men; to the extent criticism is due for omissions of nineteenth-century marginalized groups, the book does not pretend to be more than the story of one man's complicated place in American life and how some individuals through personal agency can influence events and affect societal change—or choose to avoid them. In some ways, Corcoran was a man of his time, feeling his way like many others on the path to slavery's demise. He was no firebrand fighting injustice against women or African Americans like, say, William Lloyd Garrison. Yet, as the story unfolds, in many ways Corcoran was a visionary—not just in business, the arts, and urban development. He also supported marginalized and poor people across a spectrum of class, race, and gender.

Corcoran resided at the center of a web of famous, interconnecting people throughout most of the nineteenth century, highlighting the potency of networks, commercial risk-taking, and cultural entrepreneurship that were relatively new phenomena in the nation's progress toward the modern era. Here, the past first encountered its inevitable demise: an erosion of aristocracy and deference, a declension of obedience and control, and a weakening exclusivity of banking families, merchants, and wealthy landowners controlling the levers of society, commerce, and government. Corcoran himself is a perfect example of this transition: Raised on a foundation of tight kinship bonds and connections to merchants and bankers, he leveraged expanding opportunity and a more mobile society to create broader, more complex associations that were advantageous to his goals and interests. The nation's economy was growing at a faster rate than the population, offering myriad opportunities to immigrants, investors, and entrepreneurs—even in rare cases to women and minorities agile enough to slip through the chaos of change. As fast as the economy grew in the antebellum period, it expanded exponentially after the Civil War. As a result, few individuals could expect to exert as much influence over its direction thereafter.[2] America transitioned seemingly overnight from a country too small and without enough labor to a burgeoning empire unable to contain itself.

Corcoran could only guess at the world to follow, with its myriad legal constrictions and other obstacles to economic expansion and individual autonomy that increasingly limited even the boldest entrepreneurs. From the Gilded Age forward, few individuals on their own, simply from their force of personality and power, could hope to achieve dominance and carve out multiple unique spaces for personal and public expression in the way that Corcoran did. By then, a world of specialization and bureaucratization—accountants, lawyers, and middle managers—had supplanted a more fluid commercial and communal environment, where the influence and sway of a "tipping point" allowed the footsteps of some commanding individuals to fall on largely untrodden ground.[3] Many of Corcoran's achievements likely occurred because he leveraged his interests and ambitions when, to use an old phrase, the world was younger and when growth and expansion permeated multiple sectors of society. One historian called this period the opening of American society, a significant and persistent expansion of geographic, political, economic, and social opportunity. Here, Americans' emerging possibilities generated a "revolution of choices" that promised self-fulfillment in an expanding society.[4] Men such as Corcoran, who found themselves in the right time and place, and who were the inheritors of White privilege, benefited from this rapid change and reordering of society. Such dynamism across multiple dimensions would become less possible by the end of the nineteenth century. The window to a limitless American horizon began to close.

Catalyst's Role

Corcoran was a catalyst for significant advances in American life. Even a cursory review of his story reveals his uncommon influence on the world around him.

- Corcoran played a dominant role in mid-nineteenth-century finance and banking. He helped modernize the financial securities industry, created an independent banking enterprise that lasted for 168 years, and remade the government debt market—activities for which contemporaries both praised and criticized him.

- Corcoran was an early supporter of the Hudson River School—a movement that produced a new genre of American landscape painting—and established the nation's first dedicated art gallery in Washington before similar galleries opened in New York and Chicago.

- Corcoran was committed to improving the nation's capital. With personal funds and political influence, Corcoran championed roads and aqueducts, parks and sewers, monuments, schools, churches, and orphanages. His efforts to landscape the White House and Capitol grounds, as well as the National Mall, predate such plans for New York's Central Park, typically considered the oldest urban park in a major American city.

- Corcoran was an inveterate naturalist. He created several of the nation's earliest woodland cemeteries in Washington, DC. He also helped establish the American Agricultural Society, ran a model farm, and was the president of the American Horticultural Society. He imported dozens of rare, often unknown botanicals and planted them on public lands as well as his own properties.

- Corcoran vitalized both national reconciliation and Southern recovery in the aftermath of the Civil War. He fostered a patriotic, nationalist narrative dedicated to the Union and its mythic past: supporting efforts to restore Mount Vernon, building a tomb for Thomas Jefferson, creating a portrait gallery of famous patriots (all White men), and leading efforts to complete the Washington Monument. At the same time, Corcoran worked to rebuild Southern institutions and provide—mainly but not always for White people—a measure of dignity to those impacted by the Confederacy's destruction. He helped to rebuild schools, churches, colleges, orphanages, health facilities, and plantations, and started from scratch homes for indigent women and ailing Confederate veterans.

- Corcoran skillfully constructed networks of association that combined the personal and professional; they were a key to his success and, arguably, a web of connection ahead of its time. These ties were predominantly, but not exclusively, focused on wealthy White men; Corcoran worked with whomever could help achieve his aims. He leveraged unparalleled access to presidents, judges, legislators, ministers, financiers, artists, merchants, industrialists, social workers, advocates, diplomats, and others in Washington, DC; in the nation; and in Europe. His connections to money and power, on the one hand, and to art and cultural leadership, on the other, created sophisticated and long-standing networks that Corcoran used to his advantage in politics, philanthropy, commerce, and culture. Indeed, Corcoran was frequently loyal to a fault: His connection to secessionists, Southern politicians, and leaders of the Confederacy earned Corcoran enduring enmity among some disapproving Northerners even as he leveraged ties with Radical Republicans.

- Corcoran was an important philanthropist a generation before Andrew Carnegie, John D. Rockefeller, and others spent unprecedented sums designed to build a certain public image and deflect from the rapaciousness of industrial capitalism. Corcoran gave away most of his fortune to institutions and to needy individuals—often to complete strangers. He gave generously to universities, churches, cemeteries, orphanages, and homes for the aged and poor women.[5] He was an early practitioner of delivering charity beyond one's immediate local community, targeting people, places, and causes that needed it most.

In sum, Corcoran was a rarity. He accrued an elite status with both the prewar North and South simultaneously yet retained his stature long after antebellum America vanished. His was, in its own way, a remarkable journey, as few people among the prewar Southern gentry—slaveholders and Jacksonian Democrats—transformed themselves from a suspected Confederate traitor to a confidant of Republican presidents. Corcoran lived a long and influential life that established him as a leader, at times even an originator, in multiple endeavors. Moreover, through his networks, Corcoran facilitated connections among a wealthy elite, self-conscious of its role and comfortable with its status and ability to achieve a variety of ends: public and private, political and cultural, financial and philanthropic. This group's legacy—often through Corcoran's lead—was an important foundation of the modern American capital.

1
BEGINNINGS

WILLIAM WILSON CORCORAN WAS BORN ON DECEMBER 27, 1798, THE son of an Irish immigrant shopkeeper. His father, Thomas Corcoran, came to America about fifteen years earlier and through family support and good fortune quickly achieved respectability and social influence in his adopted land. Considered a reliable and ethical merchant, Corcoran soon settled in Georgetown, a small town struggling to be a commercial port adjacent to the forthcoming capital. First Lady Abigail Adams called Georgetown "a dirty little hole," but the town seemed destined for greater things. With more than one-third of the population being owned and free Blacks by 1800, Georgetown's existence was firmly rooted in a slave society; the sale and subjugation of Black people was commonplace. Corcoran's father grew prosperous as the town flourished, and he gained recognition and privilege through appointed and elected positions. A wife, a home, and a family—and over time the acquisition of enslaved people—followed.

Thomas Corcoran arrived in the United States in his early thirties and got a leg up by working for his relations, including in the Baltimore shipping business of his aunt's husband, William Wilson. Wilson arrived in the United States in 1769 and built a successful shipping enterprise; he owned several ships that plied the Atlantic. Thomas made at least three voyages as a supercargo for his uncle, but Thomas was apparently not happy in Baltimore—and perhaps not as a sailor, either. In 1788 he decided to seek better fortunes in Richmond, Virginia. On his journey south, Thomas stopped in Georgetown, a community then only thirty years old nestled on the Potomac River, where he found several big ships in the harbor. Thomas never made it to Richmond and decided to settle in Georgetown instead.

In addition to trading dry goods on behalf of his uncle, Thomas opened a leather tannery and shoe shop on the first floor of a rented home on Congress Street, later renamed M Street, Northwest.[1] William Corcoran was proud of his father's bootstrap success and years later kept the cobbler's sign from the shop among the possessions in his library.[2]

As his success as a merchant grew, Thomas's social status rose along with his affluence. Thomas was appointed a state militia officer. President Thomas Jefferson appointed him as one of Georgetown's magistrates and a member of the levy court, a post Thomas still held when he was named one of the "midnight judges" in *Marbury v. Madison*. Among the most famous court cases in American history, the Supreme Court ruling established the constitutional precedent of federal judicial review. Thomas became a member of the Georgetown City Council, was the mayor of the city for three brief periods, and was appointed by President James Madison as its postmaster in 1815. Thomas held that post, as well as the levy court position, for the remainder of his life. He and his wife, Hannah, whom he had met in Baltimore, had twelve children, six of whom survived to maturity: James (1789), Eliza (1791), Thomas Jr. (1794), Sarah (1797), William Wilson (1798), and Martha Ellen (1807).[3]

Thomas was also involved in community improvement and philanthropic enterprises, activities to which Corcoran would also devote himself. Thomas was a founder and trustee of Columbian College, the predecessor of George Washington University in Washington, DC. In part because of his father and his connection to successive leaders of the college, Corcoran would eventually donate significant time and money to the institution. Thomas was also a founder of and benefactor of several Episcopal churches. In recognition of his success and status in the community, Thomas in 1791 led a delegation of about fifty citizens who rode out to Bladensburg, Maryland, to welcome George Washington and his escort party when the first president of the United States arrived in search of suitable land for the new capital. That same year, Thomas built a house at 3119 M Street, in the heart of commercial Georgetown, and it was here that Corcoran was born.[4] Given Thomas's status in the community, his home was frequented by the local elite as well as other notable people, including the Marquis de Lafayette. Pierre Charles L'Enfant, the visionary planner of the American capital, was also a regular visitor to the Georgetown home.[5]

Corcoran's Youth

Corcoran's early years were typical for the period. He played in the still-wooded groves on Georgetown's hills and made friends easily in the small community of shopkeepers and merchants. His later reflections, infrequently chronicled, evidenced fond memories of his boyhood. Thomas insisted on an education for his son. Corcoran was sent to the "widow Nicholson's" school at the age of five, and at seven years old he went to Thomas Kirk's academy, both well-respected educational venues in Georgetown. At twelve, he studied languages with Rev. William Allen and later spent time as a day student at Georgetown University but never graduated. As he grew older, Corcoran also studied with Rev. Addison Belt, although there is no record he was interested in the ministry.

This education appears to have been sufficient for the future businessman because, against his father's wishes, at age seventeen he gave up school and went to work at the nearby dry goods business owned by his older brothers, James and Thomas. The enterprise prospered, and the brothers were soon able to open a second Georgetown store. They installed Corcoran, then nineteen, as the new store's proprietor. Corcoran eponymously named the company W. W. Corcoran and Co. and built a steady new business. As the success of the Corcoran brothers grew, they expanded their holdings, starting up a wholesale auction house and commission business in a nearby building they purchased.[6] Auctions were, of course, a principal means of selling enslaved people, and several auction houses participated in Georgetown's slave market. As an auctioneer himself, Corcoran would certainly have been familiar with such activities, although no evidence has emerged that he personally held slave auctions. Probably through his father's connections, Corcoran in his early years is also credited with making a handsome sum from government contracts for US Army shoes during the First Seminole War.[7] Clothing such as shoes and pants made for the military were notorious for their often shoddy manufacture, although no complaints about Corcoran's contracts have come to light. All in all, the enterprising Corcoran brothers did well with their various ventures.

Success then turned to disaster when the economy fell apart. The Panic of 1819, the first significant financial crisis of the new nation, ensnared the Corcorans. Approximately one-third of the merchants in Georgetown and Baltimore failed during this time, and in February 1823, the Corcoran brothers went bankrupt.[8] They paid off their debts at fifty cents on the dollar, a respectable amount under the circumstances. In a remarkable expression of personal integrity, twenty-five years later as a wealthy banker, Corcoran sought out and in some cases hired detectives to locate his creditors from the bankruptcy to pay the remaining 50 percent indebtedness. Corcoran paid all the remaining debts plus interest, then worth some $46,000.[9]

Early Business Failure

Bankruptcy and business failure in nineteenth-century America were just as common as now. The difference is that failure in the early market economy was often misunderstood as a sign of bad character, and those willing to assume large risks were often seen as immoral and reckless, people to be avoided in commercial ventures. Just as today, firms big and small collapsed from all manner of financial and management problems. In the mid-nineteenth century, tight credit, specie shortages, and the ambiguous value of multiple circulating bank notes contributed to the period's economic uncertainty. The cost of risk was high: Upward of 95 percent of all new ventures ended up in bankruptcy.[10] The idea that eventually most business enterprises would go bankrupt was commonplace in the antebellum era. Merchants, more than individuals in other occupations, tended to face greater risk of failure.[11] With fewer options to start with, Blacks and women faced even more daunting risks than men did as barbers, tailors, and hairdressers—the work to which they were often marginalized if they could rise above manual labor at all.[12] Rare were the cases of people such as John Stanly, who owned a barbershop while still enslaved and as a free man by the 1820s owned three cotton and turpentine plantations and 163 slaves.[13] Yet, even Stanly, as one of the richest men in Georgia, faced substantial risks for failure, and the Black planter ultimately lost most of his property when he became overextended during bad economic times.

The evolution of the American mercantile system into a more robust market economy, driven by the Industrial Revolution after the War of 1812, was both a boon and a risk to aspiring entrepreneurs. Henry David

Thoreau, the nation's most famous fugitive from the capitalist ethos, believed that "the mass of men lead lives of quiet desperation" and questioned the premise of business success overall: "Why should we be in such desperate haste to succeed, and in such desperate enterprises? If a man does not keep pace with his companions, perhaps it is because he hears a different drummer."[14] Indeed, those who did not keep pace, who through failure and bankruptcy were unable to succeed in business, often found themselves destitute or beholden to others for wages. Periodicals of the time noted the increasing number of ruined lives, with many men consigned to debtors' prison or suicide.[15] In time, financial failure would be seen mainly as a consequence of economic and environmental factors, not a moral condition.[16] Nevertheless, reputation and honor were intimately tied not only to one's standing in the antebellum community but also to the price and discount at which debt holders accepted others' financial instruments.[17] Moral assessments and other personal indicators, including habits of character, as well as material assets, were included in reports by early credit companies such as the Tappan Brothers and Dun & Co. The ability to engage in commerce and obtain the "right" to incur debt was bound up in moral value as well as market value. "'Character,' opined the influential *Hunt's Merchant's Magazine,* 'to a man of business . . . is as dear as life itself.'"[18] Watching his father, brothers, and associates, Corcoran would likely have absorbed these lessons carefully on his rise to commercial respectability.

Society often blamed people's character for their difficulties even as secular individualism, entrepreneurial opportunity, and the invisible hand of the market increased economic unpredictability in everyday life. Many entrepreneurs used the shifting construct of economic, legal, and moral expectations to avoid creditors and disappear into the shadowy corners of the nation's accelerating transformation. Yet, the concept of character remained important: Like Corcoran, merchants affected by bad financial fortune worked to salvage their reputation and reclaim moral standing by repaying business debt beyond the legal requirements to do so. Enough ruined men felt a moral obligation to make their creditors whole that the term "debtor's banquet" was a common phrase in the antebellum lexicon. It described a lavish dinner held by the bankrupt businessman for his creditors in which he placed a corresponding bank draft beneath each dinner plate.[19]

Debt was the principal problem leading to business failure in this period, but it was no surprise given the illiquidity of the US monetary system. Merchants were forced to extend credit to their customers, yet they also had to rely on banks to efficiently honor discounts on bills presented for sale. With poor liquidity to start with, unpredictable business cycles, credit repudiations, and other financial problems often overwhelmed companies. High bankruptcy rates thus discouraged many businessmen from seeking new opportunities for financial independence.[20] Few entrepreneurs were able to sustain significant losses and expect to achieve success later in life. The persistent high failure rate among sole proprietorships and partnerships—a defining aspect of an individualistic and independent American identity—influenced the rise of corporate enterprises in which risk was shared more broadly.[21] Over time the trend was clearly toward wage work and an exchange of personal freedom for predictable incomes to sustain families.

Kinship ties remained important to Corcoran's career in his early years. After the failure of Corcoran & Co., for several years he devoted himself to managing his aging father's real estate holdings and took up banking work, probably with the help of local bankers and family friends: John Van Ness, John Tayloe, and John Mason. All three bankers owned people. Van Ness, a former congressman, was the president of Metropolitan Bank and later the branch president of the Bank of the United States (BUS).[22] Mason ran a small Georgetown bank where Corcoran briefly learned the trade. In 1823 Corcoran became a clerk of the real estate activities of the Bank of Columbia—his father was a director of the bank—until it failed in 1826 and was absorbed into the BUS.[23] He took over the same portfolio at the BUS until the bank was closed in 1836 as a result of President Andrew Jackson's war with Congress about centralized banking.[24] Life may have been somewhat unsettled for Corcoran in these years: In addition to several job changes, some of the family properties he managed were foreclosed and sold by the government for owed taxes in the early 1830s, shortly after his father passed away.[25]

The role of a clerk in the antebellum period was a new endeavor for young men (women were generally not accepted as business clerks until the later part of the nineteenth century). It offered a stable position in the emerging middle class and a viable alternative to craft apprenticeships or work as laborers.[26] Attaining a clerk's position or even apprenticing in a firm with clerks gave young men opportunities to learn skills for the market economy and the changing nature of commercial work. The new jobs helped them obtain better positions and broaden their horizons.[27] This was especially true in the earliest days of the expanding economy before higher education and clerkships were commonplace. Like Corcoran's experience, a clerkship typically started as an apprenticeship in a kinship network; relatives and family friends helped young men gain new positions with trusted colleagues and businessmen of character.[28] By proving their worth through diligence and honesty, clerks could often advance to partner or gain the expertise to establish their own enterprise. Aspiring clerks learned precise handwriting and patience for repetitive work such as transcription, bookkeeping, and coordinating correspondence.[29] American novelist Herman Melville, who wrote *Moby-Dick, or the Whale*, reported that a clerkship eluded him because of his poor handwriting.[30] By the middle of the nineteenth century, such jobs created more applicants than positions. A valuable steppingstone to better jobs and careers in Corcoran's early years, clerkships soon became commonplace and just another way to earn a living. The power of kinship networks declined as the market economy expanded into a regional and national structure, and as higher education trained young people for office positions and specific disciplines.

In the earliest period of professional clerkships, these new jobs gave the best-positioned men great opportunities. During his early training and clerking in business and banking, Corcoran, with the help of kinship connections, laid the foundation for some of the most important relationships of his life. Here, he met Elisha Riggs and George Peabody.[31] Riggs was a family friend who later became a wealthy financier in New York. Like the Corcorans, Riggs started in the dry goods business; he hired George Peabody as his office clerk after the two men became friends in the militia during the War of 1812. Riggs's firm succeeded quickly and expanded to New York, Baltimore, and Philadelphia. After the partnership dissolved a decade later, Riggs moved to New York and built a fortune in early investment banking. Riggs's contacts in the banking and securities fields and his access to New York capital would be critical to Corcoran's later success. Peabody opened one of the earliest American securities firms overseas, basing himself in London to broker financial instruments between the United States and Europe. These overseas connections were also important to Corcoran's eventual success, although Peabody's reputation for peddling unstable state bonds made some European financiers wary of him.[32]

Banking in the Capital

Initial efforts to build Washington's economy focused on developing inland canal traffic to the agricultural West, but these early attempts were stymied by a lack of capital. The need for commercial investment and for funds to construct the infrastructure of the federal city led to new banks, including the Bank of Columbia and a first BUS branch in Washington in 1801.[33] Three more banks were chartered in the capital before the decade's end. When Congress decided not to renew the charter of the first BUS in 1811, the Department of the Treasury deposited most of its money with the Bank of Columbia and other local banks. This arrangement boosted liquidity in the capital's emerging economy.[34] By 1814 Metropolitan Bank was flourishing, as were the other early banks. These institutions provided the government fresh funds to fight the war with Great Britain and pulled together a $500,000 reconstruction loan to rebuild the capital after the British sacked Washington, DC.[35] This local assistance was among the reasons Congress dismissed suggestions that the relatively indefensible capital on the coast should be moved inland.[36]

The reconstruction of Washington, DC, as well as the postwar improvements to the local economy, brought additional commerce to the city. A decision to locate a branch of the Second Bank of the United States in the capital spurred further growth and credit availability.[37] In this regard, Washington's banks behaved like many others in the antebellum period: With a thriving economy and little supervision, they issued increasing amounts of notes and loans without adequate backing. Easy credit and speculation accelerated until the BUS asserted itself by calling in government balances and tightening credit.[38] Thereafter, local banks were wary of the BUS's efforts to exert central control, and, ultimately, Andrew Jackson vetoed the central bank's renewal. On the upside of this monetary power struggle, the sudden banking vacuum helped Corcoran, among others, leverage new opportunities. As banks competed for government handouts, Corcoran's evident political skills and connections would make him the capital's most powerful banker.

Slavery

Growing up in Georgetown, Corcoran was immersed in the slave society created by the region's Southern elite.[39] Both Virginia and Maryland were slave states, and nearby Baltimore had a large enslaved population.[40] The capital, established in 1800, was surrounded by slave states and became a slave territory itself. The city also attracted a nearly sevenfold increase in free Blacks settling in the area in the decade after the capital's creation.[41] Washington's first slave codes went into effect in 1808 and allowed for the growth of a free Black community.[42] City fathers permitted manumitted people to remain in the city and did not require them to leave the territory, a lenient practice at the time. The city council in 1812 mandated all free Blacks to register with the municipality and carry a certificate of freedom that ostensibly protected them from slave traders indiscriminately pursuing runaways.[43] In reality, the certificate was often ignored by traders for whom the fine print of freedom did not matter. By 1827, with a steady stream of African Americans locating in the capital, the city adopted stricter Black codes, including requirements for routine curfews and the posting of a $500 bond for each free Black family. Black people—owned or free—were also restricted from entering certain parts of the city, including the Capitol and other public buildings except on specific, approved business.[44]

Enslaved people were central to an economy that relied on human bondage for nearly 200 years at that point. Slave markets proliferated throughout the area, and slave traders were everywhere.[45] For many years, owned men, women, and children were sold on what is now O Street and elsewhere in Georgetown, and even on the steps of the Capitol in the new federal city. Slave pens housing people waiting to be sold lined the edge of the future National Mall. The slave markets and the brutal conditions of slavery itself were an eyesore to many residents and visitors. Indeed, the thriving slave trade was a potent symbol of the institution's cruelty, and the affront of slavery in the capital energized abolitionists and helped outlaw Washington's slave trade as part of the Compromise of 1850. In reality, the slave trade remained viable in the capital since a vigorous market for slaves still existed in nearby Alexandria, Virginia. Overall, the number of enslaved people in the capital decreased by about half between 1800 and 1860 as the number of free Blacks steadily increased during the same period, eventually outnumbering enslaved people by a margin of three to one.[46] A strong African American community, supported by schools and churches, took root in the capital. This influx formed the nucleus of a stable Black community that would strengthen and grow in the late nineteenth and twentieth centuries.[47]

Enslaved people were certainly familiar to Corcoran; he grew up with them. Enslaved people worked in his house and throughout his community. Written evidence of Corcoran's views on slavery is scarce, but from his actions and associations over his lifetime, we can infer how his feelings toward the institution may have changed. Many wealthy and middle-class people in Georgetown and the capital city enslaved people, including his father and his brothers, Thomas and James.[48] A family slave was among the seventy-seven people in 1848 who attempted to escape bondage by commandeering the schooner *Pearl* and sailing down the Potomac River.[49] Many of Corcoran's friends owned people—and not just house slaves. One of his political allies and a close neighbor, Benjamin Ogle Tayloe (a son of banker and family friend John Tayloe III), owned several cotton plantations along with the people forced to work the fields. Important Southern members of Corcoran's network, such as Senators Jefferson Davis and John C. Breckenridge, enslaved people on large plantations below the Mason-Dixon Line. Corcoran for years maintained political, business, and social connections with many enslavers.

While the evidence viewed from two centuries distant is not clear-cut, Corcoran may have been involved in the slave trade. The papers of Corcoran's friend and business associate George Peabody contain an opaque reference to Corcoran as a slave trader when he was a young man: Peabody indicated Corcoran had ties to the "business of human chattel," but he does not elaborate on the statement.[50] If true, it might have been when Corcoran was a wholesale auctioneer at around twenty years old before the Corcoran brothers went bankrupt. There are other indicators also: Research recently revealed a receipt tied to Corcoran for an 1832 advertisement in the *Columbian Gazette* offering a private sale of slaves. The receipt for the transaction was reportedly found in the J. P. Morgan Library archives, and, if accurate, Corcoran may have placed the ad as a favor to Peabody.[51] Junius Morgan, J. P. Morgan's father, became a partner in the Peabody firm, and that could explain how such a receipt might have appeared in the Morgan papers. There are also sketchy references that Corcoran was associated with a plantation named Chalmette, in Arkansas, that was operated by his nephew James Corcoran; that plantation had enslaved people.[52] Peabody and Riggs may have been involved in the nefarious slave trade themselves; their business records contain a receipt listing slaves transported on a ship called the *Aurora*.[53]

Various legal records indicate Corcoran owned at least one person. According to census records, Corcoran owned a male slave in 1840. He also manumitted a woman named Mary and her young children in 1845, some seventeen years prior to emancipation in the capital.[54] It is unclear what happened to the enslaved man or for how long Corcoran owned any of them. There is no record of manumission for a male owned by Corcoran, and the census record does not indicate the presence of a female slave in the household. Perhaps there was a mistake in gender recorded on the 1840 tally sheet—and that slave was Mary—or perhaps she was not listed for some reason. Corcoran also provided Mary a stipend of $200 in his will, and there is no record of a stipend for any other person he owned.[55] There is no record that Corcoran owned other people, although he sold several slaves (rather than manumitting them) belonging to his father after Thomas died. Depending on the terms of the estate (or his father's verbal instructions), Corcoran may not have had the leeway to simply set free his father's people. Instead, he apparently struck a deal with the purchaser that they would not be sent to the South, where labor and living conditions were typically harsher than circumstances in the capital city.[56]

Since Corcoran left no documents clearly outlining his views on slavery, it is difficult to draw conclusions without inferences, and the data itself is not complete. Thus, we cannot be sure whether Corcoran was comfortable or uncomfortable owning a person or living in a community that enslaved people—even though he did both. The same must also be concluded about the people he sold rather than manumit from his father's estate.

Likewise, we know that Corcoran freed Mary, as well as two other women associated with her, but we have no information about his views on the matter or the circumstances that led to their freedom. In 1850 Corcoran purchased the freedom of a woman who had escaped bondage in New Orleans. Her name is not listed in the newspaper article about the episode, but she was the wife of William Williams, the free coachman for US presidents James K. Polk, Zachary Taylor, and Millard Fillmore, all of whom were friends of Corcoran's.[57] Slave traders had captured her and much of her family in Washington, DC, and hustled her to Baltimore, where they planned to return her to New Orleans. Corcoran put up the funds to free her. Here, too, we do not know if Corcoran got involved in her rescue because he believed it was the right thing to do or if he was simply helping powerful friends.

Nineteenth-Century Georgetown

Despite its early promise, Georgetown was not destined to remain an independent town. The small port was established in the 1750s by Scots involved in the region's growing tobacco trade and was incorporated in 1789 by the state of Maryland. Shortly thereafter, Georgetown became a part of the newly created District of Columbia, although for many years it remained a separate community governed under the provisions of its original charter. Most of the leading merchants and influential citizens who contributed to the town's growing prosperity during this period came from the southern tidewater area. The presence of so many natives from Maryland's plantation region gave Georgetown a distinctive Southern atmosphere—complete with the trappings of paternalism and slavery—and characterized its culture until the Civil War.[58]

After the American Revolution, Georgetown became a major exporting center for tobacco raised in nearby Maryland and Virginia. The town grew as it leveraged the burgeoning market for European tobacco products. Local merchants prospered with the "fragrant weed," and new firms were established as profits increased with little direct competition from British factors. In 1791 local merchant Thomas Johnson wrote to George Washington that Georgetown was "the best market for tobacco in the state, and perhaps in America."[59] Between its commercial attraction and proximity to the new capital, Georgetown soon replaced Annapolis as the region's mercantile and social center. Over time, the new capital would eclipse Georgetown, but the city retained its robust character through the early nineteenth century. The vigorous port economy and adjacent farming community provided steady employment for Whites and Blacks alike, although opportunities were more constrained for minorities. Still, a strong Black community grew on the support of the town's success, as evidenced by the creation of African American churches and schools as early as 1816.

While many of the early White Georgetown families with Maryland backgrounds owed their prosperity to tobacco, some residents, such as the Corcorans, succeeded in commerce by selling other products, including groceries and dry goods.[60] The Corcorans were no doubt familiar with other successful merchants in the small town, including the dry goods merchant Joseph Fearson and hardware purveyor Edward Linthicum. Linthicum was an early philanthropist, supporting the education of "free white boys" in Georgetown.[61] Fearson and another dry goods merchant, P. T. Berry, would amass considerable wealth during their lifetime, much of it like Corcoran did, by renting commercial and residential property to Irish immigrants and free Blacks.[62]

During the early years of the nineteenth century, groceries arrived on the Potomac by sailing packet from New York and Philadelphia, and were sold to retailers in Georgetown, the capital, and nearby rural areas. After 1835, when the Baltimore & Ohio Railroad connections between the capital and Baltimore were completed, the port's business suffered significant setbacks. Retailers began buying directly from wholesale firms in Baltimore and New York.[63] The economic fallout from the railroad was compounded by navigation problems when Georgetown's port and the Potomac River began to silt up. As early as 1807, civic leaders told Congress that the problem was getting worse. Between 1800 and 1830, Georgetown spent about $180,000 of its own funds to upgrade navigation, but as the improvements had little impact on the river, commerce continued to decline.[64] In a partial remedy to the problem, entrepreneurs started the Chesapeake and Ohio (C&O) Canal in 1828, but it, too, was a disappointment to city fathers and a financial drain for investors. The C&O Canal was not completed until 1850, by which time railroads had emerged as strong economic competitors. Georgetown was absorbed into the faster-growing federal city, and its charter as a separate town was repealed in 1871.[65]

Small World

In the early nineteenth century, Corcoran lived in a small world. In the communal society of Georgetown, he stayed close to home. In a still largely patriarchic community, Corcoran followed in his family's tight-knit commercial footsteps. While little is known about Corcoran's early years in Georgetown—no letters and only a few records exist from this period— the changing nature of male identity contoured his youth. As the market economy became more predominant in everyday life, expectations for White, middle-class young men shifted from an emphasis on cultivating a consensual, community-oriented persona to encouraging a more independent and secular personality.[66]

The changes could be confusing, especially since new behaviors were expected to be balanced by social expectations of continued adherence to republican rectitude. This was particularly true among the upper class, which still produced offspring tutored in the communal republican virtues of public service and selflessness.[67] Corcoran's father, Thomas, clearly exemplified this enlightened spirit in the public offices he held and the support he gave to various institutions. Corcoran emulated his father's example. Even in young adulthood, while still a man of modest means, Corcoran contributed funds to churches and the arts. His views later in life, as a much wealthier man, expressed his commitment to an increasingly vanishing republicanism: "Blessed by kind providence with larger possessions than commonly fall to the lot of man, I have regarded them as a sacred trust for knowledge, truth, and charity. My reward has been an approving conscience and the gratifying appreciation of many good and great men."[68] Corcoran was honest in admitting that others' approval motivated his behavior—one of the few times his transparency clearly revealed itself.

Corcoran's social standing was not impaired by the Corcoran brothers' commercial failing. His family's overall success and commitment to the community ensured the young man's good credentials for his rise in the banking world. He also rose quickly in the local militia, a signifier for male achievement and elite distinction. President James Monroe appointed Corcoran a first lieutenant of volunteers in 1824, and President John Quincy Adams made Corcoran a captain of artillery the following year. In 1830 President Andrew Jackson appointed Corcoran a lieutenant colonel and then a full colonel in 1832.[69] These posts were prestigious, and Corcoran was no doubt pleased with both the recognition and the resplendent uniform that accompanied the honor: crisp pantaloons, white vest, black hat, and black stock cravat. Corcoran, whom contemporaries described as tall, squarely built, and very handsome, must have cut a dashing figure and was considerably in demand among privileged society women, young and old.[70] Several coy letters written to him in 1831 by Susan Decatur, the widow of the famous naval hero Adm. Stephen Decatur, invited the young Corcoran to accompany her around town—if the young ladies could spare him. "My dear Mr. Corcoran," she entreated in one missive, "if you should find yourself destitute while the belles are at church, I wish you would come listen to my lamentations."[71]

In marrying late, Corcoran remained a favorite eligible bachelor of the Georgetown social circuit for many years—until he encountered Louise Morris. He knew, of course, that community success and business respectability required strong family roots; his letters reflect this sentiment. Yet, Corcoran was nearly forty years old—an advanced age for marriage—when he married Louise. The record remains unclear why Corcoran waited so long to finally settle down, as it was the family parlor in antebellum America where most business relationships with kin and close-knit social alliances were formed.[72] The considerable social standing of his father may have made early marriage less necessary for Corcoran, but since business and marriages were closely allied in this period, his reluctance to marry early is puzzling. Except for his courtship with Louise, there are few clues to other romances the eligible bachelor might have had. A few whispers appeared in the newspapers based on elderly reminiscences but nothing more. If there were other love letters beyond the ones he wrote to Louise, they have long since disappeared.

Courtship with Louise

It is not clear when Corcoran met Louise, but in addition to her beauty, he likely was attracted by the manners and deportment of the young woman with whom he was enamored. Louise Morris possessed a significant pedigree: The daughter of a naval hero and New England socialite, she was accustomed at a young age to the rituals of social bearing and civility that separated race and class.[73] Her letters to Corcoran are full of admonitions and cautions about manners and behavior. By contrast, Corcoran's letters extoll his love for her and his impatience about delays in their courtship. Louise sometimes had to remind the aging bachelor that his behavior required restraint. These remonstrations are ironic given the serious and dignified character Corcoran later unfailingly displayed as a banker and philanthropist. Despite her teenage years, Louise seemed more aware than Corcoran as to how their significant age differences would be judged by the insular elite in Georgetown and the capital. The letters between Corcoran and Louise reveal tensions involving age, absence due to business, children, and other issues that arose in their courtship and marriage.

The rapid population increase and the proliferation of commercial and political opportunities in the new capital city reinforced the elite's desire for physical distance, social demarcation, class distinction, and rules of decorum. This was especially important as society changed. The social community of genteel Georgetown gave way to the more confusing and chaotic society of the rising capital. From its beginnings, Washington, DC, was seen as a coarse collection of striving politicians, free Blacks, enslaved people, ambitious clerks, and con men. The new elite took several decades to form in the capital and did so partly through the effort and example of leading citizens such as Corcoran and other wealthy, ambitious men and their culturally polished wives.[74] This group was a different elite than what had typically formed in American cities; the seat of national democracy privileged an emerging social class based on power and access rather than exclusively on wealth and pedigree. Politicians de facto were the new elite; family wealth or landed antecedents—while always welcome—suddenly mattered less than raw power and political connections.

Proper social behavior in the new capital was not covered in the old etiquette books, as few people had encountered this highly fluid social structure. While incipient dangers gave rise to new etiquette books with remonstrations against trusting strangers in the perilous cities, the elites initially grappled with little guidance to adopt social mores in periods of rapidly shifting situations.[75] Guidebooks, penny dreadful novels, sensationalized newspapers, and etiquette books persuaded readers that urban strangers—the lower sorts in both race and class—frequently had immoral motives and should be avoided. Adding political ambiguity on top of social shapeshifting made negotiating a city like Washington, DC, even more problematic.[76] Herman Melville's protagonist in *Bartleby, the Scrivener* exemplifies the hazard: A mysterious and unambitious man with a murky background attains authority as a clerk in an ever-changing, unknowable city.[77] The dangerous city in the Melville tale is New York, but the fear he described revealed how many people viewed urban areas in the changing country. The danger of social counterfeits and other disreputable people populated fiction and real life.

An evolving system of complicated manners helped Northerners navigate the contours of an increasingly confusing society. Elaborate rules, less necessary in the more hierarchical and racially demarcated South, helped people negotiate emerging social contradictions "by espousing one set of values while nonverbally communicating another."[78] Admonitions for self-control and social distinction in deportment only increased as the nineteenth century proceeded, owing in part to widening contact with unknown and lower-class individuals in urban settings and rising middle-class expectations. Emotional demonstrations were particularly frowned upon as evidence of an undisciplined temperament in this era. Proper behavior was expected not only of elite peers but also from individuals of different genders, races, ages, and classes.[79]

Corcoran grew up within this rule-bound social structure, making his decision to court Louise and to flout convention somewhat surprising. His relationship does not fit the period's mores. Corcoran's brothers and friends, such as George Riggs, married at relatively young ages, although George Peabody was a lifelong bachelor. While the average age of marriage for men was around twenty-four years old during the early nineteenth century, Corcoran was in his mid-thirties when he began his courtship with Louise, and he left no record of his hesitation to marry earlier. She was still a teenager, and love and affection—rather than kinship arrangements— were just emerging as the foundation of many intimate relationships. Her family's objections to the match may have included doubts of Louise's ability to fully understand the significance and demands of an adult relationship. Moreover, friends and relatives in the close-knit community voiced concerns about the couple's age difference.

Unlike the characters in Melville's *Bartleby*, this couple was well known to each other. Corcoran came from a prosperous and privileged family. Louise was the daughter and granddaughter of naval officers. Her father was Commodore Charles Morris, a naval hero whose exploits during the War of 1812 made him famous throughout the country. He later married Harriet Bowen of Providence, Rhode Island, a scion of that city's old wealth. Morris had a remarkable record in the new American Navy. In pursuit of Barbary pirates at the Battle of Tripoli, Morris played a leading part in the destruction of the frigate *Philadelphia* in Tripoli harbor. A nineteen-year-old midshipman at the time, Morris was the first to stand on the deck of the *Philadelphia* and disable the ship so the pirates could not commandeer it. At the beginning of the War of 1812, he held the rank of lieutenant and was the executive officer of the *Constitution*. Early in the war, the frigate met a fleet of British vessels, and the enemy thought it had an easy kill; however, by a combination of skill and luck, the *Constitution* escaped the squadron, much to Morris's credit. He later rose to the second-highest position in the navy before his retirement.[80]

Marriage

The where and when of how Corcoran and Louise met are lost to the ages, although they probably met at a church or a family gathering in the intimate circles of Georgetown's small community. They were more than acquaintances by the fall of 1833, some two years before their marriage; Corcoran's scrapbook contains a long poem devoted to her that was printed in a local newspaper. Unsigned, the verse, dedicated to her by name, professes:

> Lady, forgive this tribute due to gentleness, love and you.
> And let the youthful minstrel twine around that polished brow of thine,
> this wreath of lovely florets formed but with the purest feelings warmed.
> Of youthful love the rosette dew is sprinkled o'er the flowers.
> The buds though poor they be and few were culled from young love's
>   bowers.[81]

The most controversial element of their courtship was the significant age difference. Louise was perhaps fifteen years old when they met, and Corcoran was probably thirty-five. He was still a bank clerk and manager of his father's real estate investments; his shift into private banking and great wealth were on the horizon. Indeed, Morris was not happy about what he perceived to be Corcoran's modest purse and advancing years—despite the family's Georgetown roots and strong social standing. Morris on several occasions insisted that his daughter break off the courtship with Corcoran and even sent her to Rhode Island for several months to keep her out of the banker's reach. The love letters between Corcoran and Louise reveal that Morris's resistance to their courtship was a sensitive subject. Corcoran was angry with Morris's disapproval and was hurt by the rejection and judgment that he was unsuitable as a match. Louise frequently acceded to her father's wishes to slow down the relationship, even breaking off the relationship entirely at one point.

Nevertheless, the evident affection the pair held for each other triumphed, as Corcoran and Louise, without her parents' blessing, eloped on December 23, 1835. The sudden departure from convention and custom reveals the aging bachelor's acceptance of risk, a character trait he would further develop in his business relationships. The pair went to Baltimore, accompanied by Corcoran's sister-in-law Harriet. An announcement in *The Metropolitan* newspaper indicated that Corcoran and Louise were married by the Reverend Dr. John Henshaw in Baltimore, and a copy of the entry in the church's records confirms the event.[82] Morris objected to the marriage at first, but over time he became reconciled to it, especially after the birth of the couple's first child. There is no hint of disappointment or anger in the letters Morris wrote to Corcoran while he was stationed off the coast of Brazil on the USS *Delaware* during that period. In addition to the birth of his grandchild, Morris's change of heart was probably eased by the fact that Corcoran by then was establishing a successful brokerage and banking firm.

Love Letters

Corcoran's papers in the Library of Congress contain numerous love letters from his relationship with Louise. The letters have never been published before, and they appear intact as a set even though the lovers at times implore each other to destroy the correspondence. The letters highlight their intimate connection and hopes for the future, and they contain many of the hallmarks ascribed to upper-class lovers' letters of the time, such as intimacy and dialogue evoking private, heartfelt conversations.

The nineteenth-century concept of love encouraged self-revelation to explore and test the limits of romance and commitment. Scholars suggest an absence of such sentiment in correspondence betrayed a lack of seriousness and devotion to the relationship.[83] Indeed, Corcoran's letters represent a rare peek into the emotions and reactions of a man whose writings otherwise revealed few feelings or impressions of his mind. In no other communications—neither his letters in banking and business matters nor those related to politics and the arts—did Corcoran write so freely and passionately. His love letters are in sharp contrast to his later, more formal professional letters, which reflect the careful and conservative nature of a man who sought—and attained—recognition in society's top ranks and who was writing with one eye on posterity.

Like today, courtships were rarely linear in their movement through the various components of social association, flirtation and attraction, friendship, increasing intimacy, and, potentially, engagement and marriage. Correspondence between couples was the primary vehicle for developing intimacy and free expression in an age when social association was typically chaperoned. Love letters were often the basis of the relationship itself. This was the case when couples used correspondence to explore their feelings, their similarities, their views on the world and the future, and other intimacies they shared away from the prying eyes of families, friends, and chaperones. Love letters were a foundation of romantic relationships and integral to the success of courtship.[84]

The letters between Corcoran and Louise contain several important commonalities with other lovers' correspondence of the antebellum period. Although modes of transportation and communications had improved significantly by the time of their courtship and marriage, their letters still followed an older style from when the world moved at a slower pace. Correspondence was detailed because the mail and other modes of contact were often unreliable. Communication worked, in part, through the obligation of trusted family members and friends to discreetly relay information to one another about the well-being and whereabouts of loved ones. Seen from a modern perspective as gossip, such letters were often the only way to learn about friends and relatives in an era of intermittent communication. Lost and delayed letters, which caused loved ones to fall out of touch for long periods, were common. This often raised anxiety among the correspondents and their families.

Letters of the period are somewhat counterintuitive in terms of modern norms. Men's letters tended toward complex and abstract expositions on romantic love, whereas the tone of women's letters typically was more matter of fact, even impersonal. This pattern reflects the prevailing stereotypes and gender norms of the period in which women were expected to "embody rather than articulate" the sentimental ideal, whereas men, due to their worldlier demeanor, proffered more sophisticated views and wisdom.[85] This is not to suggest that couples of the period, Corcoran and Louise included, refrained from sharing intimate details or giving each other loving advice with respect to problems they faced. But their different worldviews, expectations, and life experiences directed their discourse.

From their early letters and from the contents of Corcoran's personal scrapbook, clearly they had met at least six months prior to the first letter contained in Corcoran's papers, or as early as the spring of 1833. Corcoran's letters reveal that he was already in love with Louise by the time of his birthday in July 1834, when he turned thirty-six. [86] Another letter dated just three months later reveals that Corcoran had been in love with Louise for at least two years by that time: "Your love, my dearest Louise, has been to me a world of its own creation. It has now become a part of my very existence; and for the last two years I have loved you with an unabating intensity, which I did not believe belonged to the nature of man."[87] Louise was sixteen years old at the time.

The relationship evolved quickly from friendship to romance. This development involved substantial risks that might make their previously secretive relationship more overt and, therefore, discoverable. Clearly Louise was not initially comfortable with this course of events: "I am not quite sure that it was proper for me to commence a correspondence and am still now doubtful if I ought to continue it but I may as well confess it; we have no opportunity of speaking our thoughts and they will not be concealed so we must write them."[88]

Corcoran recognized the need to offer up his honest feelings. On the Fourth of July in 1835, he wrote: "All around me are celebrating it in mirth and revelry, I am more delightfully engaged in holding sweet communion with my love. While they declare themselves free and independent, I am sending my allegiance to the dear little empress of my soul. While they cry aloud for liberty, I glory in proclaiming myself a slave, and hug the chains and kiss the fetters, by which I am bound."[89]

His pen was clearly more elegant than hers in finding a freer expressiveness, although his analogy of human bondage as a desirous condition for romantic love in a slave society is unsettling to modern views. Corcoran's flowery words were more poetic than Louise's practical discourse, reflecting the expected norms of the time, and a different genre altogether from what he wrote as a banker:

> When bondage is so sweet, who would sigh for liberty. Liberty! To me would be death for under existing circumstances I can scarcely bear the separation. Have you in remembrance the last evening we passed together? But why my dearest love, should I ask, I know that it must be fresh in your recollection. I have dropped my pen to turn and gaze upon the spot when last you sat. How often since has my weary head been laid upon the same. When shall I see you there again echo answers when! oh! that you could come, and with thy witching smile.[90]

For her part, Louise was insecure about the relationship and worried about losing him. For all his emotional honesty, it clearly was not enough for her: "[I]f I am absent much particularly and you would remember me but as one you once loved and some other would more than fill my place."[91] Louise recognized the dangers inherent in formalizing a courtship with Corcoran and the likely disapproval of her father because she instructed Corcoran almost immediately to conceal the letters. "Guard them well for they are very precious to me. I would not part with them even to you if I did not fear the consequence of their being seen."[92]

Family Frustration

The love letters between Corcoran and Louise expressed more than sentiment; they also disclosed the practical consequences of their courtship. For example, the couple discovered very quickly that the difference in their ages posed a problem for many of their friends and family. Louise was not shy in reporting these concerns to Corcoran:

> [An unnamed friend] has been to see me. I saw her in my room, alone. She told me of the report she had heard and said she hoped it was not

true. I asked her why? She said you were too old for me! Whenever she thought of it, it made her melancholy for she did not approve of such a difference. She thought from my manner it was true and begged me to tell her if it was so. . . . I confided in her. I could not allow my friend to retain those feelings without letting her know how much she was mistaken, therefore I told her it was all true, and convinced her that my happiness entirely depended upon you.[93]

It did not take long for the Morrises to recognize and recoil from their daughter's relationship with Corcoran. Louise wrote: "On Sunday evening I was alone with mother and she said she wished me to write to her confidentially to tell her exactly what my feelings were. She repeated what she said the last time that my father would never visit at the house if we did so [if they married]! She asks that I make him some concessions." Indeed, the foreshadowing of possibilities to come were already evident: "She told me she would wish to know my feelings and decision in order that they might know what to do, for, if I persisted Father would or rather could not remain in the same place with me."[94]

Morris was fixated on the situation between his daughter and Corcoran, and his disposition was a serious concern for their relationship. "Father has been in most excellent spirits ever since he left home. I can only account for it in one way. I am going farther and farther from you," Louise wrote to Corcoran when traveling to Rhode Island.[95] Given her promise to be candid with Corcoran about all things, Louise didn't spare him the disapproval of her family.

I have had two conversations with uncle. . . . He said he feared more than he wished to know, that was, that I had really given away my whole heart. I told him his suspicions were just. He asked me if I had seriously thought of the difference in our ages and of the evils resulting from it. I told him that I had often thought of it, I had placed it in almost every light, but the evils had not made themselves apparent. He said that I deceived myself, for nature would have her way and the evils were almost too numerous to mention, that I was sacrificing all the pleasures which naturally belonged to my time of life, that our feelings must be widely different in almost every aspect and that in all probability before 20 years should have passed, I would find myself nothing more than a nurse.[96]

Yet, here was a sixteen-year-old girl with much strength of will: "I told him, that I would prefer to be the nurse of the man I loved, to marrying another no matter how brilliant the prospect be."[97]

The charge that Corcoran could not be relied on to care for and support Louise especially troubled him. Even though Corcoran was not yet a wealthy man, he was clearly offended by the accusation that he could not support a wife and family. He even suggested to Louise that he possessed more means than he had disclosed previously. "This is unkind, almost insulting. I am not the beggar they would fain persuade you. No Louise, on this point I have been particularly explicit with you and I am now compelled to say that the picture is not so dark as I had heretofore painted it."[98]

At about this time, Louise's parents packed her off to New England to put some distance between their daughter and her paramour. Her mother took Louise back to Newport, to the more insular protection of her ancestral home. Louise's letters to Corcoran from this period reveal her boredom, her desire to see him, and her frustration over her forced exile. For his part, Corcoran was increasingly upset by Louise's absence and the notion that it might go on indefinitely.

Not one word in yours [her letter] is about your return. I have flattered myself that two thirds of your visit had already been made, but, alas, disappointments seem to multiply upon me. Your Mother yesterday told a neighbor that the commodore would not go . . . for you until the last of October and that he would be absent two or three months, thus making it late in November before we meet again. I feel that my patience will not serve me until then! Can you not prevail upon your Brother to accompany you home? The very idea of your prolonging your visit beyond the . . . time cause no little uneasiness & vexation of mind.[99]

That the stress of the Morrises' disapproval took its toll on both Louise and Corcoran was equally clear. One of his letters to Louise was filled with accusations and threats, which a calmer Louise took maturely: "William you deserved a scolding for your letter of the 26th. There were some things hastily said which I am sure your calmer judgment would unsay. I never believed my father capable of such a thing and thought I had convinced you that he was not but instead of that, you express such doubts accompanied with threats and exhortations!" It was in this letter, too, where Louise first requested that Corcoran burn her letters after reading them. She had been writing him against her parents' wishes, and the letters included her true feelings, much gossip about other young couples, and her opinions about the worthiness of their courtships. "Mother does not know from me that I correspond with you. . . . If you love me, burn the copy I sent you, I would not have you keep it for the world."[100]

Corcoran was not immune to these concerns himself, and at times worried that Louise's parents were intercepting his letters to her.

> What has become of [the letter] I fear, and yet I cannot believe that anyone has dared to intercept it. If it has been, the party trespassing will have cause to regret it. They may fill the cup too full. They may proceed to a point, beyond which, forbearance would cease to be a virtue I would not my dearest Louise, that other eyes should witness the silly manner in which I pour out my warm feelings to you, though silly, they are not the less sincere. It has now reached a crisis that requires the exercise of all that firmness and decision which I believe you to possess. Demand my letter at once, for the love you bear me, do this. Let it be seen that you will not be trifled with.[101]

Louise soon discovered that she had become bitter and that her personality had changed because of her forced exile from Corcoran.

> Everybody tells me I have changed much since I left home. I have a so much more of a cold manner. Could I have experienced so many nights of sleepless misery, with none to lessen my sorrow by their kind sympathy, and have remained unchanged? No. I learned to look upon my own heart as the safe repository of all my happiness or sorrow, for I dared not hope for the sympathy of others. But even if I were changed to all the world I should remain the same to thee, love, and if cold to others, still warm, still devoted to him who means the whole world to me.[102]

Once again, she asked Corcoran to burn the letter, this time embarrassed by the frank expression of her emotions. "I wished the enclosure burnt. I cannot agree that a woman should never let her lover know the extent of love. I think there should be full and unbounded confidence between them, and if they begin with willingly and intentionally deceiving them with regard to any one thing, there is nothing to prevent its extending to others."[103]

By the time Louise arrived home in late October, much had changed. Mid-nineteenth-century courtships typically included a phase in which the woman tested her suitor to ensure his fidelity and devotion prior to marriage. This often involved a temporary dissolution of the relationship.[104] Their courtship proved true to form. After months apart and a pending reunion she had been looking forward to, Louise suddenly ended the relationship with Corcoran altogether. Pressure from her family, especially her father, influenced her decision. Louise's parents insisted that she break off the relationship with him, and she did so, writing Corcoran a heartbreaking letter designed to end it all.

> Farewell forever. Things . . . must be as they had never been. I think it would be better for both of us that we should meet as seldom as possible, and in the future we (should) meet only as acquaintances. Do not attempt to see me, for my mind is fully made up. For further information if you wish it, I refer you to Father. I return all your letters and wish my own to be returned whenever convenient to yourself. Again farewell.[105]

In hindsight, of course, we know this was not the last word, although the impact of the rejection must have shaken Corcoran at the time. His response was almost immediate.

> The enclosed was found among the letters returned to me yesterday. Can it have been written by the same hand that penned yours of yesterday? You have forbidden me to attempt to see you. I must therefore write. . . . The sudden resolution you have adopted. The change and chilling deportment towards me on Monday was not the result not of reflection . . . but feverish impulse of a mind under a high state of excitement and strong delusion. Have not the same reasons been forcibly but ineffectually urged for the last eight months? Louise . . . [b]y the love you once bore me . . . tell me how or when I have offended, and what is the nature of my transgression. This is accorded to the violent criminal, and will you deny it to me? Tell me, who has done me injustice? Who is it that has poisoned the noblest feelings of your nature? Would that my

every thought could be made known to your every feeling of my heart, every action of my life laid before you. . . . I may have deserved all this and more Louise, but not at your hands.[106]

Corcoran wrote again just a week later, sending the letter via Louise's sister.

Through the interception of your kind sister I am permitted to hand you the enclosed letter, written more than a week since . . . the correspondence between your Father and myself. . . . The incidents of the last fortnight, still appear so strange, so surprising, so like a dream that I cannot awake to sad reality. So strong were my convictions of the unwavering and unalterable attachment entertained for me by yourself, and so conscious that I had done nothing to forfeit it, that your deportment towards me on the evening after you arrived did not even arouse me to a sense of my situation. Your conversation with my sister on the same morning of the same day (for reasons already known to you) was not communicated to me until after the receipt of your last letter. You had not to learn, Louise, that every effort would be made, every argument used, to prejudice me in your estimation. These efforts have been made and alas! have but too well succeeded. That all men have their faults is true. That I have my full share of them is alike true. But that I have said or done ought in any way calculated to wound the feelings of one dearer to me than life itself, and only duly estimated when lost, as is false, as I will prove the author to be when brought to light.[107]

At least five weeks went by before he received another letter from Louise. By early December, her letters evidenced a welcome about-face. Where she had been adamant in her rejection, she had suddenly become equally resolute in her acceptance.

I am determined to marry you . . . [and] willing to give up the family for [you]. . . . Father . . . is determined not to have anything to say to me, and none in the family will speak to me. It will be better perhaps to speak to Father at once and have it settled. I would give the world to see you for five minutes tomorrow and if possible, will do so but I do not think they will allow me to go out at least until I have told them my resolve. . . .

Mother thinks we ought to be willing to postpone it for three years, when Father would consent to it, and all would be well. If you are willing dear William and think we ought to do so, let us make the sacrifice, but if you cannot, we will be firm.[108]

Corcoran's reaction was decisive. The coupled eloped and married a short time later.

Home Life

Marriage was a positive experience for Corcoran and Louise, despite several challenges the couple faced. First, they had to negotiate Corcoran's protracted business absences. Additionally, two of their three children died in infancy.[109] Their first child, a daughter named Harriet, was born just nine months after they married; she died at the age of one, in September 1837. Only the middle child, also named Louise, survived to adulthood. Childcare proved overwhelming to Louise, who frequently was forced to handle everything alone. It would only get worse: When their third child, Charles, was born, Louise was already doomed by tuberculosis. She died in November 1840, just four months after he was born. Charles, born in July 1840, died at thirteen months of age. Louise, born in March 1838, was often characterized as a delicate child, and she was the center of Corcoran's family life until her own untimely death from the same disease that killed her mother. Louise died in Cannes, France, in 1867, with her father at her side.[110]

Despite his long absences for business, Corcoran remained engaged in family life as best he could. His letters frequently apologized for being away and provided Louise with advice and encouragement. For instance, Corcoran wrote from New York to calm his wife about baby Harriet's behavior and his own absence: "Do not let the fretfulness of the baby worry you. All babies fret and ours less than anyone I ever knew, unless she has grown much worse than when I used to know her. . . . You do not, you cannot, suppose that I will remain absent one moment longer than is absolutely necessary." Yet, this was followed immediately by a warning: "Even now I cannot say when I will return."[111] Two days later that situation remained unchanged: "I am one day nearer home than when I last wrote, yet I cannot even now say when I will get there."[112]

In the meantime, the situation with the Morris family had improved. Corcoran noted in one letter that some members of her family had come around. "I should say I am happy to hear that your sister feels more at home in my house. Would to God it were so with the rest of the family? I feel persuaded that we should all be the happier for the change."[113] Soon the tide had turned, and Corcoran wrote more excitedly on the topic: "You could have communicated nothing that would have imparted as much pleasure to me, as that of the visit made you, by your Father and Mother. Whatever may be their views towards me, whether they be friendly or adverse, I have fully made up my mind to make proper concessions. You, my dear girl, know that I have never entertained an unkind feeing towards them."[114]

Corcoran appeared comfortable with married life even as Louise's letters grew more forlorn. She complained about his long business trips, and his apologies for being away grew longer and sadder. Still, Corcoran remained interested in the domestic affairs of his family and wrote about them often: "I have been trying to get you a handsome winter bonnet without success. I have not seen one that I would permit you to wear, tis so hard to reconcile me to the abominable ugly fashions," he tells Louise. Later: "I hope you will succeed in your first attempt at making Pup's toilet." A few days later, he wrote: "I was very desirous to reach home on Saturday that I might devote Sunday to love and my Louise. Do not imagine that dear baby is forgotten, my little family is ever present to my imagination and frequently, very frequently, do I visit them in my dreams."[115]

Indeed, the death of their first child occurred during his absence on a business trip, an unexpected development that truly saddened him: "I will not conceal it from you, but reflection has given me many bitter reproaches for leaving the dear little one when there was the slightest probability her taking that most horrible disease."[116] Still, business usually got the best of him, requiring the banker to balance the family with the firm: "I will use every effort to get through with my business so that I may leave New York on Sunday, but I am apprehensive that I may have to stay till Tuesday or Wednesday. In the meantime, my dear girl take great care of yourself, recollect that I am absent, and how disastrous it would be to my business for me to be prematurely called home."[117] The separate spheres occupied by men and women are clearly reflected in Corcoran's warning not to intrude upon his business dealings with domestic issues.

Some of the domestic angst the couple endured involved Louise's youth and inexperience raising children. Their correspondence mentions a housekeeper and nanny named Mrs. Gates, but it remains unclear what other domestic assistance, including enslaved people, supported the couple. Louise's awkwardness surrounding household and childcare chores was compounded by her feelings of isolation. Corcoran was often gone for a week or more, leaving Louise to struggle on without him, lonely for his company and assistance. She wrote, "I did not think I could miss you so much, that I could feel so lonely. I know it is wrong to give way to such feelings, and I struggle hard against them. Until you left, I thought I should not mind it much, it would only be for ten days and they would pass away, but now, every day seems lengthened into years."[118]

Corcoran's family frequently came to assist the new mother. "Mrs. Corcoran came in last night and urged me to spend the night with her. Your brother stopped to see how I was this morning. Yesterday afternoon Harriet wrote to me saying that Father wished me to stay with them while you were absent; that he felt very anxious about me."[119]

A growing family was also a boon to restoring good relations with Louise's father, who began to visit the Corcoran household once grandchildren appeared.

The family returned last night. Father & Mother came over this morning and caught the baby in a very pretty situation for a young lady . . . she did not have a particle of covering upon her and we were just undergoing her usual morning ablutions. I asked them who they thought she looked like. Father said he thought all young babies alike, he had often told mother if her children were mixed up in a basket with half a dozen others, she never could tell her own. It may be accounted for by his never having seen any of his own children except Elizabeth until they were six months old. He was always absent. The children have all been over. They appeared much pleased to see both myself, and the baby.[120]

For Corcoran, despite his frequent absences, this time was the highlight of his married life. Louise's health soon deteriorated, however; she died of tuberculosis at the age of twenty-one.[121]

That Corcoran never remarried remains a mystery. His growing wealth, social connections, and reputed good looks would have made the widower an obvious choice for repeat matrimony. The right marriage at middle age would have further secured his entrenchment in elite society. Nevertheless, his limited correspondence on the topic even decades later reveals a tender, emotional attachment to Louise. Neither the newspapers of the period nor his letters and other documents provide a hint of courtship or connection with anyone else—even though Corcoran lived for almost another fifty years after her death.

Whether Corcoran simply carried a torch for his young bride throughout his days or whether his consummate discretion veiled all other relationships is unknown. Corcoran remained a steadfast widower for the remainder of his life and wrote about Louise in loving, idyllic terms until his own death.

2

RISE OF THE
POLITICAL BANKER

W. W. CORCORAN GREW UP AMID ONE OF THE MOST PROFOUND
periods of change in US history, with the onset of the Industrial Revolution and the rise of a national market economy. From the textile mills of
Massachusetts to the oil fields and steel mills of Pennsylvania, the economy and life in the mid-nineteenth century became entirely different than
they had been just a few years earlier. Corcoran was fifteen years old when
Francis Lowell built his famous power looms and twenty-seven when the
Erie Canal linked western waterways with the Atlantic Ocean in a commercial continuum. The telegraph was invented when he was almost forty, the
telephone when he was seventy-eight, and the electric lightbulb began il-
luminating the darkness when he was eighty. The golden spike was ham-
mered into the ground in Promontory, Utah, creating a coast-to-coast railroad that drove a powerful new economic engine and transformed, well,
just about everything when Corcoran was seventy-one.

Some of the changes were wrought by invention, others by mechaniza-
tion, and further enhanced by economies of scale and organizational efficiency. Yet, the foundation of the new market economy was the introduction of a democratizing banking structure and easier access to capital for
investment and production. Robert Morris, no relation to Louise, in 1781
organized the Bank of North America, the first significant bank in the new
nation. Few other banks except the first Bank of the United States were created until the beginning of the nineteenth century, but states soon thereafter started issuing innumerable incorporating charters, leading to the establishment of some two thousand banks in the country by the 1830s. The
market economy may not have required massive capital investment until

large-scale industrialization after the Civil War, but the banks' new money "out of thin air" funded land purchases, new modes of transportation such as canals and steamboats, commercial production, mining equipment, mercantile activities, and public and private infrastructure, including roads and wharfs, which supported new markets.[1] Early railroads, in need of investment on an even more intensive scale, were just on the horizon.

Corcoran became one of the nation's most successful bankers and financiers in this new world. He was not the first to succeed in either endeavor, nor was he unique among his contemporaries, but his competitiveness, commercial reach, and penchant for taking risks gave him advantages lost on others who might have been unappreciative or frightened of the rapid changes. Corcoran helped modernize American banking by expanding its base and extending its reach. He assisted the transformation of investment finance from the exclusive province of a small, wealthy elite to a more democratic and accessible enterprise. He encouraged emerging powerhouse partners such as Brown Brothers & Co., E. W. Clark & Co., and Peabody & Morgan in the process.[2] Corcoran was a catalyst in encouraging bankers to leverage greater risks for returns, reaching beyond kinship bonds to develop a web of political and business connections to push lucrative deals and facilitate high-stakes transactions. Other entrepreneurs later pushed these boundaries further, but Corcoran's imprint is evident in the nation's early financial development.

Rising from a prosaic bank clerk in the mid-1830s to a confidant of presidents and one of the richest men in America a decade later, Corcoran was a testament to the American strike-it-rich mythology. To be sure, Corcoran relied on the relationships of connected family and friends in a privileged world to get his start. Even so, that old-world foundation would not reach far enough: The banker embodied the restlessness of the nation's growing commercial class, its expanding culture of individualism, and its newly cohering elite whose interests helped integrate the worlds of economics and politics. To succeed in the interconnected worlds of Washington and Wall Street that were integral to the transactions of finance and lobbying, Corcoran adopted an ecumenical character that embraced men of disparate politics, regions, wealth, and morals. Some owned people, others ran up sizable debts, and a few committed treason. Yet, many of the people with whom he made strong connections were leading citizens: statesmen enshrined in the history books, financial legends, or people whose influence and inventiveness altered the nation. In short, Corcoran probably befriended anyone who could help close a deal and did not always worry about the nuances of the relationship.

Corcoran's success also derived in part from the unique circumstances of the time in which he lived. Corcoran made his fortune in the 1840s and early 1850s (although he expanded his wealth considerably through shrewd investments thereafter) and wielded influence until the 1880s, a period in American history characterized by fewer rules, social cohesion, or economic constancy than before or after that time. His world was shedding social and economic deference, and empowering secular individualism (at least for White men) to recast the American economy in a spirit of laissez-faire dynamism. This world flourished until labor and immigration issues, big business, and government regulation again narrowed social and economic possibilities.[3]

By successfully wielding connections and influence between Washington, DC, and Wall Street among the political class, the banking community, and the rising securities industry, Corcoran became an important figure in the vitalization and expansion of the financial markets that fueled America's commercial development. This shift coincided with the rise of new men and expanding enterprises, of a growing entrepreneurial approach to commerce that became increasingly accessible to an emerging middle class, and a political culture less dependent on antecedent wealth or status.[4] In part through a financial structure that he helped build, a changing political framework, and a risk-taking personality energized by looser strictures, Corcoran championed a new approach to marketing securities that significantly broadened access to a wide range of private instruments and government funding. By adroitly bridging the private and public sectors to leverage government needs and the financial community's speculative power, Corcoran fostered fundamental change in government financing and furthered advances that others later commodified during and after the Civil War.

Antebellum Banking

Banking was an important factor in the growth of the American economy, both North and South. Historians and economists frequently portrayed

bank panics, monetary instability, and Andrew Jackson's fight over centralized banking as the totality of antebellum banking.[5] While these certainly had an impact on the pace and durability of economic development,
more recent analysis suggests this view neglected important financial influences on the national economy.[6] Part of this was the impact of growth:
An expanding economy made credit and investment opportunities more
widely available to borrowers, and new financial instruments helped increase the money supply and leverage funds to further build commercial
enterprises. This meant that the financial community was well positioned
to support—even drive—economic advancement and the government's
borrowing needs by the antebellum period.[7] Corcoran's ability to corner
markets, to provide loans and liquidity to a variety of ready borrowers, and
to make large investments of his own demonstrated the individualism and
entrepreneurship embedded in change.

Corcoran's instincts regarding financial opportunities were remarkably
good: He invested in the initial development of the telegraph and the Colt
revolver. In fact, Corcoran was the first investor in the Morse telegraph;
he gave Amos Kendall $1,000 for the first telegraph line between New York
and Philadelphia. Kendall later admitted his requests for support to many
other investors went unheeded and that Corcoran's investment in the new
technology was pivotal in obtaining additional investment and spurring
the telegraph's subsequent success.[8] Kendall had been the postmaster
general in the Jackson administration, to which Corcoran had strong ties.
Although born in Massachusetts, Kendall had lived for many years in Kentucky and, as the postmaster, blocked without legal cause the distribution
of abolitionist publications in the South.

The growth of private banking enhanced liquidity for a variety of commercial and industrial uses.[9] Even though the traditional narrative suggests that financial markets and the banking community were conservative players in the market—essentially passive supporters of change—in
reality, banks played decisive, pivotal roles as drivers of economic nation
building.[10] A growing financial structure in America's urban centers and
peripheries provided the necessary liquidity and impetus for entrepreneurial growth.[11] The emergence of strong capital markets in the early national period was predicated on robust financial institutions, including
state banks, private banks, brokers, factors, investment houses, and other
financial intermediaries.[12] Some of these entities exploited the vacuum

created by the demise of the Second Bank of the United States, but the ability of the markets to maintain stable interest rates and commodity prices across regions demonstrates the shifting economy's power and reach, as well as the growing role played by financial intermediaries.[13]

Recent scholarship suggests that antebellum financial institutions were at times more welcoming to diverse clients than previously thought. Banks over time became less restrictive, and some institutions served a clientele that extended beyond wealthy Whigs and influential merchants— a departure from the traditional interpretation.[14] Clients often included merchants, farmers, industrialists, lawyers, politicians, and many other community members. Despite populist-style claims of the time, few financial institutions were exclusive tools of individual interests or parties. Federalists, Whigs, and Democrats all found funds and established accounts through a multiplicity of banks.[15] The same is true for Corcoran's bank. In a capital with a diverse and growing population, Corcoran's bank reached beyond its famous or privileged clients, such as the presidents of the United States. Corcoran & Riggs attracted depositors and business interests of considerable diversity, from many parts of the social, economic, and political spectrum.[16] Unlike some banks, Corcoran did business with Blacks as well as Whites; indeed, the account records sometimes noted their racial distinction.[17]

Corcoran's Bank

Corcoran's success in early American banking and securities occurred literally on the foundation of the Second Bank of the United States, whose Washington, DC, offices Corcoran took over a few years after President Andrew Jackson killed the bank.[18] Distrusting central monetary authority, Jackson eradicated the most important economic stabilizer in the country until the creation of the Federal Reserve System in the early twentieth century. The bank's demise in 1836 ended Corcoran's job as a clerk. Based on his experience with real estate transactions and other investments from his work both for the bank and for his father, Corcoran soon started a brokerage house and in 1840 formed a banking firm.[19] Corcoran bought up much of the federal government's excess and deteriorated property, selling it at considerable profit in later years.[20] He started the brokerage business in a tiny storefront office only ten-by-sixteen feet wide on Pennsylvania Avenue but just steps away from the White House and the Treasury Department.[21] Within two years, Corcoran had achieved enough success to move down the street to the bankrupt Metropolitan Bank's offices. Indeed, Corcoran may have played a role in Metropolitan's demise, according to the remembrance of one congressman who implicated the banker in undermining the local chartered banks to his benefit. If true, it reveals a competitive personality that was atypical for the time and surprising given that the Metropolitan Bank's former president, John Van Ness, was a family friend and had supported Corcoran's early career. After gaining further success as a banker, Corcoran in 1845 purchased the BUS site, which remained the headquarters of Corcoran & Riggs for many years.[22]

Corcoran's bank not only handled general stocks, state debts, and similar securities but also specialized in US Treasury notes that were resold to investors or purchased for the bank's own account. The bank, started as Corcoran & Co., operated as a typical institution of the antebellum period.[23] An advertisement from 1838 reveals the banker's intentions and ambitions: "The subscriber has opened an office immediately opposite the Treasury, and adjoining the General Post Office, for the transaction of business with the general departments of the government. And for the purchase and sale of all kinds of stocks." Corcoran also noted that he would always give the highest prices for specie, treasury notes, treasury drafts, and land script.[24] A scan of similar records from newspapers of the time in both the capital and elsewhere show that Corcoran was not alone in his desire to build an entrepreneurial banking practice. While wary of and competitive with rivals, Corcoran could also be generous, serving as a reference in some advertisements for upstart firms. The banker could afford to be magnanimous: In part because of his connections and experience at the BUS, Corcoran was quickly recognized as an authority in real estate transactions, bills of exchange, and government and commercial securities, frequently outmaneuvering other companies even in the first years of his bank.[25]

Corcoran's first break came early. The banker's connection with Secretary of State Daniel Webster proved critical to his rapid rise in the financial world. While Corcoran's critics often pointed to his association with Southerners, Webster and other Northerners were vital links in his network; the banker's reliance on Jacksonians and Southern Democrats was only part of the story. Webster was from Massachusetts, the center of New England abolitionism; yet, he was complicated. Webster purchased several people but freed them under the stipulation they would receive wages from him, a portion of which they would repay him over time for their freedom. A shrewd lawyer and politician, he argued some two hundred cases before the US Supreme Court, winning several notable landmark cases that still guide American jurisprudence. Webster was an early opponent of the slaveholding Andrew Jackson, and he emerged as a "Cotton Whig" who sought to reduce sectional tensions and placate rather than antagonize Southern interests—essentially the same view that Corcoran held.[26] A man with uncommon oratorical skills, Webster remains today one of the enduring statesmen in the history books, having served as a congressman, as a senator, and twice as a secretary of state. However, he typically lived larger than his means and was frequently in debt, which may be why he was drawn to Corcoran and his bank in the first place. Webster played a crucial role in navigating the Compromise of 1850 that averted the Civil War for a decade, and he died shortly thereafter.

After the relatively unsophisticated treasury secretary Walter Forward, a Whig from Pittsburgh, failed to raise money for the government from either the domestic or foreign financial community, Webster suggested that the Tyler administration ask Corcoran to place a loan on the government's behalf.[27] Forward was a lawyer, not a financier, and his biggest problem was the nervousness of the financial community toward government debt after many states repudiated their bonds during the recession of the late 1830s. Corcoran was likely delighted to have the new treasury secretary indebted to him for a favor, because the recent abolition of the Independent Treasury System meant Forward was responsible for depositing government funds with the local banks. With assistance from the financier and family friend Elisha Riggs, Corcoran made sure to bid up the loan, offering an unusually generous $5 million, which infused much-needed confidence in the New York financial markets. The deal put Corcoran's name on the antebellum banking map.[28] Corcoran profited on the venture, as the entire loan was absorbed by investors at rates higher than his purchase price.[29] As a result of Corcoran's success in bolstering the Treasury Department, the administration thereafter had much greater luck selling securities to the financial community. By way of thanks, Forward and most of his successors gave Corcoran a place at the table, ensuring the banker obtained crucial inside information and access to bidding opportunities in subsequent financing activities. Other bankers complained about unfair practices that gave Corcoran advantages not available to most other bidders, but securities laws were all but unwritten at the time, leaving competitors without much recourse to level the playing field.

Local Banking Attributes

Although most banks of the period issued currency notes, Corcoran & Riggs did not. Currency was expensive and cumbersome to design, print, and circulate. It was also difficult to monitor appropriate reserve ratios. Corcoran's bank was small and operated with just a handful of clerks, making it difficult to handle currency. While the bank did not issue notes, it accepted deposits. Located at the center of the nation's capital, Corcoran & Riggs held the deposits of hundreds of people who lived and worked in the expanding city. These deposits included the life savings and government salaries of dozens of famous politicians over the years, including most of the US presidents from Martin Van Buren to Grover Cleveland.[30] John Tyler, a slaveholding Virginian who parted ways with Andrew Jackson and the Democratic Party over the Nullification Crisis, was critical to Corcoran's rise and was the first president to open an account with the bank—just one month after it opened. Tyler deposited his presidential paycheck, and many other presidents followed, earning Corcoran & Riggs the nickname of "the bank of presidents."[31] Due to Corcoran's growing connections, the bank held the accounts of the White House, most executive departments, and both houses of Congress. Corcoran & Riggs also managed the Smithsonian Institution trust; its first secretary, Joseph Henry, was a scientist and a Corcoran friend.[32] Doubtless no other bank could boast of the regular salary deposits of Abraham Lincoln, and it was a rare bank that simultaneously kept the holdings of free Back people. The bank held the deposits of Daniel Webster, Henry Clay, Franklin Pierce, James Buchanan, Stephen A. Douglas, Jefferson Davis, and many other politicians of the North, South, and West; of free and slave states; and of people of multiple races, ethnicities, and party affiliations.[33]

Corcoran's bank built a strong business handling bills of exchange, a lucrative enterprise that flourished after the demise of the national bank and before the introduction of modern checking services. By accepting the prevailing rate of discount on bills from banks in other states, bankers such as Corcoran assumed the remaining face value (and risk) of the instruments and presented them for redemption. Corcoran developed a reliable group of bank correspondents with whom he discounted notes, including the American Exchange Bank, Chemical Bank, Phoenix Bank, Leather Manufacturers' Bank, and Bank of America—all in New York.[34] Other banks in Philadelphia, Baltimore, and cities in Virginia offered important ties to banking centers and commercial regions that linked to his network.[35] Like many bankers, Corcoran provided loans to his best clients mostly in the normal course of business but sometimes in exchange for information or favors that benefited his interests. Over time, Corcoran became the confidant of many influential people in the capital, and his knowledge of clients' creditworthiness was indispensable to his ability to protect against risk prior to the establishment of large-scale credit operations such as Dun & Co. Corcoran's bank also operated as an early modern investment house, and it was this function, along with his propensity to provide select clients the firm's money or credit on a favorable basis, that sustained his bank as a popular institution over the years.[36] By combining the power of a bank and an investment house, Corcoran was able to purchase government securities, railroad bonds, and other financial instruments using bank reserves—often the government's own money—a century before a modern regulatory structure curbed such practices. He frequently bought securities not just for resale to other banks or financial houses but also for his own clients, the bank's accounts, and his personal portfolio as well. Many of Corcoran's allies benefited from his investment savvy through purchases he made on their behalf or the loans he advanced for them to make purchases themselves.[37]

Through extensive contacts in Congress and across multiple administrations, Corcoran successfully obtained significant government deposits and kept treasury funds long after they were withdrawn from other banks.[38] Based on the banker's connections, Corcoran & Riggs became one of the premier conduits between Washington, DC, and Wall Street. Corcoran built and benefited from strong relationships with several treasury secretaries, including Walter Forward and Levi Woodbury, a Jacksonian Democrat from New Hampshire, who often revealed to Corcoran the nature of his competitors' bids on treasury notes or the terms the government would accept.[39] His strongest connection was with Treasury Secretary Robert J. Walker, who made Corcoran the US agent for the Treasury Department during the Polk administration. In 1841—soon after he began in business—Corcoran also became the lucrative financial agent for the State Department, the result of his close relationship with Webster.

Corcoran would not have found his place in America's financial annals without Walker's help. Walker was born in 1801 in rural Pennsylvania to a Revolutionary War soldier and circuit judge, and a great-granddaughter of Benjamin Franklin. Walker was elected to the US Senate from Mississippi in 1836, despite a shady past in fraudulent Indian claims matters, and served until 1845, when he became secretary of the treasury. He was both a Unionist and an expansionist, believing in the primacy of the federal government and its manifest destiny despite its portent for sectional strife. Walker was a slaveholder himself but claimed to favor gradual emancipation and the efforts of the American Colonization Society. His relations with Corcoran were murky at times, and much hay was made over their long-term connections and his favoritism toward the banker. More than $1 million of treasury funds presumed missing during the Mexican-American War were found in the coffers of Corcoran & Riggs. President Polk later said it was among the most troubling moments of his presidency. Indeed, Andrew Jackson, Polk's mentor, had warned that Walker could not be trusted with "the nation's cash."[40] If Corcoran ever defended his actions in such transactions, it is not recorded in his papers.

Clearly, Corcoran viewed it advantageous in those early years to befriend and ally himself with politicians of all stripes—North and South, slaveholders and abolitionists, Whigs and Democrats—to further his ambitions. Presidents, cabinet secretaries, top agency officials—he created usable relationships wherever something beneficial might be leveraged. Many other people tried to insinuate themselves into influential circles and become indispensable in the same way Corcoran did, but very few succeeded. Moreover, Corcoran was not above complaining to his powerful connections when a banking situation did not go his way. "Mr. Corcoran seems to dislike the loss of deposits of the Capitol and waterworks," observed Montgomery C. Meigs, an army officer and superintendent of the

Capitol building. "He told the Secretary of War I did not deposit with him."[41] Meigs, of course, reported to the secretary of war, then Jefferson Davis.

The Network of Banking

Corcoran's early success in banking came through his ties to family friend Elisha Riggs, who introduced Corcoran to influential New York bankers and helped bankroll his initial transactions. The banker was uncommonly adept at making and keeping connections in the growing capital, but he needed ready access to capital and to demonstrate his influence in Washington, DC, to gain the confidence of Riggs's New York banking colleagues. Through Riggs, Corcoran became allied with George Newbold, the president of the Bank of America, and John Palmer, the president of the Merchants' Bank, two of the leading banks in New York's emerging financial ascendance over Philadelphia.[42] Newbold, particularly, was a leading adviser to the Jackson administration and had strong ties to Treasury Secretary Roger Taney and several of his successors. Indeed, despite his Southern slaveholding background, Corcoran maintained a close and mutually beneficial business relationship with Newbold, who was a Quaker and a member of the New York Manumission Society. Corcoran became well known to Taney's successor, Levi Woodbury, by assisting the Bank of America and the US Treasury in efforts to limit the influence of the BUS and to institute a network of "pet banks" to hold government funds. Indeed, Corcoran likely provided intelligence on the national bank's operations when he worked in its Washington, DC, branch. His actions probably helped competitors like the Bank of America gain business at the behemoth bank's expense and likely gave the Treasury Department ammunition in its war against the institution.[43]

As a result of his initial success and early connections, Corcoran by 1839 became the Washington correspondent for the Bank of America and was soon purchasing large blocks of government debt for Newbold and other New York investors.[44] Riggs did not approve all of Corcoran's requests for funds, but he provided the young entrepreneur enough liquidity to operate in the government markets. At times, the relationship seemed ready to come undone. "I have examined what you say carefully, but I cannot believe you were justified in giving so high for those notes," Riggs wrote Corcoran in December 1837 about one worrisome transaction. "Your great anxiety is the only excuse for giving so high. . . . I wish to continue with you if any good can be done."[45] The banker was already taking risks more prudent investors avoided, a character trait that would show even more strongly in the years to come.

His penchant for risk notwithstanding, Corcoran's early success was notable enough to be appreciated by bankers such as Newbold and—increasingly important—powerful politicians such as Woodbury and Webster. Corcoran possibly purchased for their accounts as well, especially for Webster, who rarely had sufficient funds. Over the years, Corcoran assisted Newbold in a variety of ventures and was an important ally and conduit of information useful to the Bank of America. "Can you do anything to aid us . . . that will add to our supply of specie for a short time. . . . A Treasury draft for half a million or a million of dollars on Philadelphia or Boston would be useful," Newbold wrote to Corcoran as their relationship matured.[46]

Investment banking, per se, did not exist in Corcoran's time, and the term did not attain its modern meaning until the 1880s. Practitioners of this business were called private or merchant bankers before the Civil War. Over time, these entrepreneurs became more than just purveyors of capital for old-line merchants and increasingly purchased securities for resale to a variety of ready clients. These investment bankers typically assumed the risks of the entire transaction, including massive failure if the price of the obligations fell and could no longer be sold at or above the original purchase price. In the past, brokers had assumed little if any risk because they sold the securities on a commission basis. They were not required to raise capital for the initial purchase, but neither were they likely to make much profit.

To strengthen his ties to the wealthy Riggs's pocketbook, Corcoran convinced the financier that his son George Riggs should join the bank instead of going to Wall Street as Elisha Riggs originally wished. The younger Riggs agreed, and shortly thereafter the banking and securities partnership of Corcoran & Riggs was formally established.[47] A small advertisement announcing the partnership appeared in the *Washington Globe* on April 14, 1841.[48] Riggs took over responsibility for the internal workings of the firm, while Corcoran, true to his talents, was the "outside" representative of the firm, building and broadening his growing network of associations.[49] Before long, the ambitious bank across from the Treasury Department was humming with activity. Newspapers described a bevy of clerks behind small screens across the front windows of the building, the principals ensconced in an office toward the back of the bank that was adorned with choice artwork, the iron safes and cabinets full of deeds and other documents, and a cloth-covered table strewn with papers in the middle of the room. Despite complaints from some competitors about the firm's sharp elbows and unfair access to government sources, Corcoran & Riggs retained a skein of respectability in its business dealings, avoiding some of the shadier banking practices of the day associated with the issuance of currency and the questionable treatment of clients' accounts. For the most part, commentators offered up praise that reflected the bank's growing reputation. "Throughout the country the firm exercises all the influence arising from a character of the highest integrity; and retains an unblemished reputation in all their transactions," said one newspaper chronicler.[50]

Reasons for Corcoran's Success

As a banker and broker, Corcoran achieved tremendous success—greater success than most of his competitors. He cultivated important ties to the New York banking and securities world. He raised capital, purchased securities on credit, redeemed notes, lined up investors, and provided intelligence to his New York sponsors about the timing, rates, and bids on government securities. To be sure, Corcoran was not the only ambitious and connected banker who gained important information from the corridors of power. The Baltimore firms of Manning & Co. and Brown & Co. were often stiff competitors who also traded on financial intelligence.[51] Still, Corcoran's financial acumen rarely failed him, especially with his skill at obtaining inside information about important business transactions. Corcoran even prospered when most investors failed during the Panic of 1873. When the Baltimore & Ohio Railroad collapsed as part of that fiasco, Corcoran—due to inside information from the company's president—made an enormous profit.[52]

Timing was also important to the success of Corcoran & Riggs. Corcoran took advantage of the national bank's collapse and the economic failures of the late 1830s to expand his business opportunities. One of the earliest bank panics occurred in 1837, during the economic meltdown that occurred between 1836 and 1840. New York lawyer George Templeton Strong captured these economic woes in his diary: "Terrible state of things out of doors. Merchants failing by the dozen. Some fear that all the banks will stop payment. We are on the eve of a change, a revolution in business matters, but it is a change that cannot be effected without shaking the whole fabric to the very foundation." Strong later wrote: "Confidence annihilated, the whole community, traveling to ruin in a body." Finally, in early May 1837, Strong wrote that the biggest New York banks had shut temporarily, including some of Corcoran's emerging associates: the Bank of America, the Merchants' Bank, and the Bank of Manhattan. "Immense crowd and excitement in Wall Street, but the military prevent any disturbance."[53] Economic failure and the vacuum left by the demise of the BUS provided important opportunities for Corcoran and his enterprising competitors.

After the BUS was eliminated, the big New York banks had even greater need for trusted intermediaries to manage securities and discounted notes, as well as to interpret information on the political environment. Corcoran built a note broker business, purchasing or redeeming for resale the notes of state banks. A profitable activity due to the era's regular monetary shortages, it became even more lucrative during the Panic of 1837, when specie dried up and banks relied almost exclusively on redeemable notes. Moreover, because of mounting debt resulting from trade problems with Great Britain, the US Treasury was forced to issue new notes, giving Corcoran an advantage in New York because of his capital connections.[54]

Corcoran was not alone in recognizing this pivotal moment. Others also recognized new opportunity in the economic upheaval of the late 1830s. Hundreds of new banks materialized across the United States, especially in the rapidly growing states and territories of the West. Some banks needed public charters before opening their doors, but other banks, such as Corcoran & Riggs, were private entities and only needed willing clients to operate.

Corcoran rarely shied away from risk; it was part of his strategy, and the press and his competitors came to expect it. By 1840, years before he would corner the government war debt market, Corcoran was purchasing large portions of the Chesapeake and Ohio Canal Co.'s stock, garnering more than 90 percent of one issue.[55] Corcoran was also willing to challenge others in court over business matters; at least two of his cases ended up at the US Supreme Court, including one involving the C&O Canal. In addition, the Supreme Court in 1854 found in favor of Corcoran a convoluted decision involving the disposition of claim shares from the Mexican-American War treaty of 1848.[56]

Banking and Political Culture

The propensity of Corcoran and others with similar motives to shower politicians with financial incentives was an important part of the political-business climate in the capital during the nineteenth century. Corcoran provided investment services to many politicians, frequently offering them the same type of inside information he provided to the New York banks. Corcoran directed his political associates to the most profitable securities and frequently provided loans, advances, and other financial incentives to help them purchase securities. Critics and rivals accused Corcoran & Riggs of being congressional pets who gained a near monopoly over government business.[57] Corcoran himself was not shy about trumpeting his attributes: "Our position and standing with the Executive and heads of departments gives us advantages in transactions with the government not enjoyed by others," and the firm typically gained "the earliest information in relation to matters and things."[58] Seen from a perspective not available in the twenty-first century, in which many such practices are illegal, the importance of monetizing inside information and trumpeting that access loudly was not lost on Corcoran, his friends, or associates.

It is no wonder Corcoran was influential: He monetized the information he acquired across several generations of politicians and businessmen. He also advanced money to important people, told them what to buy, held securities for them at the bank, and waived collateral for loans to help politicians and others build wealth and improve their financial situation. Sen. James Beck of Kentucky, among others, admitted his fortune was directly the result of profitable real estate investments Corcoran had suggested.[59] Beck owned people, was a White supremacist, and was a law partner of vice president–turned–Confederate general John Breckinridge. Breckinridge also participated in several of Corcoran's western land schemes, and the banker threw his support and pocketbook behind him when the Democratic Party split between Northern and Southern candidates for president, throwing the election to Abraham Lincoln and the Republican Party.

Among Corcoran's closest friends was Sen. Jesse Bright from Indiana. For many years, Bright was variously the chairman of the Senate Committee on the Territories, the Committee on Public Buildings, and the Committee on Claims; therefore, he was a crucial font of inside information on investment and other types of business opportunities.[60] He was first elected to the Senate in 1844 and served several consecutive terms. A leading Copperhead, he opposed the Civil War and sought immediate peace between the belligerents. Bright is distinguished for being in 1862 the last member expelled from the US Senate. A captured gun trader at the Battle of Bull Run had in his possession letters from Bright to Jefferson Davis that were related to Southern arms sales. There is no record Corcoran ever acknowledged his friend had engaged in treason, and Bright himself believed the episode was a misunderstanding. Ironically, due to the death of Vice President William King, throughout much of the 1850s and as late as 1860 Bright was the president pro tempore of the Senate; therefore, given the rules at the time, he was first in the line of presidential succession.

Over time, Corcoran engaged in a variety of significant enterprises, including land deals, with Bright and other political allies, such as Senators Robert Walker, Thomas Hart Benton, John Breckenridge, and Stephen Douglas.[61] Most of his partners in these land deals were Southerners, and some were enslavers—but not all. Besides obtaining information from his influential Senate connections, Corcoran had unparalleled access to government leaders and was often indistinguishable from the administration itself. Assisting government officials in their personal aims was mutually beneficial. John Tyler's fourth treasury secretary, George M. Bibb, admitted as much: He "used every opportune occasion" to befriend and assist Corcoran in his banking endeavors to ensure similar treatment in return.[62] Bibb was a Democratic senator from Kentucky, a lawyer, and an enslaver until he finally emancipated many of the people on his family's property.

There were many others, too. Presidents James Buchanan and Millard Fillmore often asked for Corcoran's help in making prudent investments with their funds, and he held investment funds for many influential people, ranging from explorer-politician John C. Frémont to utopian missionary Robert Dale Owen. Buchanan's inquiries are but one of many examples of this type of relationship revealed in Corcoran's papers. "Would you not deem it advisable for me to sell my stock, or a part of it, and invest the amount in some other securities? If so, what would you recommend?" the then–secretary of state and future president of the United States asked.[63] Corcoran had regular connections and similar exchanges with many members of Congress. In fact, the banker held the government's franchise for disbursing mileage and per diem allowances to senators and representatives, thus encouraging regular interactions with them.[64]

The well-connected banker was of significant help to Buchanan, Beck, Webster, and many other politicians and influential people. Clearly, not only information and favors but also money—at times—changed hands. What historians have called the Great Barbeque—a confluence of graft, bribes, and kickbacks that consumed the capital in the aftermath of the Civil War—had its beginnings in the 1840s and 1850s. Economic change ensured that genteel mercantilism would over time give way to rapacious capitalism. Railroads and industry required extensive and often aggressive financing and political intervention to compete successfully. The new era resulted in more private legislation favoring privileged companies, rapid growth in securities markets tainted by speculation and inside information, special deals for land rights-of-way, and a panoply of backroom political favors, including plain old graft.[65]

Given the political culture of the day, Corcoran could never have achieved such spectacular success without participating in the barbeque; however, it's not entirely clear to what extent he played the game. There is not much direct evidence of politicians' hands in his pocket, but then the game was played most successfully when scrutiny was avoided. It is not always clear Corcoran was comfortable with the notion of political pocket lining. He often advanced money to political allies, yet sometimes he expected repayment.[66] Corcoran also reminded associates about their obligations for the monetary advances. He cut off further dealings with several people who treated his loans as gifts and at times sued individuals to recover money and securities.[67] It seemed opaque when a loan was really a loan and when it was something more. For example, Corcoran always gave Daniel Webster's needs special attention because of his influence and friendship. Indeed, he forgave the stateman many loans the bank provided him. Corcoran was so pleased with the senator's famous "Second Reply" speech to South Carolina's Robert Y. Hayne on the floor of the Senate that his note to Webster congratulating him on the occasion also indicated that payment on a $5,000 loan was forgiven.[68] The banker's generosity became public knowledge, angering competitors and critics who portrayed it as financial collusion with a powerful politician.[69] No incidental matter, Corcoran's reaction to Webster's speech also reaffirmed his support of "liberty and union," a view that nullification was treason and that states' rights and national preservation must be saved simultaneously.

Corcoran's skills in developing political and financial relationships were critical to his success. They allowed him to retain government funds for several years after the collapse of the Independent Treasury System that supported private banks with federal money. While most competitors lost their government funds when Zachary Taylor led the Whigs to the White House, Corcoran staved off the inevitable until Franklin Pierce's administration finalized the removal of US funds from private banks.[70] Corcoran's ability to negotiate the changing reality and thornier relationships in the Whig banking world's more hostile climate is one of the clearest examples of his political skills at work.

Over time, Corcoran & Riggs became the most favored bank in the capital. In the late 1830s, Washington, DC, had four principal banks: the Bank of Washington, the Patriotic Bank, the Metropolitan Bank, and Corcoran's bank. Metropolitan was initially the Bank of America's Washington correspondent. The Patriotic Bank, correspondent for the Merchants' Bank of New York, was the recognized pet bank in the capital. By coincidence and to Corcoran's advantage, both Metropolitan and Patriotic were chartered banks, the type of institution that many Democrats and the Jacksonians especially considered corrupt.[71] Corcoran & Riggs, as a private unincorporated bank, avoided the special privilege and corruption charges that tainted other banks; it also required no legislative charter to operate. Corcoran's bank did not issue bank notes, so soft-money foes had no basis for objecting to its operation.[72] These attributes were important for new banks during Democratic administrations and one reason Corcoran continued to obtain favorable treatment from government officials. The firm started small, required minimal capitalization, made adroit investments partly on inside information, and used its proximity to the Treasury to bid on various government opportunities. As a result, Corcoran leveraged enough business to keep the firm afloat during the financial collapse of the late 1830s when many of its competitors failed.[73]

Corcoran's political savvy also gave the firm a leg up when Democratic administrations decided which banks to designate as treasury depositaries. While collateral was required to secure the government's funds, silent partner Elisha Riggs once again came to the rescue and lent the firm a substantial portion of his investment portfolio to establish the necessary collateral.[74] Corcoran also utilized inside information. His bank was permitted certain advantages to ease liquidity problems that may not have been accorded his rivals. For instance, Corcoran used state bonds in addition to federal instruments as collateral for securing federal government deposits. New York bank allies such as George Newbold also lent Corcoran funds to finance bond purchases until the government funds were deposited in his account.[75]

The importance of being selected as a treasury depositary cannot be overstated. While it took several years for Corcoran to put his Washington rivals out of business, he was helped by political attacks on Whig banks that gave the government cover to reduce his competitors' federal deposits. Metropolitan's and Patriotic's losses were clearly Corcoran's gain. Not only did Corcoran's share of federal deposits increase during this time but he also was awarded most of the government's domestic exchange business—a lucrative enterprise—while his rivals received none of it.[76] To be sure of continued favorable treatment, Corcoran provided loans to the new owners of the influential Democratic newspaper the *Globe*; at the same time, he offered loans to a range of Whig and Democratic politicians with sway over Treasury-related matters. Funds for these loans were often dispersed from the bank's government deposits.[77] Behind the scenes, Corcoran influenced the House of Representatives to investigate the District of Columbia's chartered banks. Years later, Edmund Burke, the chairman of the investigating committee and an opponent of chartered banks, remembered that Corcoran provided valuable intelligence to thwart his competitors in the capital.[78] As a result, by the end of the Tyler administration, Corcoran had essentially secured a monopoly on government banking in the capital and tied his firm to some of the most influential banks in New York. This position was officially secured in the early days of the Polk administration when Robert Walker became secretary of the treasury and made Corcoran & Riggs the sole treasury depositary in the capital.[79]

Overall, Corcoran became an increasingly powerful player in government finance. The Treasury Department frequently left large sums of securities with his bank for months at a time without redeeming them, allowing Corcoran to pocket the interest.[80] Even when Corcoran was not the beneficiary of treasury deposits or domestic transactions, his access to Robert Walker allowed him inside knowledge that was beneficial to friends, clients, and influential politicians. Numerous associates sought advantages from the relationship. "We presume you can manage to get hold of these operations . . . please make the necessary inquiries," wrote Enoch W. Clark, a senior partner in a Philadelphia firm bearing his name, to Corcoran.[81] Financiers elsewhere also relied on Corcoran for a variety of business needs. "We have been unable to get the draft on Daniel Webster accepted," wrote Gilbert & Sons, a Boston investment firm that was a correspondent bank with Corcoran. "We hold it for the present . . . subject to your instructions."[82] Even members of Congress sought Corcoran's assistance and influence. "A word from you to the President and to Mr. Walker will be duly appreciated by us," penned Robert Dale Owen—an Indiana congressman and the son of Robert Owen, the British social reformer and champion of the utopian community of New Harmony—regarding complications involving a large stock purchase.[83]

Hard-money Democrats who sought maximum separation between the government and the banks eventually prevailed, establishing a subtreasury that brought federal funds back to the government from the pet banks.[84] Corcoran tried to delay the inevitable withdrawals. He succeeded in slowing down the process with help from the New York bankers, who feared currency flow disruptions.[85] Corcoran also acted as an unofficial government spokesman by assuaging Wall Street's fears that the new system would harm banks and investors. Corcoran indicated that the government's withdrawal of funds would occur gradually over a period of years. He personally interceded when the banks in April 1846 contracted credit to protest the withdrawals. The banks then reversed themselves, easing credit, and the adoption of the subtreasury system proceeded according to plan.[86]

After the Independent Banking Act of 1846 reduced government deposits at pet banks, Corcoran was still better off than most bankers, including much larger banks in New York. Even though Corcoran & Riggs was a fraction of the size of the big New York banking houses, it retained as much in government deposits as the other banks did for most of the drawdown period in 1846 and 1847.[87] It was also among the very last of the pet banks to lose all its treasury deposits.

As treasury deposits dwindled, Corcoran held on to other government accounts.[88] While none were as large as the Treasury's deposits, they required no collateral and improved the bank's liquidity and leverage for making other business transactions. Corcoran's small but lucrative business of making interest payments on behalf of the government continued under Democratic and Whig administrations alike. Similarly, under successive Democratic and Whig administrations, the firm handled more than half of the government's debt retirement business, which provided commissions and much-needed liquidity for loans, working capital, and other operations.[89] Access to these funds was important to Corcoran's ability to act like a big bank, to influence government finance, and to strengthen his business and political connections.

Corcoran's mastery of the capital gave him an unparalleled ability to change with the times and the politics of the banking world. Whether Whigs or Democrats were in power, whether there was a central bank or pet banks, whether he offered information and funds to the bankers or to the politicians, Corcoran's bank grew bigger and his reputation stronger. In his fifteen years of active engagement with the firm, Corcoran rarely faced a significant setback in his commercial pursuits. Corcoran seemed to maneuver his way through almost any circumstance, building profits and networks all along.

While Corcoran was a growing power in Washington, DC, his presence was felt throughout the banking world, where his ability to access funds and meet market demand underscored not just his abilities but also the broadening effect of a modernizing economy. In many ways, Corcoran was acting like a modern banker. The banker's routine access to the money centers on the Eastern Seaboard from Boston to Charleston, and his strong and regular connection to banks and other economic leaders in the West and throughout the country, suggests that Corcoran was not merely a local Washington, DC, banker but also one of the nation's premier financial entrepreneurs, helping others to finance their way to a more stable future and democratizing economy by reaching beyond immediate horizons.

The transportation and communications revolutions allowed the banker to connect to the larger commercial world beyond local and limited markets. Corcoran was a leading exemplar of the future of banking and the transformative market economy itself, serving as a lynchpin that kept the modernizing banking system and the accelerating economy working effectively and profitably.

3

SELLING THE WAR

LITTLE HAS BEEN WRITTEN OVER THE YEARS ABOUT HOW THE United States paid for its wars and military conflicts, and what has been written is generally outdated and whiggish, a fancy way of saying that the best preordained outcome, well, happened. Of course, that is not always the case, but it is true about the Mexican-American War, where important financial developments then have had long-lasting significance for the United States.[1] The nation's approach to funding public debt for that conflict—guided in large part by Corcoran—helped pave the way a decade later for the Union's efforts to fund the Civil War. This approach helped create or influence some of the period's most important financial developments, including the structure of investment banking, the broadening of securities markets, the greater stability of international financial connections, the growing relationships between financiers and the government, and the increasing utility of professional networks.

By the time of the Mexican-American War, Corcoran had successfully leveraged his talents as a financial and political insider to build a small but highly influential and profitable banking house. Corcoran was so successful and politically connected that his bank was often seen as a part of the government, and he was viewed as its spokesman on important financial and monetary matters.[2] Corcoran frequently accompanied Treasury Secretary Walker to Wall Street to market the government's securities to the financial community. Both Wall Street and government officials increasingly looked to Corcoran for insight and inside information on actions that the administration was contemplating in a run-up to the war. "You have a golden key for unlocking the mysteries of Walker-dom if not

Polk-dom," wrote Robert C. Winthrop, the Speaker of the House of Representatives to Corcoran.[3] Similarly, at the start of the Mexican-American War, the powerful New York banker George Newbold wrote: "I must beg of you the favor to communicate . . . the substance of what you would say if opportunity allowed."[4] Corcoran's reputation in both the government and the banking community was instrumental to what was arguably his principal financial legacy—funding most of the Mexican-American War, which, in turn, led to large territorial gains for the United States in victory over its southern neighbor.

The Mexican-American War occurred between 1846 and 1848 after Mexico contested the US annexation of Texas in 1845. The US victory in the struggle resulted in a huge territory the size of western Europe—about a million square miles—being added to America's southern and western borders. President James K. Polk had campaigned on the promise of manifest destiny and the nation's expansion. The war garnered many detractors, but some Southerners welcomed the idea of expanding into Mexican territory (as well as Cuba and other areas) to create more slave territory for the country.

There is no record of what Corcoran thought about the war even though the banker was close to Polk and to Walker, both of whom favored expansionist policies. Yet, Corcoran certainly knew an opportunity when he saw one and was well positioned with Wall Street and Washington to leverage it. Given his connections to the Polk administration, probably no one better than Corcoran could orchestrate a plan to raise money to fight the war.

Although Corcoran's success and its implications for government finance have been little studied, they had a significant impact on the creation of modern securities markets. Corcoran took an entrepreneurial approach to war financing on behalf of the government. The banker crafted an inventive form of public sector capital development, bridging the narrow, personal banking approach used to fund the War of 1812 and the market-driven effort undertaken for the Civil War. For the War of 1812, Stephen Girard raised money mainly on a kinship basis, through his own bank and wealthy friends in the Philadelphia area. Fifty years later, Jay Cooke directed a Civil War bonds campaign that was among the first mass marketing efforts in the country.[5] Between the two approaches, Corcoran encouraged a strong government securities market by taking risks averred by others and by leveraging connections that furthered mutual ambitions and minimized competition. To some, Corcoran's approach was too risky. George Riggs, Corcoran's business partner, felt the firm was too exposed to potential losses in government securities and resigned from the firm. He was replaced by his younger brother, Elisha Riggs Jr.[6]

The War of 1812 Model

Philadelphia banker Stephen Girard is regarded as the principal financier of the War of 1812. There were many similarities between the careers of Girard and Corcoran since both attempted to gain business by leveraging government information and influence. Nevertheless, their approaches to the government's war-financing needs diverged significantly, and, ultimately, Corcoran had the greater success. Girard was a wealthy merchant who brought back to the United States his far-flung European interests when the Continent's economy stalled during the Napoleonic Wars. Just as Corcoran did twenty-five years later, Girard built a private bank that challenged the chartered, commercial banks.[7] The second war with Great Britain provided an unprecedented opportunity for bankers to earn profits on government investments. Girard sought a portion of the government's loan of 1813 and was part of the small, initial syndicate that purchased the obligations for resale.[8] However, Girard cornered less than one-third of the loan, and other wealthy individuals, such as John Jacob Astor, subscribed to large shares of the loan also. Not only did Girard fail to monopolize the loan of 1813 but he also refused repeated entreaties from the government, including personal requests from Treasury Secretary Albert Gallatin and, later, Treasury Secretary Alexander J. Dallas to subscribe to larger shares or to manage subsequent loans.[9] Administration officials personally asked Girard to take part in the loan operations and to loan the government money to aid the war effort. Girard refused, declining to support the Treasury Department with either his funds or his financial expertise. Girard's interests and goals apparently had little to do with generating revenue from government obligations or establishing insider credentials with the administration; rather, Girard's goal, which he failed to achieve, was to trade assistance to the government for its assurance that his bank would be treated on par with the chartered, commercial Philadelphia banks and that the Treasury would force the other banks to accept his currency notes. Despite the nation's urgent war needs, Girard refused to lend the government money because the Treasury had not met the conditions he requested regarding his bank. A standoff ensued: Dallas refused to intervene on the banker's behalf and declined to give Girard special accommodation in how his bank was treated. When Girard was unable to get what he wanted from the administration, he walked away from government finance.[10] His bank continued to hold government funds, but Girard rarely worked collaboratively with the government thereafter and was generally unsupportive of its war needs.[11]

Corcoran and War Finance

In contrast, Corcoran had substantial influence on public debt finance and maintained mutually beneficial interactions with the treasury secretary. Traditional views suggest investment banking arose in the United States with Jay Cooke and the sale of government bonds during the Civil War.[12] In reality, investment banking was already established by the War of 1812, when Girard and his associates bought and sold government obligations in a limited and geographically constrained manner. The view that underwriting government obligations did not gain prominence until Jay Cooke arrived on the scene overlooks the impact of the transportation revolution and the economic role of banks on the growth of public debt finance starting in the 1820s.[13] These instruments were used to fund roads, canals, early railroads, wharfs, and other public infrastructure. Moreover, the broadening reach of financial connections, the proliferation of capital needs, and the vast increase of banks and other financial firms during this period gave Corcoran, his allies, and competitors access to a much broader group of potential investors. As a result, well before the Civil War the federal government raised funds through debt finance operations although with sometimes unsatisfactory results—such as when Treasury Secretary Forward attempted to raise money in the 1830s. The situation improved after Webster persuaded Corcoran to help the government, giving it impetus to expand funding opportunities when the Mexican-American War began a few years later.[14] Bankers such as Corcoran, who bought significant shares of state and federal debt obligations starting in the 1830s, leveraged a growing securities market fueled by a rapidly expanding economy; from there they quickly latched on to the larger requirements of public finance during wartime. Corcoran and other financiers sold to each other as well as to the investing public, marking one of the clearest differences in funding approaches between the War of 1812 and the Mexican-American War. This development not only helped to broaden the base of the government and commercial securities market but also made possible the popular public subscription campaign that partly funded the Union's military requirements during the Civil War.

Corcoran, beyond building a significant domestic market for government debt, helped renew European interest in American securities. The continent had been burned by losses when US investments crashed during the financial crisis of the 1830s. Corcoran himself described the importance of the endeavor in the autobiographical portion of his published letters, speaking in the third person: "This was the first sale of securities made in Europe since 1837, and on his return to New York he was greeted by everyone with marked expressions of satisfaction; his success being a great relief to the money market by securing that amount of exchange in favor of the United States."[15] So important were Corcoran's efforts that his contemporaries saw them as a watershed event in selling securities overseas and renewing faith in the American markets. "Mr. Corcoran has unquestionably done more, much more, than any private individual to sustain the credit of the government, and he is justly entitled to great praise, and to the thanks of all, for the able and judicious manner in which he managed the business," wrote two dozen bankers, including some competitors who suddenly began eyeing the new market Corcoran opened.[16]

Corcoran's actions pointed to a new—if riskier—approach to securities marketing that created a foundation for modern debt finance. A New York journalist who subsequently reviewed Corcoran's role in the nation's financial maturation wrote, "When Mr. Corcoran returned to America, he received, in New York, a brilliant ovation from the bankers and capitalists of that commercial metropolis, who hailed him as the fortress of American credit on the exchanges of London and the Continent of Europe."[17] Another observer made clear that Corcoran—and not, as some suggested, Treasury Secretary Walker or President Polk—deserved the credit for international finance improvements.[18]

Corcoran played an important part in the rise of international finance and the development of a robust American securities market overseas. His close connection to international firms such as the Baring Brothers, the Rothschilds, Peabody & Morgan, and other financial luminaries underscored the power of leveraging risk across networks and highlighted the increasing importance of international finance patterns and capital flows.[19] J. S. Morgan became the junior partner in George Peabody's London firm, which evolved into J. S. Morgan & Co., the firm his son J. P. Morgan increasingly managed as his father's health declined. Corcoran's persuasiveness in selling government debt instruments abroad, combined with his connections to European bourses and the US government, showed a sophisticated understanding of international finance and diplomatic skill that few domestic firms evidenced.[20] Indeed, Baring Brothers, the Morgans, and George Peabody had all warned Corcoran that the loans could not be sold outside the United States. Corcoran believed otherwise and arrived in London with little notice; a few weeks later the whole business was wrapped up, both in London Paris.[21]

Government's Response

Throughout the Mexican-American War, Corcoran managed the placement of government loans at the best rates for himself and his clients, principally through his access to Treasury Secretary Walker and based on his tolerance for risk. Corcoran also helped support government financial policy on behalf of the Polk administration when American banks and other investors first rejected efforts to fund the war.[22] Treasury Secretary Walker, similar to many of his predecessors, had unstable relationships with Wall Street and the banking community.[23] Walker had participated in various business deals with Corcoran over the years but apparently was unschooled in financial policy.[24] Walker seems not to have recognized the negative impact of government operations and his own approach to the banks on the market or on investors' tolerance for risks.[25]

Disenchantment with the government's financial policies was compounded by Walker's missteps in structuring the initial wartime securities. In July 1846 Congress authorized loans valued at $10 million.[26] Walker began issuing notes at low rates and gradually increased the interest, but the financial community barely responded.[27] By the fall of 1846, the government had only $4 million left in the Treasury, and war demands were growing steadily. Clearly the administration would have to change its approach. Walker, on advice from Corcoran and others, suspended deposit withdrawals from the pet banks, and the president approved a loan at 6 percent, closer to the more generous level Wall Street originally anticipated. However, Walker refused to make concessions to the banks and instead authorized a large loan to the major banks at just 5 percent. The banks in New York and Philadelphia uniformly rejected his offer. Only after Corcoran gave further advice both to Walker and to Secretary of State James Buchanan did the treasury secretary relent and offer the higher-yield 6 percent loan.[28]

By itself, Walker's capitulation was not enough to ensure the loan's success. It only succeeded because of intermediaries such as Corcoran, who convinced Walker to relax loan policies and eliminate the need for specie as a loan requirement; that action sparked considerable interest in the loan.[29] Corcoran not only achieved a handsome profit but, just as importantly, also gained experience, good will, and additional network connections in the emerging investment community during the sale of the first war loan. In the meantime, he advanced funds to friends and influential members of Congress to purchase the securities for themselves, at times at par or below the market price.[30] Through generous access to capital, thanks to his New York banking connections, Corcoran captured most of the loan. He also successfully routed competitors who later sold heavily from their portfolios in a failed attempt to undercut his profits and break his hold on the market.[31] His success in capturing and reselling most of the government debt at a solid profit was recognized throughout the financial sector. "They [Corcoran & Riggs] have made a princely fortune by taking the whole of the last government six per cent loan," a clearly envious Philip Hone confided to his diary.[32]

The 1847 Loan

Despite its early success, Corcoran & Riggs encountered growing pains. The partners disagreed over how to handle the new war loan floated by the Treasury Department in 1847. Riggs and his father, Elisha, were more conservative bankers than Corcoran and worried that risky financial practices and sharp elbows might harm their reputation. The Riggses were old-school bankers and clearly believed the firm needed to earn its place through conservative business practices, acquiring a proportionate share of the loan to the bank's size and status, and accumulating experience and a positive reputation incrementally.[33] Their view clashed with Corcoran's more aggressive tactics. As with the 1846 loan, Corcoran hoped to corner the market for the 1847 loan, an aggressive business practice that unnerved his partner and many competitors. Corcoran persevered. The firm leveraged its connections with Walker to obtain much more of the loan than the conservative banking world thought prudent for the upstart firm: Rather than the modest $1 million or $2 million that some bidders offered, Corcoran bid—and captured—almost $15 million of the loan, virtually the entire offering.[34] He succeeded in cornering most of the loan because, as Whig papers jealous of his connections made clear, he probably gained inside information from Walker and others in the Treasury Department.[35] As a result, Corcoran was willing to risk more because he likely learned the loan amounts could be funded through installments and that not all of the money was required upfront, per the usual procedure.[36] Such information clearly provided the small firm a significant competitive advantage and allowed Corcoran to take a majority portion of the loan.

Corcoran's actions garnered exactly the type of notoriety that worried the Riggs family: Competitors charged that Corcoran unfairly and unethically gained inside information from the administration. Elisha Riggs even tried to keep his own connection to the dealings secret; he complained that the young banker mishandled the overly speculative dealings with Walker, a charge Corcoran denied.[37] No records suggest that Corcoran had second thoughts about the deal or worried about its impact on his reputation. Newspapers waited for the plan to fail and followed the market price assiduously, anticipating the overextended firm's imminent bankruptcy. Corcoran & Riggs was starting "to look blue," said one paper, using an antiquated term for nervousness.[38] Another blamed Walker's corruptibility: "Corcoran & Riggs are . . . permitted by Mr. Walker to traffic in public securities and enrich themselves and their friends at the expense of the government."[39] The corruption allegations provoked several fights on the floor of the House of Representatives, as members of Congress at times debated whether Corcoran was the "government banker" or whether the Treasury was being fleeced by "sharpers and shavers."[40] On the other hand, such accusations belied the positive press the banker frequently drew elsewhere (at times in papers Corcoran subsidized): "Mr. C. is apparently about 50 years of age, stout built, healthy, and rather near-sighted. His manners are cheerful, dignified and polished, and his integrity of the highest order."[41] Another newspaper insisted "that the breath of suspicion has never rested upon his fair frame as a businessman, or as a gentleman in private life."[42]

Their discomfort notwithstanding, Corcoran's partners in the loan deal must have been pleased with the outcome. Capturing such a large portion of the 1847 loan allowed them to control significant amounts for their personal accounts as well as for their firms. Selling at high premiums allowed Corcoran to leverage the notes with little need to borrow, but when interest rates increased and the war dragged on, Corcoran was forced to borrow funds to cover the spread.[43] Walker frequently came to Corcoran's rescue: The Treasury Department often postponed loan installment requirements, further aiding the firm's ability to manage the portfolio. The banker's ability to leverage a variety of investment firms (and individuals) to coordinate the loan, combined with a better reception for the securities than in the previous year, made the process of disposing of the 1847 notes an easier and more profitable undertaking. The firm earned more than $250,000 from its sale of the loan, far beyond its profits to that point combined.[44]

The 1848 Loan

The 1847 loan was a harbinger of the 1848 loan—at least at first. Once again, Corcoran prevailed because of his access to inside information and his penchant for leveraging risks beyond most of his peers' acceptable norms. To help sell the 1848 loan, Corcoran relied upon and even expanded the brokerage connections he had previously developed to sell the 1847 loan.

The administration again authorized a large loan to replenish reserves in case the war with Mexico, which was quickly becoming a guerrilla war, dragged on. Moreover, Walker was encouraging slave territory expansionists who were bent on the annexation of Mexico and Cuba, and wanted a surplus available in case opportunities to purchase land arose. Walker originally sought a loan of $23 million, but when a peace treaty with Mexico ended hopes of annexation, the loan amount was reduced to $16 million.[45] Corcoran again was able to corner most of the loan, in this case about $14 million, by working closely with other bankers. As usual, he likely gleaned inside information about his competitors' bids.[46]

Events turned out a little bit differently this time. In fact, Corcoran's success in absorbing a large, risky loan was problematic. Although he had amply demonstrated his prowess at connecting the investment banking and political worlds to his advantage, concerns about his sharp elbows remained. The worriers included his business partner. While George Riggs had reluctantly supported Corcoran's outsize loan capture in 1847 despite misgivings about the risk and his reputation, financial conditions in 1848 were not as good as the previous year. Riggs worried the firm's position would be precarious if the loans could not be quickly absorbed. Newspaper commentators were dubious of the venture and again predicted failure.[47] Moreover, Corcoran proposed buying a large portion of the new loan when the firm still had significant portions of the old loan on its books.[48] Whether this was foolhardy or brilliant depended on one's perspective, but obviously Corcoran had enough inside information about the loan to assure himself, if not Riggs, that the risk was worth taking. Corcoran, as the firm's senior partner and its policy-making principal, brushed aside concerns and bid the loan. In response, Riggs quit the firm. Elisha Riggs, who still served as a source of capital and acted as a silent partner, replaced him with young Elisha Riggs Jr. as a partner with a 25 percent interest to handle the firm's internal matters. George Riggs did not return to active management of the firm until Corcoran retired. The business breach between the two men had no effect on their personal friendship, which continued for the remainder of their lives.[49]

The real problem was not with the firm but with the financial community. The favorable market from the 1847 loan had largely disappeared by 1848. Many things contributed to this situation, including a less robust economy and the fears of some financiers that the American money market was saturated from the previous loan and that the remaining capital wasn't sufficient to absorb the new loan.[50] Observers also warned that, as before, the disgruntled firms Corcoran beat out to clinch the new loan were artificially depressing its market value to hurt the banker.[51] Corcoran soon discovered his own loan sales were lagging and that as money grew tighter, demand fell, and the price dropped. He was forced to stop selling his portion of the loan, preferring to gamble that the price would rise later, rather than selling at lower prices in the meantime and risk his future profits.[52]

The European Market

As the American capital market dried up, Corcoran, in cooperation with Walker, decided to sell the 1848 subscription in Europe.[53] Such a strategy brought considerable risk: While success in Europe could boost loan demand and the price, the government had tried to raise money in Europe to help support treasury notes just a year before with little success. Plus the previous war loans were sold almost exclusively in the United States. There was little precedent for the Europeans to support the American government in its wartime capital needs. The European financial community had a long memory. For years, they had been hesitant to engage in the American market after many state bonds defaulted in the depression of the late 1830s. Some European financiers, such as Baring Brothers, also felt that the American approach to raising public funds was risky. Corcoran's strategy was even riskier and untried. He wanted to float a large loan and divide it among a variety of financial backers, both strong and weak investors. The Europeans typically targeted much smaller loans among a few well-known backers, taking a more conservative and traditional approach such as the one Stephen Girard used to fund the War of 1812.[54]

Corcoran recognized that the American market for public debt instruments was faltering and would remain weak unless funds from elsewhere, such as England and France, could be enticed to support the deal. He convinced Walker to supply him with a $5 million advance from the Treasury to support the loans. Walker also made Corcoran an agent of the US government for the purposes of selling the loans abroad, and the banker departed for Europe with letters from the government, the British ambassador, and John Davis, a former Whig governor of Massachusetts whom the Barings respected for his efforts to negotiate the repayment of state bonds that had tripped up the venerable investment house.[55] Corcoran attempted to convince Daniel Webster to accompany the banker, but his age precluded the trip.[56] Ironically, at the same time Corcoran was trying to hold bond prices steady and convince the European financial community of the merits of the offering, his own firm, among others, panicked and began selling in the thick of a bear market. It took Corcoran months to reverse the damage done by his timid partners and peers.[57]

In the meantime, guided by his old friend George Peabody through his London financial contacts, Corcoran hosted several weeks of negotiations in London and Paris with influential European financiers. Under Corcoran's guidance, Walker agreed to allow interest from the contract date, not the purchase date—a move that increased profits for the prospective holders. Corcoran also indicated he would release his remaining block slowly to support the price. The British, who had been opposed to the mission from the start, eventually agreed to take more than $3 million of the portfolio although at stiff terms that left Corcoran essentially at a break-even point when exchange rates were factored into the deal.[58] Still, that counted as a success: Failure to convince the British would have left Corcoran, his firm, and his investors with huge losses; instead, Corcoran turned a dubious financial transaction into a significant achievement. His efforts to attract European investors transformed the deal into a diplomatic mission that the British financial community was obligated to support to maintain good relations with the United States and gave American investors breathing room to absorb the old loan and keep the new loan out of the market for a while. Over the ensuing eighteen months, Corcoran earned handsome profits for himself and his investors; he also reaped the benefits of the contacts he made in the European financial community. Indeed, Baring Brothers, which had not supported Corcoran's entrance into the European market, become his principal business partner on several international business deals.[59] The British banking stalwart and frequent competitor—in business for nearly 250 years until it failed in 1995—became a willing ally once it saw the results. "All goes on smoothly here, and the demand for United States stock runs away with all we have or wish. Our business relations with you have opened under . . . happy auspices," the powerful London bankers wrote soon after the successful sale of bonds in Europe.[60]

Corcoran's own words, written in the third person in his autobiography, reveal how pleased he was with the financial gamble:

Mr. Bates of the House of Baring Brothers and Company and Mr. George Peabody [told him] that no sale could be made of the stock and no money could be raised ... and they regretted that he had not written to them to inquire before coming over. He replied that he was perfectly satisfied that such would be their views and therefore came, confident that he would convince them of the expediency of taking an interest in the securities; and that the very fact that London bankers had taken the securities would make it successful.[61]

Corcoran was uncannily accurate, since that was exactly how the risk scenario played out. The banker ended up selling millions of dollars of the loan to six major London houses: Baring Brothers, Peabody & Morgan, Overend Gurney, Dennison and Company, Samuel Jones Lloyd, and James Morrison. The US markets, relieved that the Europeans were supporting such a large American transaction, resumed their activities and bid up the share price. When Corcoran eventually sold most of his remaining shares, he more than made up in America what he squeezed out at the break-even price in London. He returned to New York on the *Britannia* in October 1848 as a Wall Street financial hero, not to mention a savior of his own coffers.

The investment success Corcoran secured in England further solidified his ties with important financiers, including Joshua Bates, the senior partner at Baring. Bates was an American but, like George Peabody, spent most of his life in London. Born in Massachusetts, Bates was a very religious man, an abolitionist, and a strong supporter of the Union cause in the run-up to the Civil War. He was also the principal philanthropist behind the Boston Public Library. Corcoran's old friend Peabody also helped to expand the banker's overseas network. Peabody was somewhat of a recluse and more ambivalent about the Union cause—an oversight that would come back to haunt him later in life. Peabody's junior partner, J. S. Morgan, and Morgan's son J. P. in time would have immense influence in expanding the European financial world that Corcoran pried open. Indeed, Corcoran, in a matter of weeks, appeared to be more successful than Peabody and Morgan had been over a period of years in encouraging European investors to look positively on American debt obligations. In the end, the conservative Peabody, essentially the founder of the House of Morgan, relied on Corcoran to show the way to improved international financial relations.

War Funding Legacy

The Mexican-American War was arguably the best government-financed debt until modern times. Unlike the American Revolution and the War of 1812, the US government was not forced to rely on one or two wealthy merchant bankers and a handful of banks to hold the loan. Nor did it require a vast public campaign such as the one Jay Cooke created to sell war bonds in the North during the Civil War. In large part through Corcoran's efforts, the government during the Mexican-American War sold its debt obligations at either par or above the securities' value and provided solid rates of return. Importantly, the government obtained specie rather than rapidly devaluing paper money for its needs. Unlike other major conflicts the US government financed, the Mexican-American War neither sapped the economy nor drained other resource investments. The nation maintained the gold standard, and the federal government did not impose taxes on its citizens. In these important ways, the Mexican-American War remains unique among US war-financing programs.

The biggest change from previous war-funding efforts was the introduction of large-scale investment banking. Corcoran and other bankers and investment houses supported the government's war needs by purchasing and reselling public debt obligations. This approach became possible in the 1840s because of the burgeoning market economy's increased financial flexibility and liquidity, as well as new transportation and communications modes that allowed more rapid transactions and connections. War-financing requirements intensified the marketing of securities as an institutionalized endeavor that, until the war, had been more ad hoc and limited in nature. The growth of commerce, particularly the development of capital needs for railroads and other industrial enterprises, made the older kinship-dominated investment structure increasingly inefficient and obsolete. Indeed, Corcoran's broader vision for marketing significant blocks of debt to large and small institutions alike and, later, for reselling to individuals eventually became standard practice in the industry.

An essential difference between funding the War of 1812 and the Mexican-American War was the role and reach of networks. This system required an increased reliance on financial intermediaries and strangers tied to distant parts of the commercial world to succeed. Corcoran recognized this new world and leveraged it. By comparison, Stephen Girard during the War of 1812 relied almost entirely on his wealthy family and intimate banking connections for the minimal support he provided to the government's war needs. The trust, immediacy, and reciprocal nature of relationships prevalent in a nascent market economy familiar to Girard had resolutely given way to a broader world of market exchange and competition by the 1840s. Corcoran certainly traded on the trust and intimacy of personal contacts to attain his financial goals, but he did so on a much broader playing field than Girard had. Moreover, the extensive public marketing campaign Jay Cooke later engineered to finance the Union's Civil War needs still had its roots in the older banker's approach.

Despite Cooke's marketing innovation, there were considerable differences in the approach to finance between Corcoran and Cooke. At least one observer of the time gave most of the credit to Corcoran. By the time of the Civil War, the banking houses of Corcoran & Riggs and Jay Cooke & Co. were within sight of each other near the White House.[62] Corcoran and Cooke were both treated more favorably by government officials in ways that were not made available to others. Rumors of corruption swirled around Cooke, not unlike the accusations leveled at Corcoran. Nevertheless, Corcoran's challenges were larger and his return greater. All of Corcoran's loans were made when currency was restricted to specie, but Cooke was able to negotiate in national paper, allowing him more liquidity leverage. With Corcoran, all government loans were absorbed at or above par, and each loan was taken at a premium. As a result, all debts were paid fully in cash. Many of Cooke's creditors after the Civil War received just twenty cents on the dollar due to the outstanding loan remainders. Newspapers at the time, while grumbling at Corcoran's near monopoly of the loan, also recognized the profit the government achieved through Corcoran's transactions as opposed to the losses it sustained in financing the war of 1812.[63]

Corcoran worked all the angles. He laid the groundwork with powerful bankers across the geographic and political structure to assist the administration in meeting national war-financing needs. Corcoran assuaged the investment community, often convincing members—despite Walker's efforts—that the deals were in their and their country's best interests. Corcoran was among the few bankers who could legitimately speak for the treasury secretary. Most of all, Corcoran was a consummate dealmaker, using his knowledge and contacts to beat out most competitors.

Increasingly, his insider status in government circles regardless of the political party in power made Corcoran among the most respected and sought-after bankers and investors of his era. Walker himself noted his dependence on Corcoran for the success of the government's financial policies in the Mexican-American War: "Throughout this whole period, [Corcoran] proved himself not only an able financier, but a devoted patriot, always advising such counsel as was best calculated to promote the interest of the government."[64] Of course, he rarely failed to promote his own interests as well.

The success that Corcoran, with support from Walker, achieved in creating a stable market for debt obligations established a new enthusiasm among investors both in the United States and in Europe. The growing confidence in American securities came in time to help fuel the great capital needs that started with the railroads and heavy industry in the 1850s and ran on into the Gilded Age. The energized markets financed billions of dollars needed for commerce, transportation, and communications advances, and for the new factories and industries that would usher in modern America. Moreover, in restructuring how financial instruments were marketed, Corcoran and other influential bankers laid the groundwork for the modern securities markets that would emerge after the Civil War. It was this world—the world of orderly credit markets, investor confidence, and extensive public-private cooperation between bankers and the government—that the Morgans, Cooke, E. H. Harriman, Abraham Kuhn, Solomon Loeb, and other Gilded Age financial entrepreneurs inherited.

4

AMERICA'S LOBBYIST

DURING THE SUMMERS OF 1877 AND 1878, WELL-KNOWN PORTRAIT painter Cornelia Adèle Fassett set up a studio in the Supreme Court's chamber, located in the US Capitol, while the court was in recess. Fassett sought to memorialize the electoral commission's 1877 meeting in the historic chamber. The painting was completed in 1879 and eventually sold to Congress for $7,500—much less than her asking price. The crowded painting depicts 260 people, most of whom never attended the commission's hearing. Yet, there is Corcoran, seated in the first row just below the commissioners, a respectful acknowledgment of his influence and status in the proceeding and in the halls of power.[1]

The nod to Corcoran was appropriate. After all, the banker was among the earliest and most enduring professional lobbyists of the mid-nineteenth century. More than that, his pervasive influence in the activities of legislative committees, executive agencies, and other parts of the government suggest that lobbying as a lucrative occupation started earlier than is typically assumed. It is difficult to draw conclusions about the early days of lobbying; most such practices involved secrecy, backslapping, and—often—bribes to achieve their aims. Lobbying in the capital prior to the Gilded Age was an especially opaque profession; it is difficult to generalize about this period.[2] Historians typically peg the rise of lobbying to the Gilded Age as a necessary lubricant to the machinery of policy and regulation overseen by legislatures in the rise of railroads and industry. Accurate to a point, in that Gilded Age lobbying and corruption became notorious and ubiquitous, Corcoran was already a well-known lobbyist for various clients in the 1830s, decades before such activities were widely practiced. By the 1840s and 1850s, Corcoran had many clients, suggesting that lobbying, while perhaps not yet widespread, was a viable enterprise in the antebellum period. As a result, lobbying had more significant antecedents in this era than previously acknowledged. The Gilded Age was infamous for corrupt lobbying and bribery schemes such as the Crédit Mobilier and Whiskey Ring scandals. Lobbying itself likely dates to the dawn of the republic, but a growing economy encouraged its utility in securing appropriate outcomes for those who could afford to hire the right political influencer.

What began in obscure statehouse cloakrooms was ultimately reproduced in the capital. The quiet antebellum start of this persuasive profession was transformed by the unprecedented government spending during the Civil War and the easy access to lucrative contracts. An observer toward the end of the Civil War described the scene: "There were lobby agents, male and female, ready to give the influence they boasted for a consideration. . . . There were men and women who could engineer private bills through Congress and could tell to a dollar how much it would cost to pass them through both houses. There were anxious and hungry contractors ready to pay a hundred thousand dollars for a chance to make a million."[3]

Corcoran's adroit utilization of networks was a key to his success in lobbying endeavors as much as it was in banking. His connections to money and power, on the one hand, and to art and culture, on the other, created important and long-standing connections across multiple fields that Corcoran used to his advantage years before such actions became commonplace.[4] Many imitators followed in Corcoran's footsteps, especially during the Gilded Age and thereafter, gaining enormous success and wealth as lobbyists, but few if any of them spanned the decades, political factions, and breadth of issues in the way this early lobbyist did. A neighbor of the banker's described his influence this way: "Mr. Corcoran by his magnificent entertainments, threw all others in the shade. In General [President Franklin] Pierce's time, Mr. Corcoran wielded a great influence in Washington. His splendid dinners are well remembered, with a file of senators on each side of the table."[5]

Corcoran never held public office or any other position in American politics. The closest he came was serving as the head of the organization dedicated to completing the Washington Monument or acting as a backroom adviser and bankroller to several Democratic presidential aspirants, most notably James Buchanan and Samuel Tilden. Nevertheless, Corcoran was among the country's most influential men in the privileged circles of government offices and the capital's drawing rooms. Despite his Southern pedigree, enslaver past, and sharp business elbows, he maintained the confidence and trust of many people in the nation's powerful political and business elite for decades. Corcoran leveraged his significant wealth, along with insider information, into considerable influence with the Whig and Democratic Parties, and even with the Republican Party at times. Some of the banker's activities, and how his influence was perceived by others, were documented in correspondence of the time. Yet, most of his success as a lobbyist depended on stealth and backroom influence. Many of Corcoran's actions on behalf of himself or others are lost in the obscurity lobbying practitioners prefer.

Leveraging Networks

Corcoran's success rested on his skill in developing and leveraging networks. Indeed, many of his influential associates were helpful to him not only in politics or business but also throughout his many other endeavors, where they assumed critical roles in a variety of activities. His business associates later became colleagues and advisers for his art gallery, his political friends became the capital city's advocates, and those involved in his philanthropic and civic ventures were members of the city's elite. Some connections unraveled during the Civil War, but most remained intact. Corcoran's mastery of peer networks sustained his connections even during difficult times and helped restore his reputation after the war. For better or for worse, perhaps loyal to a fault, Corcoran often picked up his relationship with many Southerners and Confederates right where they left off before the war. Northerners seemed generally unfazed by Corcoran's activities; most people probably found their own advantages in associating with him. Indeed, his connection with Union general and Republican president Ulysses S. Grant flourished at the same time Corcoran was spending summers with Confederate general Robert E. Lee.

Corcoran needed strong networks to succeed in the lobbying business. This departure from existing norms was a harbinger of the emerging world. Most elites of the time still relied on kinship relationships rather than on peer networks, especially in establishing and maintaining business and financial relationships.[6] They operated within a construct of age-old traditions predating the acceleration of transportation, communications, large-scale capital requirements, and industrial development. Trust and business operations rarely extended beyond family members and longtime friends. These practices built many successful family dynasties in America.[7] Many bankers followed in these traditions, including the Riggs family with whom Corcoran built his banking house. The Riggs family—father, sons, nephews, cousins—were involved as partners and employees from the start of the family's participation in the firm. Corcoran himself relied on his close family friend—Elijah Riggs—to help establish the firm, but he quickly expanded beyond kinship networks into peer relationships and other connection patterns. Corcoran's only son did not live to maturity, and his brothers, nephews, and son-in-law were uninvolved in the banker's various enterprises. Indeed, he had little to do with his brothers commercially after the failure of the family dry goods business. Corcoran clearly decided a kinship network was not as important or effective as a more modern peer network for achieving success in banking and lobbying.

Corcoran's Difference

Corcoran recognized the promise inherent in the more individualistic and entrepreneurial order emerging in mid-nineteenth-century America. He was well suited to excel at a time when competence mattered as much or more than kinship. Even early in his career, Corcoran was an intimate of powerful people. There were numerous reasons behind Corcoran's ability to befriend almost everyone who mattered in the capital: He was the wealthiest man in Washington, DC, for decades and represented the pinnacle of elite society because of his connections to capital and culture. For a generation, Corcoran's parties and dinner table were renowned throughout the city, and his invitations promised not only delightful evenings but social recognition as well. One secretary of the treasury lamented after leaving a Corcoran dinner party that he wished the nation's Treasury were as full as he was.[8] A cultivated Englishwoman remarked after attending one of Corcoran's parties that it was "the grandest dinner I ever partook of on either side of the Atlantic."[9] Horatio King, President Buchanan's post-master general, even wrote verse lauding the banker's fetes: "At Corcoran's party, the other night tis said, the news comes all the way from Quaddy, they drank twice 90 gallons of apple toddy."[10] Corcoran's invitations were, in fact, a social designation, a tangible proclamation of arrival, a valuable tool to newly elected congressmen or recently minted army officers eager to climb career ladders or to become part of the Washington, DC, establishment. A Corcoran party was an important introduction for new members of the diplomatic corps. Moreover, a night at Corcoran's mansion was useful even to the most seasoned politicians for whom a few minutes with the president—many of whom frequented his house just across Lafayette Square from the White House—might earn support for a pet project. Luminaries of the privileged elite at his parties ranged from Gen. Winfield Scott to Edward Everett, from Daniel Webster to Jefferson Davis, from President Millard Fillmore to Washington Irving, and from Henry Adams to Roscoe Conkling.[11] Men of different political parties, even adversaries, mingled in Corcoran's parlor. Men destined to play historic and opposing roles in the Civil War sat down to dinner in the banker's Moroccan-inspired dining room.

His parties were grand and widely attended. "Corcoran had a magnificent ball last night . . . though excessively crowded. I suppose there must have been invited from twelve to fifteen hundred," wrote Elisha Riggs Jr. to his father in describing Corcoran's annual party honoring George Washington's birthday.[12] One newspaper reported that a Corcoran party the previous night ranked as "the most magnificent of the fashionable season."[13] His parties were always packed. "It went even above the President's receptions," declared one chronicler after a Corcoran gala in 1855.[14]

Corcoran often brought together important and interesting people who might benefit himself and others. He had the ear of presidents even before he became a wealthy and influential banker. He was among the select few who accompanied President John Tyler on an inspection of naval facilities, even though he had no known experience in the topic.[15] As Corcoran gained prominence, he gained greater access, further expanding his networks.

Corcoran exercised significant leverage and influence in the Whig and Democratic Parties, especially before the Civil War. While principally a Democrat, he had plenty of Whig friends and associates, such as

Daniel Webster. He financially supported both parties' newspapers and befriended numerous Washington publishers, most likely to ensure favorable treatment of himself and his concerns.[16] Corcoran provided funds to support Buchanan's presidential aspirations as early as 1852. Buchanan lost to northern Democrat Franklin Pierce, who in turn beat Whig candidate Winfield Scott. That all three politicians were associates, dinner companions, and recipients of the banker's financial services and information reflected Corcoran's adeptness at tending to his networks. He later played a major role in Buchanan's 1856 presidential campaign and his successful election as president.[17]

Lobbying Connections

Corcoran developed and sustained connections of people influential in finance, art, and politics. On the national political scene, he counted as a friend and confidant almost every US president from Andrew Jackson to Grover Cleveland, except perhaps Abraham Lincoln. Even Lincoln, however, banked at Corcoran & Riggs. Corcoran was personal friends with Millard Fillmore, James Polk, James Buchanan, and Franklin Pierce. He befriended many of the most powerful representatives and senators of his time, dozens of former and current cabinet members and other administration officials, diplomats, and Supreme Court justices. Even Republican presidents, such as Grant and Rutherford B. Hayes, sought Corcoran's views on important topics and came to his parties and dinners. His ability to gain the confidence and friendship of important men of all political parties, regions, and factions over several political generations made him a unique and valuable ally to the capital's powerbrokers and dealmakers— and to the people who paid for favors and persuasion.

Corcoran had a vast group of political allies. From the North, he counted many as friends and associates:

- Edward Everett—a Whig US senator, a governor of Massachusetts, a secretary of state, a president of Harvard University, and a famed orator who spoke for two hours at Gettysburg Cemetery immediately preceding Abraham Lincoln's two-minute address—was a Unitarian minister but gave a speech supporting the institution of slavery that thereafter sullied his reputation.

- Daniel Webster—a Whig US senator, a secretary of state under three presidents, and one of the most famous orators in American history—was a principal influence on the Compromise of 1850. He alienated many people in the North by accepting as part of the deal the Fugitive Slave Act, which required runaway enslaved persons to be returned to their owners.

- Robert Winthrop—a Speaker of the House of Representatives, a successor to Webster in the Senate, a governor of Massachusetts, and a direct descendent of John Winthrop's—was also close to George Peabody and helped manage the expatriate's American philanthropic trusts. Winthrop's muddled views on slavery in a strongly abolitionist state denied him reelection to the Senate.

Corcoran likewise was on intimate terms with many men from the South:

- Robert E. Lee—the Confederate general and president of Washington University (later Washington and Lee University) with whom Corcoran often summered in rural West Virginia—owned people and inherited numerous slaves from his family estate. He accepted the dissolution of slavery after the Civil War but opposed racial equality for African Americans.

- John Slidell—a Democratic US senator from Louisiana until the Civil War and thereafter a Confederate diplomat charged with obtaining recognition and financial aid for the South in Europe—largely failed in his mission to France and settled in Paris after the war ended. For years while Slidell was in Congress, he and Corcoran lived just a few houses apart in Lafayette Square—the senator rented a home from Corcoran—and visited each other almost daily.

- Jefferson Davis—a Democratic US senator from Mississippi, a secretary of war under Franklin Pierce, and the president of the Confederate States of America—was a regular at Corcoran's dinner table for many years. Davis owned more than a hundred people on his plantation and argued against secession until the Southern states left the Union.

- Robert Walker—a Democratic US senator from Mississippi and the treasury secretary in the Polk administration—was a staunch defender of slavery and an enslaver himself. Nevertheless, he supported the Union and was Lincoln's emissary to Great Britain to oppose the Confederacy. Walker and Corcoran were close associates and business partners in many ventures.

The rising West also proffered Corcoran numerous allies:

- Henry Clay—the youngest-ever Speaker of the House of Representatives and a US senator from Kentucky, was known as the Great Compromiser for his role in keeping the Union together as the forces of secession gathered. Clay owned about fifty people on a planation in his home state.
- George Bibb—also a Democratic US senator from Kentucky and a predecessor to Walker as treasury secretary—was instrumental in favoring Corcoran's bank in the early years of the firm. Bibb was an enslaver who was appointed treasury secretary when he was nearly sixty-eight years old and was widely considered incapable of doing the job.
- Stephen Douglas—a Democratic US senator from Illinois and a presidential candidate—was Corcoran's confidant and frequent business partner, especially in land and railroad deals related to the western territories. The Douglas family owned people, and during the 1858 Lincoln-Douglas debates, the senator famously equivocated on slavery's morality.
- Jesse Bright—one of Corcoran's closest friends and a Democratic US senator from Indiana—holds the distinction of being the last member expelled from the chamber. In 1862 he was accused of treasonous activities against the Union when letters bearing his signature outlining the sale of firearms to the South were found at the Second Battle of Manassas. He was a states-rights champion and enslaver on his Kentucky farm. Bright had long been the chairman of important Senate committees involving lands, railroads, public buildings, and claims activities that benefited Corcoran and his business connections.[18]

While his closest confidants were clearly of Whig and Democratic persuasion, and many of the Democrats were enslavers, Corcoran also built important relationships with Republicans.[19] These connections became especially useful after the Civil War, when he returned to Washington, DC, from abroad amid the rise of Republican governance. Corcoran made business deals, traded information, and mended political fences with many Republican politicians, former union generals, and other power-brokers. Despite his decidedly murky past, he built loyalty with Republicans because of his wealth, stature in the community, network leverage, and philanthropic activities. While his access to inside information and his role as a powerbroker was not what it had been before the Civil War, Corcoran still retained considerable influence in the new era. Even such prominent Republicans as Lincoln's secretary of state, William Seward, and Sen. Charles Sumner, the leader of the Radical Republicans, remained Corcoran's friends and associates.

Finally, Corcoran's close contacts extended far beyond the political and business connections that might further his wealth and professional ambitions. His cultural and philanthropic endeavors, as well as his reputation as a wealthy, propertied gentleman interested in gastronomy, art, public spaces, Southern culture, horticulture, and the general welfare, created additional associations with which the banker influenced the capital and the country. In this regard, Corcoran's reach, as evidenced simply by the range of people with whom he corresponded, was prodigious:[20]

- Dorothea Dix and Corcoran worked on sanitation, philanthropy, and urban development projects. He provided funds, connections, and other resources to assist the healthcare pioneer in her efforts to improve public health and urban conditions.
- Joseph Henry, Andrew Jackson Downing, J. B. French, William Storey, James Renwick, Walter Ulrich, and other architects, scientists, and urban design proponents worked with Corcoran to build and improve his properties as well as the capital's public spaces.
- A host of artists and collectors ranging from Albert Bierstadt to William T. Walters sought Corcoran's patronage and views on art. Artists and collectors throughout the country recognized Corcoran's gallery as among the era's most important cultural anchors in the capital.
- A panoply of individuals and civic organizations interacted with Corcoran on a variety of charitable endeavors. The wider his renown for good deeds became, the more Americans across the spectrum of race, class, region, and politics sought his assistance. These requests ranged from former enslaved people seeking a few nights' lodging to

House Speaker Henry Clay seeking funds to aid the growing temperance movement.

- Notables from Jefferson Davis to William Tecumseh Sherman discussed ways to remedy and repair the nation's sectional problems. Throughout the national crisis and its aftermath, Corcoran was recognized for bridging faction, region, and party, whether at his dinner table or in the congressional cloakrooms.[21]

Banker to Lobbyist

One of Corcoran's most important roles in the nation's capital was in interpreting and influencing the government's actions. As the senior partner of Corcoran & Riggs, Corcoran spent little time in the office managing the daily affairs of the bank; his influence made him too valuable to engage in mundane operations.[22] On most days, Corcoran was either negotiating business in other places, such as New York, Baltimore, and Philadelphia, or discussing political and financial matters with his allies in the capital city. His proximity to the power brokers was critical to his reputation for producing meaningful results for his clients. Lobbying seemed a natural extension of his financial talents.

In truth, Corcoran had always been a lobbyist on behalf of himself and his associates.[23] Over time, the banker began to leverage information and connections on behalf of others, and there was no shortage of parties interested in the information or assistance he could provide. Some of the requests were mundane, such as when William Appleton of Boston asked Corcoran to secure for him a Washington, DC, church pew.[24] Many individuals sought Corcoran's help in obtaining specific employment or other favors. "What is the probable success of this operation? If you think it can be advantageously made, to whom would you recommend their confiding as an agent?" George M. Dallas, the vice president of the United States, asked Corcoran regarding loan subscriptions by the Pennsylvania Railroad.[25]

Ironically, some of the most powerful and connected members of Congress often asked Corcoran what news he could glean regarding pending government actions. Even when the writer was an important politician in his own right, the letter often showed the superior behind-the-scenes power and influence Corcoran wielded. "I am extremely anxious to know whether the late news from the Rio Grande is likely to involve an extra session of Congress," asked Robert Winthrop, who as the Speaker of the House presumably would have had a better insight into the schedule of his own chamber than Corcoran did.[26]

Claims Business

The government claims business was among the most lucrative areas in which Corcoran's lobbying ability produced significant results. There were many types of claims, although most involved some combination of land, contracts, and pension rights. Claims against the government were typically decided by individual acts of Congress, usually designated as private relief legislation. Prior to the Civil War, the federal judiciary had little involvement in the redress of claims, and arm-twisting in the halls of the Capitol was the most effective method for achieving a client's objectives. Sometimes persuasion was sufficient. Other times more tangible action was required, such as offering recalcitrant legislators a portion of the claim. Prior to the government's shifting claims to administrative and judicial venues for resolution in the late nineteenth century, Congress decided thousands of claims each year. The results of congressional action could be extremely lucrative for the winning claimants and for Corcoran, who usually took a percentage of the final award as his fee.[27] Lobbyists such as Corcoran, adept at the whispered word at the right time, could also block a client's competitors by helping to divert claims to legislative dead ends. The same was true, of course, for other legislative activities where the banker had a stake.

The claims business kept Corcoran busy well beyond his banking and investment interests. The types of claims for which clients hired him ranged from the settlement of Indian lands to disputed mineral rights, from Mexican-American War claims to military pensions. Fees for coordinating and consolidating claims and for lobbying on behalf of claimants were lucrative, usually involving 10 percent of the claim or more, and it was not uncommon for lobbyists such as Corcoran to take a part interest in land as compensation in those cases where it was a component of the claim.[28] Once again, Corcoran used network allies to pursue his claim targets. As early as 1839 he leveraged his association with the commissioner of Indian affairs, who steered the banker toward the most solid and secure claims in his portfolio, allowing the banker to focus his attention on the strongest cases most likely to be paid out.[29] Combined with his contacts at the Treasury Department, which audited the claims, Corcoran's connections helped him develop and sustain a strong business in lobbying and merchandizing government claims. No surprise, Corcoran was also on excellent terms with the successive chairs of the Senate Claims Committee and the Indian Affairs Committee, which for a time conveniently included Jesse Bright.

Many of Corcoran's important connections also sought his help. At various times, his claims work was requested by such notables as the Blairs from Maryland, a powerful Democratic family with important party connections; Pierre Chouteau, a founder of the city of St. Louis; Treasury Secretary Robert Walker when he was a US senator; and Sen. Thomas Benton and his famous explorer-politician son-in-law, John C. Frémont. Corcoran worked to convince key members of Congress or the administration of the various claims' merits, often provided advances and loans to many claimants, and coordinated the payments when they were resolved on behalf of his clients.[30] Known and trusted by so many Washington, DC, insiders, the banker was often selected as the agent to pay out claims even when he had not been involved in the case. For this, too, he received a fee.

Such involvement often wrapped the banker up in legal disputes and government inquiries.[31] The claims business was notorious for dishonesty and graft, as the politicians and government officials responsible for making the decisions often had significant stakes in the outcome. Frequently all that was necessary to obtain the desired results was a modicum of logrolling and influence from men such as Corcoran to get the claims resolved and paid.[32] But sometimes more effort was required. Prior to the legendary graft and corruption of the Great Barbeque, the antebellum claims business was among the least scrupulous ways to earn a living in the capital. Success depended on ensuring that all interested or useful parties to a claim's disposition gained something tangible from the outcome. Lobbyists such as Corcoran provided favors, payments, loans, or other tangible rewards to dozens of interconnected individuals—all looking for a handout. Thus, in the claims arena, Corcoran was least successful in maintaining his gentlemanly, ethical reputation critical to the period's expectations. Indeed, one associate of Corcoran's, to whom the banker had funneled money for his defense against federal charges of forgery and perjury related to claims in a silver mining case, committed suicide in the courtroom upon hearing the verdict that he would spend ten years at hard labor.[33] Several hundred thousand dollars of the award ended up in the coffers of Corcoran & Riggs. While the incident did not affect the banker's ability to obtain business, Corcoran seems to have reduced his reliance on individual claims matters thereafter—sticking with group claims instead—probably because the risk to his reputation was not worth the remuneration he received.

Corcoran also lobbied extensively for state debt and other credit obligations that needed special legislation to trigger a payout. The banker performed these duties principally on behalf of other clients—businessmen, speculators, members of Congress—but also for his own account. Corcoran helped convince the federal government to assume the debt of Texas as part of the Compromise of 1850.[34] A virtual "who's who" of the capital was involved in the effort, as a raft of politicians either owned a portion of the Texas debt or saw political advantages in having it assumed by the federal government when the security's value plummeted. Henry Clay and Daniel Webster, both Corcoran associates, were proponents, as was John Davis, the former Speaker of the House. Corcoran and George Peabody attempted to purchase a large block of the debt at low rates but only partly succeeded. As the price rose, Corcoran made gifts of the debt obligation—or provided interest-free loans—to friends and politicians such as Davis and Stephen Douglas. Prospects for the federal assumption of the debt became complicated by conditions that Texas insisted be attached to the Pearce Act, the legislation approving the new state's monetary passage into the Union. Texas sought to change the conditions under which holders of the debt would be repaid, a move that would have disadvantaged the debt class owned by Corcoran and his associates. As a result, Corcoran and others with the same debt class attempted to thwart the incoming state's efforts. Treasury Secretary Thomas Corwin, Attorney General Reverdy Johnson, and several other government leaders received loans from or had various obligations waived by the banker in connection with the Texas debt issue. Corwin was an Ohio Whig senator and a governor before becoming treasury secretary. He became a Republican soon after the party was created in the 1850s and, at the height of the secession crisis, proposed a constitutional amendment banning the federal government from interfering with slavery. For his part, Johnson was the defense attorney for the slave owner in the landmark case *Dred Scott v. Sanford* that ruled African Americans were not citizens, but Johnson was personally opposed to slavery and led the fight to prevent his home state of Maryland from seceding during the Civil War.

Corcoran's generosity to Secretary Corwin was a likely response to the secretary's generous praise of Corcoran and his desire to make him the government's Texas agent to handle financial issues. "I have had more opportunity to know Mr. Corcoran than any of the bankers or dealers in stocks in this part of the country. From all I know of that class of men, I would prefer Mr. Corcoran. He is a gentleman in social life, an honest and honorable and highly intelligent man in business affairs. I should trust him to any extent," Corwin explained.[35] Attorney General Johnson was also close to George Peabody and later advised the expatriate banker on philanthropic endeavors. It was hardly surprising, therefore, that the final deal favored Corcoran, Peabody, Corwin, Johnson, and their allies. The persuasive lobbying efforts paid off handsomely with a profit of about 20 percent, although the time and funds tied up to persuade politicians on behalf of the deal chewed into that return.[36] Among the many deals Corcoran helped his clients clinch, the Texas debt episode reveals Corcoran's reach, persuasiveness, and pocketbook in achieving his lobbying ends.[37] Indeed, he rarely lost.

Collins Shipping Line

Another complex lobbying effort involved the Collins Line.[38] Corcoran—on behalf of himself, Elisha Riggs and his son George, members of Congress, and various financiers—helped businessman Edward Collins develop a North Atlantic shipping enterprise. Corcoran probably became involved out of a desire to support his associates, as it is not clear that the banker had a significant stake in the company. Collins was a business partner with Sen. John Slidell's brother, and Corcoran probably supported the project due to his friendship with the senator. Collins, whose family had been involved in the maritime business for years, sought to develop a profitable mail and passenger shipping line between America and Great

Britain, principally to compete with Samuel Cunard's successful transatlantic shipping operations as well as with American shippers such as Cornelius Vanderbilt.[39] Working through Corcoran, Collins sought a federal mail subsidy for his company, claiming the government would be more than repaid by the diversion of postal fees from Great Britain to the United States. In part because of Corcoran, this effort was successful, and on his last day in office, President Tyler signed legislation authorizing the postmaster general to negotiate overseas mail contracts. Over the next few years, Collins won from Congress and the Polk administration a ten-year contract worth $385,000, part of which was paid in advance to subsidize shipbuilding costs.

All went well for Collins at first. The firm established the New York and Liverpool United States Mail Steamship Company, and Collins built several steamships to carry the cross-Atlantic traffic. Some of the best-known investment companies took substantial portions of the securities supporting the venture, many of which had been both allies and competitors to Corcoran, including Brown Brothers & Co. and Matthew Morgan & Co. Collins, Elisha and George Riggs, and George Peabody took the largest positions.[40] Once the venture proved profitable, Collins sought to increase the government's mail subsidy. Yet, upstart competitors, such as the Ebony Line, eyeing similar routes and profits objected to unfair treatment for the Collins Line, and a pitched battle ensued in Congress for government support to the nascent shipping lines. Corcoran's hand can be seen in the vigorous support for the venture chronicled in the *Union*, the principal Democratic newspaper in the capital.[41] Collins sent several well-connected men from New York to help persuade Congress in his favor, an indication of the growing reach and utility of the lobbying business. The new players included William Wetmore, a former clerk of the House, and Benjamin French, a future head of the Public Buildings Office. Corcoran knew both men well. They focused on the House of Representatives, and Corcoran, with greater influence among senators, concentrated on the upper chamber. Not all of Corcoran's usual associates were swayed. Stephen Douglas, typically a strong ally of the banker's in business endeavors, supported the Ebony Line. Collins also had to contend with Cornelius Vanderbilt, who resented the government's attempts to subsidize new competitors to his detriment. Vanderbilt tried to bargain with Collins but to no avail.[42]

The commodore was no match for Collins and his lobbyists; Collins even berthed the sumptuous yacht *Baltic* in the Potomac, the better to entertain wavering legislators.

In the end, persuasion, and probably bribes, achieved the desired results. Congress passed legislation that increased the subsidy to $858,000, nearly three times the original amount, through 1854.[43] A member of the US House, noting that the chamber had approved legislation it had rejected previously, ascribed the change of heart to bribery.[44] Whatever the reason, it was great for Collins. The company did well by all measures, bringing in profits of between 30 percent and 40 percent; Corcoran reported some $600,000 in 1853 alone.[45]

Then in 1854, it all fell apart. One of the Collins's steamship liners, the *Arctic*, with his wife and daughter aboard, sank in a collision, and another ship was lost at sea. An effort to revive the government subsidy succeeded in Congress but was vetoed by President Franklin Pierce.[46] Nervous investors, including the Browns, sought to dump their holdings and demanded payment in cash. Corcoran insisted that insurance payments, the government, and bondholders had the first claim on assets and compelled the Browns, who carried some of the insurance, to buy out his bonds. At the end of the affair, Corcoran may have come out of the Collins fiasco better compensated than anyone else. In 1858 the subsidy expired, and the Collins Line went bankrupt, with the remaining ships sold to pay off debts. Thanks to the government subsidy, Corcoran's colleagues recovered their original investment and received some 7 percent profit for their efforts.[47]

These early lobbying efforts, with their share of speculation and secret financial exchanges aimed at obtaining legislative and administrative favors, demonstrate the increasing power of the lobbyists and influence peddlers, whose sway over the levers of politics grew rapidly after the Civil War.[48] Congress and federal agencies were slow and cumbersome, and the complex development needs of industrial capitalism overwhelmed a structure that still operated on a transactional basis. Largely void of regulatory and bureaucratic efficiency and neutrality, the public sector had difficulty deflecting corruption.[49] From the pursuit of corporate charters to mineral drilling rights, from land and contract claims to railroad rights-of-way, decision points at both the state and federal level were regular targets of intense lobbying efforts; their success brought great wealth and market advantage to a variety of commercial ventures.

Until after the Civil War, few permanent lobbyists were in the capital. As the needs of business expanded, lobbyists such as Sam Ward became fixtures in the capital and made careers in the art of influence peddling. Through a confluence of factors, Corcoran was among the earliest and most successful lobbyists for much of the nineteenth century, and his ability to act as a conduit for all parties behind the scenes cemented his reputation as a notable rainmaker well before the Gilded Age.[50] No one else bestrode the center of American politics and commerce in quite the same way Corcoran did. It explains not only his success as a lobbyist but also his ability later in life to survive in a Northern, increasingly radical Republican capital after the Civil War. Even President Rutherford B. Hayes recognized his influence. Corcoran spent considerable effort and money attempting to defeat Hayes, but the president visited him shortly after his inauguration and appeared at almost all the banker's birthday parties.[51] As he did with Democrats and Whigs before Hayes, Corcoran often joined the Republican president for entertaining excursions in addition to more serious White House conversations. Hayes even asked Corcoran to join him in his private rail car to attend the Maryland state fair.[52] In connecting Corcoran's own good to the public good, Sen. Jesse Bright probably got it right: "God has made but few such gentlemen as Corcoran. He appears anxious to reward genius and merit wherever he finds it and . . . in advancing success he promotes the public good."[53]

Land Speculation

Corcoran's position as a Washington insider and inveterate networker put the banker at the center of mid-nineteenth-century efforts to capitalize on the nation's geographic expansion. Efforts to corner land and railroad rights-of-way all but consumed emerging entrepreneurs, many of whom attempted to leverage the federal government and statehouses. People with sufficient capital and a vision of the nation's future took advantage of its prodigious westward expansion. Early on, Corcoran was one of these men. The banker became a significant investor in western lands and pursued his ventures in the new territories and states in the same fashion he pursued other activities. Corcoran leveraged business and political connections in both the capital and other parts of the country to create a broad array of investment opportunities. Many of the well-connected or wealthy men who joined his land and railroad ventures were already involved with the banker in other financial or political pursuits. Among them were a host of familiar names, including George Riggs, Elisha and Romulus Riggs, Robert Walker, Stephen Douglas, Jesse Bright, John Breckenridge, John Slidell, and August Belmont, among others.[54]

Corcoran was heavily involved in buying, selling, and holding for his own and other accounts a variety of railroad paper as well as state and local bonds in the new territories and states. In the 1850s, for instance, Corcoran held a considerable position in Illinois investments. He owned these bonds in conjunction with Rep. Thomas Bayly of Virginia, an important congressional leader, despite the politician's corrupt reputation and his ownership of approximately thirty Blacks who worked his Accomac County plantation.[55] Indeed, Illinois investments were not only an important part of the banker's portfolio but also of his ties to that state's Sen. Stephen Douglas, also an enslaver with whom Corcoran had substantial connections. Douglas held an account at Corcoran & Riggs from 1846 until his death in 1861, and the banker often made suggestions or advanced funds to help "the little giant" strengthen his portfolio.[56] To that end, Corcoran even held discussions with the Illinois delegation on ways to optimize the state's indebtedness and its impact on railroad bonds.[57] Securities dealers, bankers, and politicians routinely asked Corcoran for his advice regarding the timely issuance and investment value of state railroad debt instruments and for inside information that might guide personal financial decisions.[58]

Corcoran became one of the largest investors in western lands, a significant achievement given the frenzied speculation in America's expansion. In conjunction with others in his network, he purchased large amounts of property throughout the new states and territories. Some of the land was acquired via the claims process, while Corcoran obtained other tracts through bidding processes that likely seemed irregular to some other investors.[59] The banker's strong relationships with the Treasury Department and with Secretary Robert Walker gave him advantages in submitting bids for defaulted federal lands in states such as Texas, Missouri, Michigan, Mississippi, and Illinois.[60] As early as 1839, Corcoran had purchased Illinois property with Amos Kendall and received significant long-term rent from the land. Using his knowledge of the claims business, Corcoran and Romulus Riggs obtained 40,000 acres of military tract land in Illinois that had been set aside for veterans of the War of 1812.[61] Corcoran also owned more than 103,000 acres of other western lands acquired principally through Treasury Department bids, although not all the conveyed lands were free and clear of older claims and titles.[62] He purchased a variety of lots in at least eight rapidly growing cities, including New York City. Corcoran joined with Sen. John Slidell and August Belmont to acquire thousands of acres in Iowa and Wisconsin. He even provided funds to Walker to purchase western lands; the treasury secretary was so successful he boasted to James Buchanan that, in some cases, his investments had increased nearly a hundredfold.[63] During and after the Civil War, some Southern investors associated with the Confederacy, such as Slidell and Breckenridge, found many of their lands and other assets confiscated by northern cities and states.[64] Corcoran ran into similar problems at least once, but it seemed not to deter him. After the war, the banker resumed purchasing western lands and made significant investments in Oregon.[65]

Corcoran also took a leading role in a speculative venture to purchase land and promote the city of Superior, Wisconsin. With the help of Senators Douglas and Breckenridge, among others, he bet on the city as the eastern terminus of the northern transcontinental railroad. The banker supported the shares of Breckenridge, Douglas, Walker, Bright, and several other politicians to push the project forward. Ultimately Duluth supplanted Superior as the principal terminus but not before the venture provided some solid speculative profits to the Corcoran group.[66] It also provided unwanted publicity. The *Detroit Advertiser* complained that the land was owned by rebels or those, like Corcoran, who were in "open sympathy" with the South. That newspaper and others advocated that the government confiscate the property from the group.[67] In 1863 the US marshal for Wisconsin seized some of the property, roughly half the original town of Superior, including land owned by Corcoran.[68] Land also was confiscated from many of the original Corcoran group of investors, including former senator and vice president John Breckenridge and a former governor of South Carolina, William Aiken Jr., who was arrested on disloyalty charges by the secretary of war.[69]

The Politics of Politics

Corcoran routinely mingled business and politics. He provided investment services, including loans and investment advice for presidents, senators, and many other influential politicians. Corcoran's efforts on behalf
of President James Polk are just one example: The banker managed the
president's financial accounts and made investments for him. Polk and
Corcoran presumably both prospered from the arrangement; however, at
one point after Corcoran had invested about $3,000 in government secu-
rities on behalf of the president, Polk decided it was not appropriate for
him to personally profit from such activities. He instructed Corcoran to direct his portfolio elsewhere: "I do not doubt my lawful right to make such
investments, but in view of my official position, I deem it proper to relinquish the stock."[70]

During the same period, Secretary of State James Buchanan regularly
advised the banker about important pending changes in the federal government's financial programs. Corcoran used this inside information for
his own benefit, but in the process, he also refined Buchanan's investment
portfolio to leverage greater gains anticipated from the government's actions.[71] When Buchanan became the US ambassador to the Court of St.
James, Corcoran promised in his absence to handle Buchanan's business
affairs. In return, during Corcoran's European travels in 1855, Buchanan
went to great lengths to have the banker received in elite business and social circles.[72]

The backslapping went both ways, and Corcoran was not shy about en-
listing his associates to maintain and improve his own position when necessary. Many men in Washington, DC, and elsewhere were beholden to
Corcoran for some favor or advice, and they were happy to help pay their
literal or figurative debt by assisting him. When Zachary Taylor's election
in 1849 turned the White House over to the Whigs, some of Taylor's associates sought to remove Corcoran & Riggs as the government's pet bank in
favor of a banker who was a more *reliable* friend to the Whigs (they clearly
didn't know Corcoran). He immediately began a letter-writing campaign
and drafted several important New York bankers and merchants to persuade the new administration to keep the government's banking structure unchanged and Corcoran's favored status intact. Indeed, William
Astor, who became the richest man in America in 1848 upon the death of

his father, John Jacob Astor, was one of many men who wrote on Corcoran's behalf. A leading merchant in the China trade and a large holder of New York real estate, Astor insisted on Corcoran's retention as the government's principal banker. Astor implored the administration to ignore "efforts being made to injure [Corcoran & Riggs. They have] . . . high standing as men and bankers." Astor also recognized Corcoran's efforts to sustain the government's creditworthiness: "Mr. Corcoran has unquestionably done more, much more, than any other private individual to sustain the credit of the government, and he is justly entitled to great praise, and to the thanks of all, for the able and judicious manner in which he managed the business."[73] Corcoran also had members of Congress write to the administration to help demonstrate his value to the government.[74] These efforts had the desired effect: The Taylor administration retained the banker, keeping intact his virtual monopoly in government securities and banking in the capital for years to come.

Electoral Politics

Corcoran, as one of the wealthiest men in America and connected with dozens of current and former Whig and Democratic politicians and the newspaper publishers who supported them, held an unrivaled position to influence electoral politics. As the clouds of sectional conflict gathered in the 1850s, Corcoran supported politicians who were defenders of the Union but sympathetic to the South and the states' right of self-determination.[75] Buchanan, then a Democratic senator from Pennsylvania, fit that description. After the Compromise of 1850, Corcoran gave money to Buchanan for his 1852 presidential campaign.[76] The Baltimore Democratic convention endured forty-nine ballots before the delegates awarded the nomination to Buchanan's rival, Sen. Franklin Pierce of New Hampshire. Pierce easily won against the Whig nominee, Gen. Winfield Scott, a hero of the Mexican-American War and a regular at Corcoran's dinner table. Pierce—like Buchanan, a Northerner who supported states' rights—had a rocky presidency, and his popularity in the North plummeted after he supported the Kansas-Nebraska Act that helped wreck the Missouri Compromise. He also supported the Ostend Manifesto that Southern expansionists, including Robert Walker, hoped would help create more slave territory in

Cuba and elsewhere south of the border. Corcoran's papers do not reveal whether he supported the territorial expansionists who sought more room for slavery to grow, but true to form, he was on cordial terms with Buchanan, Pierce, and Scott. They were all part of his network.

By the time of the 1856 presidential campaign, Corcoran had ostensibly retired from banking and devoted much of his energy and finances to supporting Buchanan's nomination.[77] Working with Senators Slidell and Bright, Corcoran recruited delegates for Buchanan—then serving as the US envoy to Great Britain—even before the ambassador returned to the United States.[78] Bright proved his loyalty to Corcoran and Buchanan by engineering a switch of the entire Indiana delegation, which was previously committed to Senator Douglas of Illinois, to support the Pennsylvanian.[79]

Corcoran's hand was also evident behind the scenes of the Democratic convention. In a remarkably modern approach to electoral politics, he went to Cincinnati several weeks before the convention to work with Buchanan's day-to-day campaign managers and provided political advice, contacts, and financial support to influence delegates. Corcoran paid for delegates' rooms, food, and liquor, and—just before the convention—brought in hundreds of Buchanan supporters to demonstrate in the candidate's favor and to persuade wavering delegates of his popularity.[80] How much Corcoran's efforts were responsible for Buchanan's success is difficult to measure, but after sixteen ballots, Pierce dropped out, throwing the nomination to Buchanan. His election to the presidency several months later was undoubtedly the high point of Corcoran's king-making activities, although he retained influence in Democratic circles for the rest of his life. At nearly eighty years old, Corcoran was a member of the Congressional Democratic Committee and a notable player and contributor in Samuel Tilden's 1876 presidential campaign.[81] Many Democratic-leaning newspapers could also trace their origins to his largesse, including the *Daily Patriot* (Washington, DC). Objections from the opposition decried it "lamentable to see an old man made the mover and tool of a class of unscrupulous destructives who care only for his money."[82]

Some legislators considered Corcoran's expectations on political payback for anointing Buchannan excessive. Senator Douglas complained that Corcoran wanted to exclusively control the incoming administration's political patronage. Many in the party were concerned that Buchanan now owed more political debts than was healthy for an incoming president. On

the other hand, stalwarts such as Millard Fillmore and Edward Everett relied on Corcoran to guide the new president away from party influences
and to "keep him straight."[83] Republican-leaning newspapers, such as the
New York Tribune, were particularly sensitive to the prospect of undue influence. The paper named Corcoran as a confidant of the president's and
a significant influence on potential cabinet choices. The *Tribune* also accused Robert Walker of being too close to Corcoran to become secretary
of state.[84] Whether this criticism had an impact on Buchanan's choices or
not, Walker did not get the job. Friends and associates also encouraged
Corcoran to ensure that Buchannan was sensitive to their own personal
and professional concerns. "I am relying upon you to see that my absence
from [Washington] does not prejudice my interests . . . with Mr. B.," wrote
Senator Bright.[85]

If anyone could watch over Buchanan by proximity alone, Corcoran
could. They were sufficiently close by the beginning of his presidency
that Buchanan often stayed in Corcoran's mansion. The banker lent him
servants, a cook, and a coach and driver during his stays in the capital.
Buchanan even lodged with Corcoran prior to his inauguration instead of
the traditional suite at the Willard Hotel. At midnight on March 3, 1857, the
night before the inauguration, a band played "Hail to the Chief" outside
Corcoran's mansion until the president-elect appeared at the window to
acknowledge the musicians.[86] While the friendship between the two men
became strained during Buchanan's presidency due to his policies over the
South's imminent secession, clearly Buchanan preferred the society of the
banker to that which was forced upon him by his presidential duties. Before their relationship soured, Buchanan relied heavily on Corcoran for advice and comfort. "I will call to see you at 9 this evening. I have had a very
worrying day," he wrote the banker in one instance.[87] No record reveals
whether the pair were on intimate terms, although Buchanan has often
been referred to as the nation's first gay president.[88]

Growing tension over sectional disputes ended the longtime friendship
between Corcoran and Buchanan; they appear to have stopped talking or
corresponding once secession began in earnest. Corcoran, as with many
Democratic faithful, was furious about the party's fracturing into Northern
and Southern wings, and he principally blamed Senator Douglas. Douglas
had been the main driver behind the Kansas-Nebraska Act that eviscerated
the Missouri Compromise, and his stance at the Democratic conventions

in 1856 and 1860 further undermined party cohesion. Since he supported states' rights, Corcoran decided to back the Southern wing of the party and rejected Douglas and the party's Northern wing. The conflict required many people, Corcoran among them, to make tough choices. Nevertheless, Corcoran's principles predominated, and the banker threw his influence and money behind the political aspirations of Buchanan's vice president, John Breckenridge of Kentucky, who was also part of his network. Gossip of the time whispered that Douglas's defeat came at the hands of Corcoran, who spent upward of $1 million at the Charleston convention to sway delegates.[89] Corcoran's former banking partner, George Riggs, became Breckenridge's national campaign treasurer.[90]

After Lincoln was elected president, many Democrats believed the cause of states' rights would suffer, and Southerners increasingly talked of secession. When Buchanan in the closing months of his term failed to meet the South's demands and thereby defuse the conflict—despite what many Northerners saw as his undue leniency toward the South— Corcoran, along with many others, broke with the president.

The Civil War meant that the days of Corcoran's unrivaled network and capital mastery were ending—at least for a time. The conflict tore much of the country apart, and Corcoran's usual ability to influence all parties behind the scenes or to act as a powerbroker became increasingly difficult. With Lincoln and the Republicans in power and the conflict in full swing, Corcoran's customary access would be diminished—but not destroyed.

5

CULTURE AND
COMMUNITY

THE NATIONAL MALL, THE WASHINGTON MONUMENT, THE US
Capitol, the White House and Lafayette Square, the Corcoran Gallery of
Art, the Oak Hill Cemetery—Corcoran influenced all of them and more.
Indeed, without the philanthropist's vision and entrepreneurial enthusiasm in the mid-nineteenth-century capital, some of our most recognizable national heritage, symbols, and iconography would either be absent
or, at least, different today.

Corcoran helped develop and lead American urban culture at an important juncture in the nineteenth century amid the contours of an expanding capital. In doing so, Corcoran helped shape a cosmopolitan construct
in which wealth and position, traditions, and loyalties were not the sole
transmitters of elite acceptance and identity. In early America, White privilege was conveyed mainly by accumulated wealth and family pedigree in
townships and urban centers such as Philadelphia, Boston, New York, and
Charleston. Yet, Washington, DC, presented a new vision and emerging
national experiment, and except for the nearby Georgetown gentry, there
was little social structure around which the elite at first cohered. Beyond
the city's newness, notions of traditional deference and elite comport-
ment were further scrambled by universal White male suffrage, in which
men of limited means gained equal political standing with the wealthy—
and could even hold political office.[1]

The absorption of new elements into the existing elite, a factor in
Gilded Age social dynamics, occurred in the capital earlier than in other
urban centers. The capital city witnessed the coalescence of a privileged

bourgeoisie in this period, in part defined by Corcoran's influence. Corcoran in the mid-nineteenth century gained prominence as a purveyor of American culture. Through the leverage and opportunities provided by his wealth and the influence of his ideas and interests, the banker helped bring to the nation's capital a level of sophistication and modernity that likely would have developed more slowly absent his dedication to the city's refinement and improvement. Corcoran helped summon this elite coherence before such efforts were commonplace in other urban centers. By encouraging refinement in the arts and in the social graces of gastronomy and entertainment, and engagement in urban development, public beautification, architecture, patriotism, education, and poor relief, as well as other areas, Corcoran helped form the outlines and aspirations of a modern elite that would not fully mature in most cities for a generation.[2]

Corcoran was not the only one among his peers who acted as a guide for important social and cultural developments in the capital. Other influential city residents in the mid-nineteenth century—and other urban centers—also championed civic progress. Corcoran often found ready partners willing to join him in urban refinement efforts, but his leadership and signal contributions made a significant difference in many cases. His privilege and dedication alone do not account for the contributions the banker made to an impressive number of areas, and few of his contemporaries in this era left comparable legacies in the scope of their activities and achievements.

More than 150 years ago, Corcoran helped build an American capital that we still recognize today. "Bourgeoisie" is a term the elite of that era would not have recognized or applied to themselves, but they understood the distinction of their identity: They were the vanguard of an economic, political, and cultural awakening in the nation's growing cities.[3] More than simply White, rich, or powerful, the bourgeoisie through their behavior and influence built institutions, organizations, and cultural structures that resulted in monumental architecture, parks, orchestras and museums, libraries, charity organizations, and a host of other elements of American public life that remain as part of the nation's social and cultural construction. The elite formed common bonds to achieve objectives that helped remake and refine the built and social environment to reflect their values and improve cities according to their views and expectations.[4]

People such as Corcoran served as cultural mediators and advanced Americans' interaction with expressions of refinement that—especially in venues such as parks—were often accessible to all.

Elites acted similarly in most urban centers, such as New York, Chicago, and San Francisco; the pattern is largely the same in Washington, DC, as well.[5] With a social and political structure in the capital that from the start accommodated a transient population, a local elite still emerged that took particular interest in the city's development and in its social and cultural institutions.[6] America's national elite, including founders such as George Washington and Thomas Jefferson, encouraged the real estate prospects of the city and planned for a capital that mirrored Paris.[7] However, until after the Civil War, the individuals most associated with improvements to the nation's capital tended to be part of the local establishment.[8] Men who owned large tracts of land, such as John Van Ness, and bankers such as Corcoran and Riggs, along with some wealthy doctors and lawyers—rather than incoming politicians—often swayed the direction of the physical and cultural development in the capital. Their interest in the city derived from their status as permanent residents rather than their political dominance. As in other cities, the Washington elite created socially exclusive neighborhoods and new institutions for the arts, music, education, and sciences. In Boston, Beacon Hill evolved as the center of the mercantile elite; Rittenhouse Square appealed to the same class in Philadelphia; and Union Square and lower Fifth Avenue in New York were the center of that city's financial and commercial elite. Lafayette Square, a former cherry orchard, became the most fashionable area in the capital city, and Corcoran's mansion, and the homes that he built and rented to some of Washington's most influential people, were right in the middle of it.[9]

Philanthropic Impulse

Few people exemplify the philanthropic creed more than Andrew Carnegie, the Gilded Age steel tycoon who became one of the greatest benefactors in American history. Carnegie gave hundreds of millions of dollars to the arts, education, and libraries, which symbolized the positive civic good capable from the extraordinary wealth prevalent in industrial capitalism.[10]

While more generous than some, Carnegie was not alone in his efforts to better the society around him. Leveraging vast amounts of money unfathomable to their mercantile predecessors, industrial magnates and wealthy financiers such as Carnegie, Henry Ford, John D. Rockefeller, and J. P. Morgan dispensed fortunes to a variety of causes. Whether they engaged in these activities to enhance their reputation and erase the stigma of capitalism's ugly side is a matter of debate. Still, their munificence aided specific endeavors designed to improve American life in various venues and spawned a new field of not-for-profit enterprises devoted to charitable giving.[11] The modern era of philanthropy traces its beginnings to the large fortunes amassed during the Gilded Age. The philanthropic impulse in this period explains how large-money foundations and other charity enterprises arose during the development of the Progressive Era's civil society. In turn, this activism presaged the role of the public sector and the federal government in supporting social needs and the recognition that societal concerns often had outgrown local communities or the nonprofit sector's ability to support them.[12]

Elite concern with the poor and disadvantaged represented a long tradition of American community obligation.[13] This tradition stressed modest financial contributions and voluntary actions from a wide swath of the community to assist those in need; the wealthy were expected to give their share and lead the endeavors as a model to others. The extraordinary gifts of the Gilded Age magnates and the modern era's public sector assistance were off in the future.[14] Yet, some philanthropists, including Corcoran, recognized unfulfilled needs and sought to broaden the contributions of charities to solving social problems. Corcoran the benefactor effectively expanded the notion of local charity by attempting to find more encompassing and direct responses designed to ease poverty and suffering.[15] To be sure, Corcoran was in some ways a classic, self-conscious benefactor in the nineteenth-century mold. Like many upper- and even middle-class individuals, he felt obligated to support those less fortunate, such as orphans and the poor. He provided firewood to help warm Georgetown's destitute in winter and funds to feed them throughout the year. Corcoran rebuilt the capital's orphanage, gave it land, and helped create a new facility to house the residents and support their care.[16] Such efforts were common among the socially conscious elite in most urban centers of the nation in the mid-nineteenth century; this largesse would become better organized as part of the social gospel movement a few decades later.

Much of Corcoran's assistance to poor relief and other charitable efforts fits in this traditional mold. Some of his other philanthropic activities reveal a more modern style. The benefactor was perhaps a generation ahead of his time in targeting large sums to worthy projects in the arts, religion, and education. Some projects were local, but many had a broader trajectory and influence, advancing both the traditional, community-centered approach to assistance as well as modern institutional endeavors that anticipated more complex arrangements. Yet, even as he broadened from community to regional or national projects, Corcoran did not embrace the more organizational and bureaucratic approach that developed after the Civil War, preferring to use the networked, entrepreneurial style with which he was more comfortable.[17] Benefactors who fit this mold typically embraced egalitarian ideals, religious freedom, civic virtue, and entrepreneurial activism—the sum of which furthered a philanthropic creed emphasizing the importance of individual Americans' contributions in charitable causes.[18]

Some of Corcoran's activities had little in common with the typical charity of the era. In addition to funding poor relief, education, and the arts, which were common and expected outlets for elite expression, Corcoran championed a variety of infrastructure projects that did not fit the mold. He used his funds, resources, and connections to help build the Washington Aqueduct, several roads, public gardens, monuments, and cemeteries, among other contributions.[19] Moreover, the banker's concern for the war-torn condition of the South after the Civil War led him to donate resources to a variety of relief and improvement projects on a regional scale. In this way, Corcoran acted more like a modern nonprofit organization that targets the Appalachian poor, agricultural migrants, and so on, rather than operating in the localized manner of the period. Corcoran's vision encompassed a broad mission to rebuild and improve the South through relief projects, education, and infrastructure assistance in places ranging from Richmond, Virginia, to Charleston, South Carolina, and a variety of small towns in between. In this way, Corcoran articulated a model of good works with both old-style and modern characteristics that showed what was possible for the nonprofits and government programs that followed.[20]

Corcoran's Philanthropic Vision

Corcoran rarely left a record explaining the choices for his charity. Some, such as landscaping, likely sprang from his sincere interest in and avocation of horticulture. Others, including art, were educational and uplifting in nature, and they hinted at a posture of privilege and patrimony. Nevertheless, Corcoran's support of the capital city in which he spent most of his life grew as he gained wealth, prestige, and influence. During the middle of the nineteenth century, few other people had such a broad impact on Washington, DC, and his effort to improve the capital was a remarkable early model of urban development. His interest in landscaping the White House and Capitol grounds, and the public expanse that would become the National Mall, predated similar plans for New York's Central Park, typically identified as the first planned urban park in a major American city.[21] His support of American art, promising artists, and a rising cadre of American architects contributed to a structural and cultural foundation that others later built upon. A cavalcade of public works, such as roads, waterworks, schools, meetinghouses, churches, orphanages, and other projects, resulted from his vision and checkbook. Few Americans of his own era or thereafter appear to have provided charity and endowment to such a range of institutions. Lesser known are the similar good works he provided on an individual basis to an untold number of people in need; most of the recipients were known only to him.

While most of Corcoran's philanthropy came after his Civil War exile, he also made significant contributions before the war—even before he became wealthy. In 1834 Corcoran led a group of local citizens interested in building a theater. They purchased a site on Pennsylvania Avenue at E Street and built a Greek revival structure that opened in 1835 as the National Theater. Completed just in time for President Polk's inauguration, it held a grand ball in his honor. Shortly thereafter, it was consumed in a fire that destroyed most of the block. Indeed, it was not a lucky location, as four subsequent theater buildings were also destroyed by fire on that spot.[22] In 1843, while still building his banking firm, Corcoran helped raise money for a new high school for boys in the capital. The school's other benefactors included several influential men with whom Corcoran would have a lifelong association, such as James Buchanan and Robert Walker.[23]

For many years, Corcoran dispensed benefactions large and small. The banker donated money to churches and provided loans to houses of worship—including St. John's, Congress Street Methodist, and Trinity Episcopal Churches, and the Church of the Ascension and Saint Agnes—that he never collected.[24] He donated start-up money to the Agricultural College of Maryland. He purchased deeds to forfeited land and presented them to the defaulter as paid. On laying the cornerstone for Washington's new Church of the Ascension, the Reverend Dr. John Elliott offered thanks to Corcoran with unrestrained praise: "Need I repeat his name in Washington, need I repeat it in America or where the Atlantic breaks upon the continent? Go listen to the widow's prayer and you will hear it and the orphan boy, he has heard it."[25] After the Civil War, Corcoran also gave large sums to Southern churches. He donated thirty-six thousand acres of Texas land to the Episcopal Church in that state and eleven thousand acres for similar purposes in Mississippi.[26] Corcoran also gave $10,000 in bonds and Virginia lands to the theological seminary associated with the Episcopal Church.[27]

In 1848 Corcoran gave $10,000 to the poor of Georgetown, his hometown, and made regular gifts to support the fund thereafter. His charity was remarkably diverse: Donations ranged from funds provided for a priest to visit his native Ireland to an organ donated to the Western Lunatic Asylum in Staunton, Virginia.[28] Corcoran subsidized the publication of a treatise on art by the head of Columbian College. Every January, he commemorated the New Year by giving each clerk at Corcoran & Riggs $5,000. Even while residing in France during the Civil War, Corcoran in 1865 provided land and funds for the Washington City Orphan Asylum; he had previously donated sufficient funds so that the orphanage and the city did not have to ask Congress for money.[29] Corcoran made these generous contributions after he and Mayor John Walker Maury first battled with a reluctant Congress to provide funds. Maury and Corcoran also were early supporters and lobbyists on behalf of the Washington Aqueduct, and the two arm-twisted Congress into providing funds for a local insane asylum, the predecessor to St. Elizabeths Hospital. Maury and Corcoran were associated through the Metropolitan Bank, of which Maury became president when John Van Ness died (even if, as reported, Corcoran had a hand in the bank's eventual demise). Maury owned six people, whom his wife manumitted after he died at the young age of forty-six.

Over the years, Corcoran made substantial gifts of money, land, and buildings to Columbian College (later George Washington University), and he served for a period as the president of its board of trustees.[30] He also provided funds to the University of Virginia, the College of William and Mary, the Virginia Military Institute, and the college that became Washington and Lee University.[31] Corcoran also provided $160,000 to establish a commercial market for the Washington, DC, community.

The banker's charity increased along with his wealth, and by the late-1840s (when the government war loan business was booming), his reputation as a benefactor was already well known. Newspapers at the time were ebullient in noting Corcoran's contributions. The *Georgetown Courier* wrote: "There seems to be no limit to the judicious benevolence of Mr. Corcoran."[32] Other wealthy men also took notice. George Peabody, himself recognized as one of the major benefactors of the nineteenth century, wrote Corcoran: "I cannot keep pace with your noble acts of charity; but one of these days I mean to come out, and then if my feelings regarding money don't change and I have plenty, I shall become a strong competitor of yours in benevolence."[33]

Equally notable was Corcoran's reputation of giving funds not just to institutions but also to individuals in need. He provided monthly stipends to numerous individuals who depended on his charity for their living expenses.[34] Corcoran regularly provided money in the capital and many other places to ensure the poor had wood and coal for winter heating. He provided significant sums to support Hungarians who fled that country's 1848 revolution and financed the trip for more than a dozen immigrants to join their relatives in the western United States. "You acted nobly by the Hungarians," George Peabody wrote Corcoran once the gift became common knowledge.[35]

By some accounts, Corcoran spent $5 million annually on charity and philanthropy, a tremendous sum for the period; suggestions are that he ultimately gave away three-quarters of his wealth.[36] Indeed, Corcoran's reputation for charity was so well known that a swindler sought to bilk unsuspecting people out of money while using a fake letter of introduction from the philanthropist.[37] While Corcoran is well remembered for his beneficence to organizations, especially the ones he established himself, he is less remembered for his assistance to ordinary individuals. In his own day, however, the recognition of his charity and its frequent anonymity were apparent throughout the city—even the country. One newspaper, the *New York Daybook*, described how a group of youths who had been mischievously destroying a fence outside Corcoran's home stopped their vandalism and rebuilt it on the spot when one of them realized that the owner was the well-known philanthropist. "Many deeds which we are not permitted to make known show the gentleman in an honorable and enviable light," the *Daybook* wrote.[38]

By the time of his death, Corcoran was receiving nearly a hundred requests every day for assistance.[39] To deal with the crush of inquiries, Corcoran created a preprinted form to politely refuse most requests. "In reply to your communication," the form read, "I beg to state that applications for relief from pecuniary embarrassment have become so numerous that the mere acknowledgement of their reception would occupy a considerable portion of my time. In the exercise of a necessary discrimination, I have endeavored to meet, as far as practicable, these multiplied demands; but have ultimately reached a limit which a due regard to my own interests and conscience will not let me exceed."[40] Over time, Corcoran was forced to discontinue his regular strolls around town to avoid being stalked by overzealous supplicants. As one observer wrote: "I could fill a column with his deeds and benevolence to individuals unsolicited and performed so quietly and gracefully as to have only been known to the recipients."[41]

Corcoran attended to the needs of individuals not just in the capital but also in other places burdened by hardship. As the *Richmond Dispatch* noted in describing his beneficence after the Civil War, "This reminds me of a number of personal good offices done by this kind man to quite a number of parties whose misfortunes were shipwrecked by the war. They were mentioned to me by a friend, himself a beneficiary."[42] The breadth of his charity to individuals was not just unusual but spanned races and classes, and often was quite personal in nature.[43] As the *Boston Journal* wrote after the war, Corcoran "has ever been a free giver to the destitute and has supported a large number of persons both white and black, many of whom he used to know in their better days."[44] Another newspaper remarked that Corcoran helped build churches in the African American community and contributed to minorities' charities, but such acts were not well recorded.[45] This generosity may be why a committee of prominent African Americans apologized to Corcoran for insulting remarks civil rights leader Frederick Douglass once directed toward the philanthropist.[46] If anything, the extent and breadth of Corcoran's generosity only expanded in the aftermath of the Civil War, as the benefactor sought to help and heal the country, its people, and its institutions.

The Growing Capital

The capital Corcoran knew as a young man was transformed by the needs of commerce, population growth, and nation building by the mid-nineteenth century. Starting as a rudimentary outpost with primitive comforts and graces, Washington, DC, evolved, in part due to Corcoran, into a modern, sophisticated city. While the capital never became what the founding fathers and its French city planner fully envisioned, neither did it remain the backwater that foreign visitors had often denigrated.

Even as the grizzly bears that Meriwether Lewis brought home from his western expedition graced the White House lawn in cages and bison roamed the future National Mall, the capital slowly took familiar form. Washington began to prosper from the start, and it grew rapidly as the ashes cooled from the British Army's burning of the city's public buildings in 1814. The Treasury Department in the first years of the new capital reported higher internal revenue duties paid in the city than from the combination of several states.[47] As military purchases increased in response to the war, new banks opened, and the US Navy employed local men to construct war ships. The strong economy continued after the war ended, and the capital's leading citizens built a large brick building as a temporary meeting place for Congress. Indeed, the burning of the public buildings by the British served as a catalyst to improve the city and expand it, and foreign visitors observed a city rising from the ashes, increasing in prosperity.[48] Starting with the rebuilding of the Capitol and the White House, Congress also provided money for a variety of other public projects, including the US Botanic Garden at the foot of Capitol Hill.[49]

As a pillar in the community representing the established roots of Georgetown society and the city fathers of the new capital, Corcoran was in a unique position to influence the growing city's development. Public infrastructure was an important element of this expansion. As noted previously, among the critical endeavors he supported, Corcoran helped persuade Congress to build a new water system for the capital. The city's antebellum water supply was thought to be inadequate and unhealthy. Congress recognized the need for a better water supply after a fire in 1851 destroyed part of the Capitol that housed the Library of Congress.[50] Congress directed the War Department to develop a new water supply for the capital, and Montgomery C. Meigs, a young army lieutenant, was selected to lead the design.

This project was the first of many that Meigs would oversee in the capital; over several decades, he exerted considerable influence on the capital's infrastructure. Meigs has been called the most connected, influential engineer ever seen in Washington, DC, but he often failed in obtaining a consistent flow of funds for important projects.[51] As the capital could hardly function without a safe, reliable water system, Meigs was successful in getting initial appropriations for the aqueduct, but he was often forced to rely on Corcoran and others to maintain steady legislative support.[52]

A grand celebration was held in 1853 to kick off the project. Luminaries ranging from President Franklin Pierce and Secretary of War Jefferson Davis to the mayors of Washington and Georgetown were ferried by steam packet to Great Falls, the location of the headwaters supplying the capital.[53] Although Meigs, with Maury and Corcoran's help, got the aqueduct flowing, the project still had dry spells. Congress's short attention span was a perennial problem. Despite the on-again, off-again character of its construction, the Washington Aqueduct was long considered one of the most successful infrastructure projects in antebellum America and typically rated as second only to the Croton Reservoir project in New York City.[54]

Washington Landscapes

Besides the aqueduct, Corcoran also helped effect changes in the city's urban design by improving streets, lighting, and landscaping. The National Mall would eventually become one of the most recognized vistas in the world, but in the 1840s, the area was often impassable and dangerous. Corcoran was largely responsible for getting the project to develop it underway. After discussions with city fathers, landscapers, and politicians, Corcoran convinced President Millard Fillmore to upgrade, illuminate, and landscape the White House grounds, significant portions of the

Mall, and the Capitol grounds. Corcoran was joined in this effort by Smithsonian secretary Joseph Henry, who focused on the area around the new Smithsonian Castle in the center of the Mall, and Walter Lenox, the city's mayor.[55] At the request of the president, the three men formed a commission, helped draw up project plans, and selected a landscape architect. Corcoran helped Henry plan and beautify the area adjacent to the castle and saw to it that some two hundred to three hundred trees, including rare varieties that he selected and purchased with his own funds, were planted as part of the effort. Congress allocated funds to protect the area with a fence, a common practice for lands in major urban areas that were designated as public grounds. The fence also had the practical advantage of corralling the bison that roamed the Smithsonian's parcel of the Mall.[56]

Corcoran was considered the driving force behind the Mall project. He used his influence to secure funds from Congress and recruited leading landscapers. Again digging into his own pocket, Corcoran persuaded America's premier landscape architect, Andrew Jackson Downing, to manage the project.[57] Commissioner of Public Buildings Ignatius Mudd noted that it was at the behest of "several prominent gentlemen of this city" that the president asked Downing to design the project.[58] Newspapers of the time were more explicit. "From the beginning Mr. Corcoran has taken the deepest interest in this work and . . . it was mainly through his personal solicitation that Mr. Downing was persuaded to undertake it," wrote the *New York Evening Post*. "It could not be in better hands."[59]

Corcoran had already recruited Downing to create the gardens of his Lafayette Square mansion in 1849, and he probably discussed the Mall project with him at that time.[60] Downing was enthusiastic about the prospects for the Mall and planned a series of winding paths, separate gardens, small lakes, and other naturalistic elements to beautify the still rustic capital and serve as a Victorian model for American landscape development.[61] Indeed, Mudd was as enthusiastic about the project as Corcoran, Henry, and Downing were, and the public buildings commissioner supported their concept of one continuous green space stretching from the Capitol to the then-unfinished Washington Monument. "These [land parcels] are so situated, and so connected with each other, that they present an extensive landscape, and when viewed from a favorable point, cannot fail to strike the observer as the most beautiful and interesting feature of the federal metropolis," he wrote.[62] The project was almost complete when disaster struck: Mudd died suddenly in 1851, and Downing drowned in a steamboat accident in 1852 with his vision unfinished.

Despite the tragedy, the project moved forward. Downing's protégé, B. F. Saul, was appointed the famous landscaper's successor. Corcoran had his hand in the selection, as he was already supporting the young aspirant with horticultural commissions. Saul's work in the next few years was well received, as John Blake, a subsequent commissioner of public buildings, in 1857 noted that "the work for the continuing improvement of the Mall is now progressing rapidly . . . and will doubtless add very much to the appearance of the Mall, which is destined to be one of the most interesting features in the plan of the city."[63] Nonetheless, part of Downing's vision was never realized. While Downing had hoped to create a harmonious, uninterrupted park, the design was altered to include buildings and roadways that cut the greenway for better access across the city; otherwise, the original plan remained the same. Enough of the project was complete by 1859 that *Harper's New Monthly Magazine* extolled the Mall's promise:

> During the fierce heat of summer, it is pleasant to see the large concourse of people which pours into the Capitol Grounds or those around the President's Mansion sitting under the shade of the trees while the Marine Band furnishes the choicest of music; and it requires no poetic enthusiasm to picture the coming day when the Mall stretching from the Capitol to the margin of the noble Potomac shall be one continuous shade, covered with glorious foliage, and vocal with the rippling of fountains and the song of birds.[64]

As an avid horticulturalist, Corcoran often selected and purchased the rare trees and shrubs from around the world that graced his projects. Working with Downing, then with Saul, Corcoran suggested new styles and specimens of horticulture for the Mall, the White House and Capitol grounds, Lafayette Square, his own gardens across from the square, and his country estate just outside the city limits.[65] While many of the specimens Corcoran obtained from around the world died or were destroyed over the years, some remain. The banker was strongly committed to improving the landscape in and around the capital. After Downing died, he provided Saul work space and financial help. He supported the gardener for many years, offering commissions for landscape designs for his homes and public spaces. He even gave Saul a generous corner of his S Street property on which the botanist established one of the earliest successful greenhouse and nursery operations in the country.[66]

In 1857 despite the steady lurch toward Civil War, Corcoran also was largely responsible for establishing the American Horticultural Society, of which he became president. Corcoran even attended the American Agricultural Society congress in 1862 during the Civil War; he was named in the original congressional charter of the society and was the vice president of the organization.[67]

Oak Hill

Corcoran clearly admired the Victorian landscape sensibility and appeal of naturalistic settings and buffers in urban environments. This likely led to his interest in cemeteries. Corcoran purchased and developed the land to create several cemeteries in the nation's capital. The best known was Oak Hill, created from "Parrott's Woods," a vacant Georgetown plot that Corcoran purchased for $3,500 in the late 1840s.[68] He put more than $50,000 worth of improvements into the property and established Oak Hill as one of the earliest examples of America's natural cemetery movement that placed the deceased in parklike settings rather than in rows of churchyard headstones.[69] This was no random aesthetic development but a reaction to increasing concern about urban health and city sanitation problems. Fearful of the unhealthy atmosphere thought to exist in dense, inner-city burial grounds, some European cities as early as the 1810s created expansive cemeteries in country settings or, at the least, away from dense urban areas. In 1831 the city of Boston created Mount Auburn Cemetery on seventy-two acres along the Charles River, becoming the first American example of the natural cemetery movement that gained popularity over time.[70]

To create his vision for Oak Hill, Corcoran relied on architect James Renwick, who designed a small, intimate chapel for the sylvan property. The chapel was the very antithesis of Renwick's most famous religious structure, St. Patrick's Cathedral in Manhattan. The Oak Hill Chapel was designed in Gothic style and influenced by the work of English architect Augustus Pugin. The fence was copied from the enclosure surrounding Mount Auburn Cemetery, and the gateposts are copies of the same feature designed by Renwick for the entrance to the Smithsonian Castle, which he also built.[71] Renwick designed the cemetery gatehouse as well, and Corcoran personally imported rare plantings from Australia to the Amazon to adorn the cemetery grounds. One observer compared the cemetery positively to Mount Auburn, Green-Wood, and similar contemporary sites, insisting Oak Hill "outstrips them all."[72] The *National Intelligencer* suggested it "was not surpassed by any other cemetery in the country."[73]

Oak Hill covered many acres of prime Georgetown real estate that had been rolling hills, farms, and orchards, but the location was still not far enough away from the population center to suit at least one physician who protested its development. Georgetown doctor Louis Mackall opposed the new cemetery, citing Oak Hill's anticipated "deleterious air" and "putrid effluvia" as likely dangers to residents. Mackall at some point must have overcome his initial misgivings, as he was buried in Oak Hill in 1876.[74] Corcoran apparently held no grudge against him.

Corcoran and his family were buried at Oak Hill, along with other notables, including Secretary of War Edwin Stanton and John Nicolay, Lincoln's personal secretary.[75] Corcoran's mausoleum of Italian marble was designed by Thomas U. Walter, the architect of the Capitol (who had previously designed the banker's famous Moorish dining room), and included a cherub with a finger pointing upward to the flight of the departed spirit, a common Victorian funerary tribute.[76] The tomb was situated on the highest point of land in the cemetery, itself upon the highest point of land in Georgetown. In a letter provided to the cemetery's board of managers after his death, but dated April 24, 1871, Corcoran wrote of his love for this special place:

> In my own individual case, many circumstances concur to invest this spot with a peculiar and melancholy interest. It is contiguous to the town that gave me birth . . . its hills were the playgrounds of my childhood, that pure uncalculating season to which, in the conflict with the stern realities of life, memory so often and so fondly reverts. Beneath its shades lies some of the companions of my youthful days; and others, with whom in riper years I had contracted friendships that death alone dissolved.[77]

In a rare emotional revelation committed to the record, Corcoran also wrote about friends and loved ones buried at Oak Hill and fondly recalled his wife Louise: "Here repose the relics of one, sacred to the tenderest, purest feelings of my heart, whose presence threw an ever cheery light around me."[78] Even in matters of death, Corcoran's networks mattered: Oak Hill Cemetery was the final resting place of Treasury Secretary Robert Walker and Smithsonian secretary Joseph Henry, as well as the temporary resting place of others, including the sons of Jefferson Davis and Abraham Lincoln. Lincoln's son Willie was buried at Oak Hill and later laid to rest in Springfield, Illinois, along with his father after the president's assassination.[79]

For years after Oak Hill was established, Corcoran remained engaged and committed to the original vision of his benefaction. He was upset to learn that the cemetery's superintendent and his associates had likely received kickbacks from stonemasons and that the account books were a mess. New directors were installed, the superintendent was chastised, and Corcoran was lauded for his contributions.[80] Still, the benefactor remained concerned about the aesthetics of the cemetery and implored the board of managers to remain faithful to his original vision of a landscaped sylvan refuge. Corcoran was concerned about the numerous burial plots that increasingly covered the acreage. He insisted that the ban on headstones be adhered to, that no interments be placed within a hundred yards of the streets, that no enclosures should encircle the lots, and that nothing but foliage be visible from the approaches and the streets. "[T]he whole history of my connection with the Cemetery, from the original establishment to the present hour, precludes the supposition that I could advocate the adoption of any course, detrimental to its interests," he wrote to the managers.[81]

At times, the respect and deference usually accorded to Corcoran in his philanthropic endeavors was challenged by others' efforts to control the cemetery's development.[82] Corcoran established Oak Hill as a gift to the city of Georgetown, and it embodied the Southern legacy of that city. Most of the men and women who found perpetual repose at Oak Hill were Corcoran's friends and relatives, or members of the Southern-leaning political and social elite. Northerners typically found final peace in Rock Creek Cemetery. A dispute among lot holders and managers at Oak Hill revealed the decline of deference and showed that the nation's sectional conflict remained unresolved in many places, including a Georgetown cemetery. By the end of the Civil War, Corcoran's beloved cemetery had taken on a decidedly Northern cast. Numerous monuments to Union soldiers dotted the sylvan lots, unsettlingly close to his own family plots. Of umbrage was a monument just several feet away from the Corcoran plot memorializing Lt. John Rogers Meigs of the Union army; his image in uniform was carved to show him fallen in battle.[83] Meigs was the son of Brig. Gen. Montgomery Meigs, Corcoran's onetime ally on various public works projects. To reaffirm his vision, Corcoran took back control of the cemetery and its board of managers—despite the increasing presence of Northerners and Grant administration acolytes on the board. It was not easy. Only after a heated showdown, including an unruly lot holder screaming in Corcoran's face and Corcoran's nephew threatening to use his cane against the man, was the original order restored.[84] Today, Corcoran's vision remains surprisingly intact, as Oak Hill continues to be a sylvan respite amid a changed and congested capital.

Corcoran retained an interest and influence in important urban landscaping projects throughout his life. Forty years after Oak Hill, the Mall, and similar projects, Corcoran was among the first city fathers to advocate draining the Potomac flats and creating Rock Creek Park. Even in his final years, he could be found at the city commissioners' office discussing park plans or pursuing the subject with President Hayes.[85] Park proponents viewed the green swath of land as an essential barrier to urban sprawl and a natural buffer to ensure the safety of the capital's water supply. Its 1,754 acres were a significant piece of undeveloped real estate and brought Corcoran and other supporters into conflict with city developers.[86] The main credit for championing Rock Creek goes not to Corcoran but to Charles Glover, which is only fitting. At the end of the nineteenth century, after the deaths of Corcoran and Riggs, Glover became the president of Riggs Bank and the chairman of the board of trustees for the Corcoran Gallery of Art. Efforts to create this major park began in 1866 and culminated in 1890, when Congress established Rock Creek Park. Even in death, Corcoran's networks still endured.

Corcoran's Real Estate

In addition to parks and cemeteries, Corcoran had significant influence on the capital's built environment. Corcoran became Washington's largest property owner in the period just before the Civil War, and he kept that distinction, despite the war and his European exile, for many years. He owned large swaths of land at the city's outskirts and anticipated the direction of Washington's growth. Corcoran owned entire blocks of property in the heart of the capital on which he built office buildings, hotels, and other structures, including warehouses, greenhouses, and inns.[87]

Corcoran was among the first elite leaders in America to encourage and sponsor a wide variety of architects and architectural styles. In fostering architectural expression, he replicated his successful support for various artists and art forms that broadened the horizons of taste and accessibility. Corcoran sponsored architectural projects from at least a dozen well-known or emerging architects—a precursor to the bourgeois practice decades later of expressing wealth and style by championing a genre of artistic or cultural taste. Corcoran engaged many important and up-and-coming architects and builders of the mid-nineteenth century, including Thomas Walter, James Renwick, Robert Mills, William Storey, and others who made significant contributions to the era. One is hard-pressed to find another benefactor in this period who equally encouraged the work of the emerging American architectural and design profession. Corcoran used their talents to build or improve most of his projects, including his home, country estate, rental properties, cemetery, art gallery, home for indigent women, office buildings, and the public properties he influenced.[88]

Corcoran's most important real estate investment was his home. Corcoran's mansion and three acres of grounds became a showcase for the arts and for other refined tastes, such as paintings, rare books, gastronomy, furnishings, and landscaping. In the mid-1840s Corcoran and his daughter moved to this prestigious address on Lafayette Square across the street from the White House.[89] Except for his Civil War exile, Corcoran lived in the house until he died. Lafayette Square was an increasingly prestigious section of the capital and for many decades was an address favored by the elite.[90] The square's residents ranged from New York senator and Secretary of State William Seward to writer and presidential scion Henry Adams. The mansion was built in 1828 and purchased by Sen. Daniel Webster around 1840, after the original owner defaulted on two deeds of trust. At least one treaty was negotiated in the house—the 1842 Webster-Ashburton Treaty with Britain that set the permanent boundaries between Maine and Canada.[91] Webster paid just a portion of the purchase price to obtain the property and apparently never paid any more than about one-third of the price in total. The statesman was constantly in debt and found the house too expensive to maintain. Corcoran purchased the mansion for the same amount Webster paid, in essence bailing the senator out of debt. Corcoran frequently assisted the statesman financially and clearly supported the senator through real estate transactions as well.[92]

Corcoran quickly changed the federal-style house into something much grander with the help of James Renwick, who redesigned the house into an Italianate mansion.[93] He also added two wings and a showy, Moorish dining room created by Thomas U. Walter.[94] The library and study was Corcoran's pride and joy, the inner sanctum where in later years he received most visitors (especially charity supplicants) and where portraits of family members and friends, such as Daniel Webster, graced the walls. The room had a substantial book collection, richly carved fireplaces and heavy draperies, an array of famous autographed letters, and even the shop sign from his father's Georgetown shoe cobbler business. Corcoran's bedroom was described as elegant but subdued, and his private art showroom still contained a variety of paintings years after most of his collection was transferred to his art gallery.[95]

Then as now, famous architects could be a handful, and Renwick did not always deliver the projects as promised. Corcoran had a strong interest in the particulars and grew increasingly worried: "If the work for the library and dining room is not begun at once, I fear they will not be finished for the winter."[96] Corcoran's frustration and dedication to detail were obvious the next year as well, when he wrote again: "Please hurry on the balusters, and inside stairs, and Emery is in need of the drawings of the front steps and balustrade above the bay window and the iron brackets to go under the windows."[97] Corcoran was often away on business, and his redoubtable secretary, Anthony Hyde, filled in, reliably expressing equal concern: "Some matters about the house are satisfactory, and some otherwise, he wrote to Renwick."[98] Despite the occasional frustrations over construction, the effort and expense were apparently worth it, both to contemporaries and posterity. "The style of the house is very well conceived," wrote the *Republic* in 1880, "of good, solid execution and well understood and tastefully designed details."[99] Commenting on the home's later demolition, the Commission of Fine Arts confirmed the historic views: "The Corcoran residence represents a very significant loss, both to history as well as design. For Washington, D.C., the property was an early forerunner of principles later associated with the Ecole des Beau Artes . . . and was a complement to the site as much as products from succeeding and more educated designers."[100] In 1854 Corcoran's home caught fire and was damaged but rebuilt; it was demolished in 1920 and replaced by the headquarters of the US Chamber of Commerce.[101]

The original grounds to the mansion were expansive, stretching for several blocks along Sixteenth Street. The open space gave the amateur horticulturist plenty of room to build greenhouses and develop gardens, as the grounds covered three square acres at the time Corcoran asked Downing to develop the gardens and landscape plans. Some of the plantings were sufficiently rare that the American Forestry Association selected his specimens for original documentation, including a Norfolk Island Pine tree, a South Pacific native and one of the first in the country. Corcoran for many years also maintained an orchard on his property.[102]

Corcoran's country estate, Harewood, located just outside the city, was also worthy of note. Purchased in 1852 from the estate of Rev. John Brackenridge, the founder of the First Presbyterian Church of Washington, Harewood was set on two hundred acres of rolling land adjacent to what today is the Catholic University of America and the nearby Washington Hospital Center. The estate included forty acres of grounds designed by Andrew Jackson Downing, John Hennessy Saul, and his son, B. F. Saul; they are now part of the US Armed Forces Retirement Home (Old Soldiers' Home). Corcoran's property on the city's outskirts, like his downtown home, contained rare botanical species that he had shipped in from all over the world.[103] It was apparently quite a sight. "The ends of the earth have been brought together. Norway and Brazilian trees nod to each other. American vines twine over Australian shrubs; Italian myrtles whisper to rhododendrons from the Blue Ridge," wrote one visitor to the property.[104] The estate also contained a small hunting lodge, a red Seneca sandstone building with a mansard roof.

Corcoran's imprint on the physical development of the nation's capital unfolded in other ways as well. While he was not among the city's earliest real estate developers, a distinction that probably belongs to George Washington, the banker used his wealth and knowledge about the capital to buy and sell land and property to his advantage.[105] Corcoran recognized the growing need for office space, a relatively new phenomenon in which companies and government agencies needed room to house the middle managers and bureaucrats responsible for overseeing expanding national operations. Corcoran in 1847 purchased land and demolished existing buildings at Pennsylvania Avenue and Fifteenth Street and constructed one of the first commercial buildings in the capital.[106] With Renwick as the architect again, Corcoran built a forty-room, five-story office building in Greek-revival style that was rented to business tenants and the federal government to house offices for an overcrowded Treasury Department.[107] About the same time, Corcoran erected a building as a social hall and library for working men (which he later dedicated as the medical school for Columbian College). In 1853 alone, he began construction on eight new properties. In 1875 Corcoran razed his first office building and built in its place a six-story Renaissance revival building that was more than double the size of the first office building.[108] In addition to government agencies, most members of Washington's art community maintained studios in these office buildings at little or no rent, thanks to Corcoran. The 1875 office building was demolished in 1917 to make way for the Hotel Washington.[109]

Lafayette Square

In addition to his interests in residential and commercial real estate, Corcoran supported the development of bounded neighborhoods and streetscapes. While Pierre Charles L'Enfant had envisioned the idea of a large park across the street from the president's house in the capital's original plans, Corcoran was arguably the individual most responsible for influencing the aesthetic of Lafayette Square. Originally called President's Park, the parcel was developed in the same period as Washington Square Park and Gramercy Park in New York City, long considered early models of American city planning. Gramercy Park was essentially a swamp in 1831 when Samuel Ruggles, a developer and champion of urban open spaces, purchased Gramercy Farm. The land was enclosed in 1833, and landscaping began in 1844. Ruggles sold lots starting in the late 1830s for homes to surround the park, but the Panic of 1837 scrambled his plans. The building of stately brownstones did not really begin until the 1840s.[110]

The time line for Washington Square Park in New York City was similar. The area began as a potter's field cemetery during the eighteenth-century and early nineteenth-century yellow fever epidemics and was far from the center of town. The cemetery was closed in 1825, and the city bought the land in 1826 to serve as a militia parade field.[111] Stately Greek revival homes started rising on the park's borders in the 1830s, and Washington Square became an increasingly desirable address in the ensuing decades. The famous arch memorializing America's first president was not added until 1890.[112]

Development of President's Park started slightly earlier than exclusive residential enclaves in other major urban areas possibly as a result of L'Enfant's master plan, which envisioned a park adjacent to the White House.[113] The executive mansion was an important anchor for the area, but the square developed slowly at first. It was not until 1818, more than a decade after the White House was finished, that the first residential homes were built on the park's perimeter. The pace then picked up. By the early 1820s, the homes of Dolley Madison and Stephen Decatur were fixtures on the square. Both a parish house for St. John's Episcopal Church and the house that Corcoran would later purchase at 1611 H Street were built in the late 1820s. More houses were built on the square in the 1830s, and by the early 1840s, the soon renamed Lafayette Square started to acquire the exclusive character common to bounded enclave projects of the time.[114]

It is no coincidence that much of the square's refinement occurred in the years after Corcoran became a resident. Corcoran's interests in landscaping, real estate, and architecture contributed to the square's development, and much of the quadrant's aesthetic remains intact today. Although fences of various kinds were erected around the square over the years, efforts to landscape the area did not began in earnest until 1851. President Fillmore, on Corcoran's advice, commissioned landscape architect Andrew Jackson Downing to beautify the square.[115] Downing had his hands full, as he was landscaping the Mall at the same time. Congress provided an appropriation for the upgrades, and Corcoran donated a variety of exotic plantings from his collection to help landscape the area. Given Corcoran's political leanings, and an assist from Mayor John Walker Maury, it is no surprise that the park soon gained sculptor Clark Mill's prominent statue of Andrew Jackson astride his horse, a heroic Southern general, enslaver, and Democratic president.

From the start, Lafayette Square became one of the most enviable—although, at times, notorious—addresses in the capital. Decatur's death in his house at the northwest corner of the square after a duel, the murder of Phillip Barton Key (son of Francis Scott Key) in a lover's triangle, and the attempted assassination of Secretary of State William Seward on the night Lincoln was killed certainly raised the area's profile. Still, the square was especially beautiful at night when the lamps at its edges and around the White House were lit, according to observations at the time.[116] Dozens of eminent politicians, military officers, literary figures, senators, diplomats, financiers, socialites, and even a spy or two lived on Lafayette Square over the years. After Dolley Madison's death, her home was inhabited by Maj. Gen. George McClellan, the commander of the Army of the Potomac during the Civil War. After Decatur was killed by a fellow navy commodore, a succession of secretaries of state lived in his house, including Henry Clay and Martin Van Buren. The foreign ministers of France, Russia, and England, as well as politicians such as James Blaine, Gideon Welles, Charles Sumner, and William Marcy all lived on the square, mainly in homes built or owned by Corcoran.[117] Indeed, Corcoran even purchased lots on either side of a home Sumner purchased at the corner of Lafayette Square and Vermont Avenue to push up the value.

Corcoran, who retained Renwick again, built at least eight new houses, all in the vicinity of his home on Lafayette Square. Several of the homes Corcoran constructed were directly on the square; Henry Adams during his residency there lived in several of them.[118] Other Corcoran properties were occupied by the academic beginnings of George Washington University.[119] Corcoran in 1845 erected a rental property between his mansion and the homes that would eventually connect the residences and friendship of John Hay and Henry Adams, property that was later transformed into the Hay-Adams Hotel. Indeed, Hay, a private secretary to President Lincoln and a future secretary of state, bought the land for his home from Corcoran, who had originally planned to erect an apartment building on the plot. This neoclassical residence housed many notable individuals over the years, including two of Corcoran's most important associates—the newspaper editor and Democratic Party booster Thomas Ritchie and his friend Senator Slidell.[120] Ritchie bought the house at 1607 H Street from Corcoran, who purchased it back from his estate when he died.[121] Slidell lived in the house for many years thereafter (until the Civil War), followed by Lincoln's navy secretary, Gideon Welles, and Henry Adams. Indeed, the square was a small community: US Navy captain Charles Wilkes, who purchased the Dolley Madison house across the square from Slidell, caused an international incident during the Civil War when he forcibly removed Slidell and other Confederate diplomats (including Corcoran's son-in-law) from the RMS *Trent* on the high seas and sent them to a Union brig outside Boston.[122]

Corcoran also built several hotels in the fast-growing city, the most prominent of which was the Arlington Hotel. Established in 1868 on the site of the current Department of Veterans Affairs' headquarters on Vermont Avenue, Northwest, the Arlington was considered the capital's most exclusive hotel during the last third of the nineteenth century.[123] Reminiscent of the Louvre in its Second Empire style—like several other projects Corcoran built—the Arlington was viewed as an extension of the Capitol and a home away from home for kings, ambassadors, and other elite guests. The residence of dozens of senators and congressmen during legislative sessions, it was the only place J. P. Morgan stayed when in Washington, DC, having his own permanent, privately appointed suite.[124] Grover Cleveland stayed at Corcoran's hotel prior to his inauguration and held formal receptions there for the diplomatic corps, the Supreme Court, and other political luminaries.[125]

Corcoran clearly believed in the future of the capital, and his ability to anticipate its growth and capture profits from it supported his desire to improve the city. For example, Corcoran sought to fix the capital's streets, and after the Civil War, he became one of the first people in the country to experiment with asphalt.[126] Since the new road material was essentially unknown until the late nineteenth century, Corcoran was instrumental in testing asphalt to determine its utility under various traffic and weather conditions. The road around his Arlington Hotel, as well as around his home at Lafayette Square, was laid in asphalt and represented one of the earliest uses of the material in the United States. This project was surely a testament not only to Corcoran's continuing interest in municipal improvement late in his life but also to his still-strong connections. Not just anyone could rip up city streets at the center of the postbellum capital, within view of the White House, and put down a brand-new surface material.

6

THE COLLECTOR

ONE OF CORCORAN'S MOST IMPORTANT CONTRIBUTIONS, PERHAPS his greatest legacy, was in the art world. As with the other fields in which he left his mark, Corcoran was ahead of his time in the creation of his art gallery and the generous support he gave to American painters. To be sure, his wealth and status had much to do with his art associations. Collecting art and supporting emerging artists were among several ways that urban elites began to differentiate themselves from other parts of society.[1] Corcoran became an undisputed leader in establishing an elite foundation in the capital that bolstered upper-class refinement and helped guide expectations of behavior and cultural boundaries before the Gilded Age.

The extent to which the founders of Washington, DC, anticipated the capital city might encourage the arts was, at best, implied. The founders hoped the American capital would emulate the capitals of Europe, replete with beautiful monuments, stately streets, a national university, and imposing public buildings.[2] The Louvre in Paris, the National Gallery in London, and, indeed, the foreign capitals themselves had no American counterparts. The country was, for the most part, too new and rustic to exemplify artistic refinement. Washington was not alone among American cities in lacking European polish or the Continent's hallmarks of culture and civility.[3] Cities in the antebellum United States, to the extent that they had museums at all, exhibited haphazard collections of relatively random items. The most notable example was Charles Willson Peale's museum, founded in Philadelphia in the late eighteenth century. Containing Thomas Jefferson's donation of the minerals collected by the Lewis and Clark expedition, the museum also displayed portraits of contemporary Americans, dinosaur fossils, stuffed birds, and similar ephemera.[4] Ultimately, Peale gave up on the art collection entirely and focused his museum on the increasingly popular genre of natural history. The museum did not survive the antebellum period, and after Peale's death, the collection was largely sold off.[5]

Throughout most of the antebellum period, museums tended to be structured on the Peale model, and similar collections by P. T. Barnum and other purveyors of curiosities typically mixed a variety of items and genres the curators thought could best be marketed to the public for a profit. As the natural sciences took on greater prominence and professionalism, scientific academies proliferated. Some of the new groups set aside rooms to showcase the natural world; many of these sites gradually evolved into museums. Barnum and similar entrepreneurs organized and expanded their collections, which eventually became famous sideshows and circuses. Their vision of presenting museum-quality materials rarely materialized.[6]

Meanwhile, serious art was often dismissed by the academies as imitations of nature that were overly emotional or sensual in character—thus, not appropriate for polite society. The sentiments of Smithsonian secretary Joseph Henry, Corcoran's friend and a scientist, exemplify this view. Henry reported to the Smithsonian's board of regents that "it is no part of the plan of the Institution to form a museum merely to attract . . . the casual visitor."[7] He saw little room for art within the terms of James Smithson's bequest and ultimately shipped the Smithsonian's art collection to Corcoran, making the banker's privately funded, public gallery, which opened in 1874, the closest thing America had to a national art gallery until the 1930s.[8]

Art Scene in Washington, DC

The only artist of significance to settle in the capital during its first decades was Charles Bird King, a portrait painter and student of Benjamin West's. King opened a small room adjacent to his studio to display his paintings.[9] His was probably the first collection of paintings in the city, according to George Watterson, the third librarian of Congress, who described the studio in 1847.[10] Most of the paintings were by King, but the display also included several paintings by William Dunlap, Thomas Sully, and Samuel F. B. Morse.[11] The studio became an early gathering place for artists, some of whom would later make a name for themselves, including George Caleb Bingham and Eastman Johnson.[12] King also painted several portraits of Native Americans that were displayed in the halls of the War Department until they were transferred to the National Institution, located in the Patent Office Building. These paintings were transferred again in the 1850s to the new Smithsonian Institution and were among the paintings that Joseph Henry sent to Corcoran.[13]

Washington, DC, was often characterized in the antebellum era as a sleepy town and not as a capital city worthy of the nation. Art historians often opine that the capital lacked an arts culture until the mid-1850s.[14] Whether coincidental or not, in this period Corcoran began collecting paintings in earnest, amassing in about a decade one of the country's most respected collections of European and American art. Moreover, while Corcoran was not the earliest supporter of American landscape painting, he was among the most steadfast and acquisitive patrons of this new genre.

To the extent the capital's art scene was viewed as provincial, it did not account for the contributions of beautification projects and public art in the Capitol building and elsewhere. The process of rebuilding the Capitol, the White House, and other public buildings after the War of 1812 brought American and European artists, painters, and sculptors to Washington, DC. In the Capitol alone, artistic expression ranged from the Revolutionary War scenes rendered by John Trumbull to the famous *Apotheosis of Washington*. The fresco in the Capitol dome was painted by Constantino Brumidi, who had painstakingly restored Raphael's frescos at the Vatican.[15] Sculptures, fountains, columns, frescoes, art, and architectural detailing increasingly adorned the growing city and its public spaces.

The biggest art project was the Capitol itself. The art program for the building's reconstruction was directed by Montgomery Meigs, who was now the chief engineer of the US Army and Corcoran's collaborator on the construction of the Washington Aqueduct.[16] The Capitol's art program was at its height in the mid-1850s, the same period that Corcoran was most actively acquiring paintings for his collection. Meigs's management of the Capitol's art program was often controversial. Architect of the Capitol Walter Ulrich wanted American artists to adorn the building in a simple style that emphasized the nation's republican and agrarian roots. By contrast,

Meigs had a vision grounded in Victorian decoration and Renaissance style, and with support from his mentor, Secretary of War Jefferson Davis, took control of the program from Ulrich.[17] Meigs, an engineer and graduate of West Point, had no formal art training. Nonetheless, he fostered an aesthetic for the Capitol's decoration and design that survives in large part to this day. The modern US Capitol contains a profusion of large Italian-style frescoes, marble and tile floors, bronze Florentine-style doors, and abundant paintings, murals, statues, and pediments.

Meigs quickly received criticism from the art community and members of Congress who objected to the absence of American artists' works in the halls of Congress.[18] The chief engineer responded by seeking out American painters and sculptors, and he solicited advice from Corcoran and others knowledgeable in the artistic realm. Indeed, Corcoran was among the first people to see the completed *Apotheosis of Washington* fresco, as the engineer recorded in his journal that "Mr. Corcoran came with his daughter and another lady to look at the fresco painting today," shortly after it was completed.[19] Meigs was aided by artists Corcoran supported, including Hiram Powers and Emmanuel Leutze. Gouverneur Kemble, a wealthy industrialist and former Democratic representative from New York with a significant collection of Hudson River School paintings, also advised Meigs.[20] In response to the controversy, Meigs commissioned some American artists' work for the Capitol, but he eventually lost control of the program. Detractors criticized his grandiose vision and efforts to steer commissions to favored artists. President James Buchanan formed a commission on the Capitol's art program that criticized Meigs's approach. Given Corcoran's friendship with Buchanan and his reputation in the art world, likely he was consulted on the problem, but there is no record about his thoughts on the matter. Nevertheless, the commission found Meigs guilty of designing an art program focused on "an effete and decayed race which in no way represents us" and displayed "gaudy, inharmonious colors."[21] About the only thing the commission approved of in Meigs's project was the decoration of American landscapes, including the birds and animals depicted in the Capitol's corridors.[22] Secretary of War John Floyd eventually sacked Meigs, banishing him to a lackluster foreign post. However, the redoubtable engineer regained his post at the Capitol with the help of congressional Republicans once Lincoln became president.

Corcoran and Other Collectors

In addition to the program of artistic embellishment for the capital's public buildings, some of the city's wealthiest residents began purchasing art in the antebellum period as an expression of their wealth and social status. There were other early collectors elsewhere in the country, including Luman Reed of New York and Robert Gilmor of Baltimore. How much influence these collectors had on Corcoran's decision to collect art or the genres he pursued is not clear, and his papers do not reference their collections. Yet, the capital in this period gained a small but important group of collectors. In addition to Corcoran's assemblage, which was displayed in a newly built wing of his home on Lafayette Square, important art collections were also in the private homes of George Riggs, J. C. McGuire, and Robert Chilton.[23] Riggs owned an original Thomas Gainsborough portrait. McGuire, a wealthy dry goods merchant and auctioneer, had thirty-six paintings and three hundred drawings by American artists.[24] Over time, all four of the capital's early collectors gravitated to American paintings, particularly the increasingly popular Hudson River landscapes of Albert Bierstadt, Thomas Cole, John Frederick Kensett, and others. Corcoran's parents were not unfamiliar with portrait painting. Both sat and had their portraits painted in oil on canvas by fellow Washington resident Charles Peale Polk.

There is conflicting evidence about exactly when Corcoran began purchasing art. By one assessment, Corcoran began collecting in the late 1830s. Other scholars suggest Corcoran did not begin collecting art until around 1850, but this seems not to accord with the evidence. Corcoran may have purchased an oil painting by Flemish artist Jan Brueghel from Commodore Stephen Decatur, who died in 1820. This could be true, but Corcoran was only twenty-two years old at the time and without the financial resources he would accumulate later. It also leaves a gap of about twenty years until his next purchase, and there are no references to the painting in either man's papers. However, Corcoran and Decatur were friendly; after Decatur's death, Corcoran became a financial adviser and confidant to his widow. More likely, Corcoran obtained the painting from Susan Decatur sometime in the 1830s.[25]

Corcoran purchased a few paintings from Mount Vernon in the 1840s as his interest in art grew. By the early 1850s, Corcoran had amassed a considerable collection of American and European paintings and sculpture; the collection was sufficiently large that he had to expand and adapt his home to contain it. The collection was already gaining recognition, and artists were eager to be represented in the gallery. As early as 1850, noted American artist Daniel Huntington wrote to Corcoran about how much the gallery meant to him: "I am very desirous that the two pictures, which are perhaps the best and certainly the most pleasing I have ever painted, should have a place in the collection which you are forming."[26]

Even by the 1840s, Corcoran's collection was well known in the capital, and requests to view it were so frequent that Corcoran opened his home twice a week for visitors to peruse his paintings. Most newspaper articles describing the expanding capital mentioned Corcoran's home and private gallery as "must-see" attractions for visitors. In this regard, Corcoran went further than other early American collectors such as Reed and Gilmore, who on an ad hoc basis allowed people interested in art into their homes. Corcoran formalized the early American private house gallery, setting aside certain days for viewing the collection, creating special rooms, and holding events to encourage public viewership.[27] Corcoran's art collection, even in its early years, was well regarded. "His hall of paintings contains some of the first specimens of Italian artists seen in our country; to view them it seemed like walking in the splendid palaces of Rome," wrote an anonymous reviewer at the time.[28] Another reviewer commented that the first thing that will "strike a careful observer is the infinite variety of exquisite pictures."[29]

Corcoran's approach to collecting art is typically described in one of two ways: The first view is that while he purchased some European masters according to the popular taste of the time, Corcoran principally collected American art of a nationalistic vein.[30] The second view is that Corcoran had little original approach at all and was unduly influenced by the opinions and purchases of artists, collectors, and dealers.[31] Some of the earliest paintings Corcoran purchased were European in origin; he selected them during trips to the Continent in the 1840s and 1850s. "Corcoran pursued his interest in art with the same combination of diplomacy and opportunism that marked his business career," one art historian wrote on Corcoran's efforts to create a gallery. "Taking a cue from his European associates, he began in the late 1840s to collect European landscape and portrait paintings in a serious manner."[32] Indeed, friends in Europe at times

selected paintings for Corcoran to purchase; among them were the financier George Peabody, the art collector William Walters, the famed scientist
Baron Alexander von Humboldt, and the chargé d'affaires at the American
Embassy in Rome. Corcoran was in contact with other collectors as well,
including the Boston financier and a founder of the Metropolitan Museum
of Art Samuel Gray Ward.[33]

Whether Corcoran was a cultural visionary or not, the reality is that he
created an environment in which art and painting were supported and
encouraged in the capital city. This was an important milestone because
critics still chastised the city even after the Civil War for its lack of quality art outside of a few modest house museums and the Capitol building itself.[34] Corcoran's ability to bankroll promising painters, his prominence and leadership in the Washington Art Association, his decision to
collect American landscape paintings at a critical time in that genre's development, and his determination to build the first museum dedicated exclusively to art by almost any definition make him an important figure in
the development of American culture. As with other collectors who shifted
from European art to American landscapes, Corcoran likely recognized in
this new genre the power of a sentimental and nationalist view.[35] In collecting this uniquely American genre, he was either lucky or clairvoyant in
his choices of the works of Frederic Church, Asher B. Durand, Bierstadt,
Cole, and Kensett.[36]

As noted previously, Corcoran was an early enthusiast of American
landscapes, especially the Hudson River School. Art historians often see
in this stylized genre a reconceptualization of the country's development,
a portrayal of America that was more representational than real, more the-
matic than temporal.[37] By eliminating depictions of conflict and hardship,
painters such as Cole and Church showed the new country as a place of
promise and prosperity. As a result, painters of the period took dangerous or forlorn scenes and made them majestic and heroic. Kensett's view
of New Hampshire's White Mountains is a prime example of this artistic impulse; the serene beauty of the canvas projects a completely different view than the forbidding and dangerous representation of the area
suggested by early paintings and guidebooks—and reality.[38] This idyllic
view of America fit nicely with Corcoran's conceptualization of the world,
since much of the banker's own efforts were devoted to creating order and
beauty from a rough environment. Perhaps he shared the view that an

emphasis on promise and prosperity for the emerging nation, a new Eden, could erase the rising conflicts about race and region. Art of the period often ignored the turmoil of the 1850s and reified an imagined nation of beauty and bounty. This message was eagerly embraced by many Americans, as art historians recount a constant demand for versions of these paintings made by lesser artists, a new market for artistic engravings of popular works, and an ability to command record prices for major works by the period's best artists.[39]

Corcoran collected American art mainly from living artists. One periodical wrote that he had the "finest and choicest" gallery in the country.[40] The decision to focus on living artists was relatively new; most art patrons bought the work of dead masters whose paintings were already recognized as classics.[41] The window that Corcoran helped open for living American painters would shut again by the late nineteenth century as the nation's industrialists grabbed up famous European paintings, often eschewing American artists and subjects. By comparison, Corcoran's early purchases, in addition to European masterpieces, included Daniel Huntington's *Mercy's Dream*, which he bought in 1850 from the American artist. Huntington soon became close with the banker and had a significant influence on Corcoran's collection.[42] That same year, Corcoran also purchased Cole's 1837 pair, *The Departure* and *The Return*, which, more than any other paintings, put Corcoran on the map as a serious collector of the Hudson River School.[43]

Corcoran took risks in purchasing new art, not unlike those he took in business. This risk was present in his decision to purchase and display *The Greek Slave*, a marble depiction of a nude woman in chains carved by Hiram Powers. Art historians recognize Powers's statue as an important departure point in artistic representation as it was the first female nude accepted by the American public.[44] *The Greek Slave* also brought Corcoran's collection fame and notoriety.[45] He placed the statue on public view during his Christmas parties in 1851, shocking the Victorian sensibility of some guests.[46] The controversial statue offended some parts of Washington society, yet artists, critics, and some members of the public saw it as a sign of the country's growing maturity in matters of art.[47] The original sculpture had won immediate attention at the Great Exposition in Paris in 1851, and Corcoran obtained the first of five copies that were made. He purchased his version from a Louisiana hatmaker who won the statue in a charity auction.[48] Corcoran never wrote about his purchase of the statue, and it is not clear if he ever considered its multiple representations. The statue drew the ire of some Northern abolitionists who thought it was meant to glorify slavery, and British cartoonists in an issue of *Punch* satirized it by colorizing the slave's visage and providing her with exaggerated African American features.[49]

Early Impact

By the 1850s Corcoran was steadily buying American art. Charles Lanham's 1855 catalog of Corcoran's collection listed just twenty-three paintings. An updated version of the catalog two years later contained eighty-two entries, about one-third of which were American in origin.[50] In addition to the work of Cole and other well-known artists, Corcoran also purchased paintings such as William Tylee Ranney's *Duck Shooting* and Seth Eastman's *Ball Playing among the Sioux Indians*. Corcoran acquired Thomas Doughty's *View on the Hudson in Autumn* and Jasper Cropsey's *Headquarters on the Hudson River*. The catalog listings ranged from Huntington's *Mercy's Dream*—"acknowledged by critics to be the masterpiece by this gifted artist"—to lesser-known items with no commentary at all.[51]

By 1855 Corcoran was clearly a well-known art collector and patron of artists. In addition to purchasing works from stars such as Huntington and Cole, Corcoran was attentive to striving artists. He purchased as much art as he could but let go as much as he purchased. "My gallery is full, and were this not the case, it would be out of my power to purchase one tenth of the pictures offered to me," he wrote to an inquirer.[52] Despite his propensity for overbuying, Corcoran helped support the needs of artists in other ways. He was a founding member of the Washington Art Association.[53] The organization was made up of more than two hundred people from major cities in the eastern United States. Washington, DC, contributed about thirty members to the group, including artists, collectors, art dealers, and art booksellers. Corcoran knew many of the members, including painters such as Charles Bird King and John Cranch, photographer Mathew Brady, and local art collectors G. W. Riggs, J. C. McGuire, and Robert Chilton. Corcoran gave generous support to the organization by buying paintings from the artists, providing work and exhibition space in his commercial buildings, and paying for exhibition expenses. Corcoran also purchased paintings from association members William Brenton Boggs, Eastman Johnson, and William MacLeod (who would later become the Corcoran Gallery's first curator), among others.[54]

As his art collection began outstripping his ability to find wall space, Corcoran engaged architect James Renwick to add a gallery wing to his Lafayette Square mansion. It was here that Corcoran first began to exhibit his growing collection to the public. A journalist who visited Corcoran's house in 1856 wrote that "attached to the dwelling and entered by a door on the left of the main entrance hall, is a unique and spacious picture gallery, well-lighted, and arranged with artistic taste. Twice a week, on Tuesdays and Fridays, this gallery is thrown open to the public when any person of genteel and respectable appearance has free admission during certain hours."[55]

Despite the success of his house gallery, Corcoran soon decided the space was unable to accommodate his expanding art collection and the growing number of visitors. In the mid-1850s, after a European tour that included a visit to the new Louvre extensions in Paris, Corcoran began planning for a new space to house his collection—an independent gallery space open to a public increasingly receptive to cultural refinement.[56] Corcoran's early efforts to collect and display art, and to make it available to the public, represented an important milestone in the capital's cultural development. His new gallery would advance the art world even further.

Battle for the Gallery

Completing his decades-long vision of an art gallery was no easy task. In 1859, at the banker's instruction, Renwick began to design the nation's first building exclusively devoted to the public exhibition of paintings and other works of art.[57] Corcoran spent about $100,000 on the building by the outbreak of the Civil War, but development then stopped for nearly a decade. In 1861, shortly after the war started, the War Department took over the unfinished building for use by the Quartermasters Corps, which was commanded by Corcoran's onetime associate, Montgomery Meigs. Meigs immediately altered the gallery building to fit his military needs, including carving additional windows and niches into the facade. For eight years, the quartermaster's brigade and other parts of the military occupied the gallery, paid no rent to the owner, and did considerable damage to the structure.[58]

Even after the gallery building was returned to Corcoran when the war ended, the government was not finished with him. War Secretary Edwin Stanton spent nearly five years attempting to prosecute the banker for tax evasion. They finally compromised when Corcoran relinquished his claims for rent from the War Department, and the government abandoned its tax prosecution.[59] Some Northern-leaning papers justified the government's occupation of the gallery and reported that it had paid back rent almost immediately—which was not accurate.[60] Other papers came to Corcoran's defense. The *Boston Courier* wrote that Corcoran was a Democrat who stood on principle, and his gift to the nation demonstrated that he loved his country.[61] Similarly, the *Express* (Boston) wrote that the government never needed to take over the gallery in the first place, and had it chosen temporary quarters elsewhere, the gallery would already be completed.[62]

Corcoran was luckier with his principal residence. Rather than see the government occupy his home, Corcoran during his wartime exile cleverly invited the French ambassador to take up residence there. The ambassador stayed for several years, giving the mansion diplomatic protection.[63] Unfortunately, Corcoran's summer estate at Harewood did not fare as well. It became a hospital for twenty-eight hundred Union soldiers and an ad hoc encampment for miscellaneous troops. The Union army, which had virtually overrun the capital during and after the Civil War, crowded into every space available. Harewood, along with the Mall around the Smithsonian, never quite recovered. The vision of a Victorian park and woodlands that Corcoran helped create for these properties was partially destroyed. Troops trammeled the sylvan paths in both places, and many of the rare trees that the financier had collected from around the world were indiscriminately cut for firewood and shelter.[64]

Corcoran moved quickly to complete the gallery once it was finally returned to him. In May 1869, Corcoran appointed a board of trustees and explained that he wished to "establish an institution in Washington City, to be dedicated to art, and used solely for the purpose of encouraging American genius in the production and preservation of works pertaining to the 'fine arts' and kindred objects." Yet, the years had taken their toll, as he revealed in his charge to the new trustees: "It is my cherished hope to have placed the proposed establishment, complete in all its appointments, in successful operation before divesting myself of the title by any formal instrument, but the years which have passed away, and the accumulation of other cares and duties, warn me no longer to indulge anticipation."[65] The banker was clearly worn out from his exile, delays in building the gallery, and struggles with the government over his property and taxes. By the time the gallery was finished, Corcoran was already in his seventies and had suffered the deaths of both his wife and his daughter. Corcoran did not reveal his inner thoughts easily, but he felt the loss of his family. Around this time, he wrote to the board of managers of Oak Hill Cemetery about his daughter, Louise: "One (child) only attained maturity, and she, who (I had fondly hoped) would remain the solace of my declining years, was early called to a brighter and a happier sphere."[66]

The gallery's handpicked board acted quickly and by November 1869 had established officers and formal committees to move Corcoran's vision forward. The board was also able to finally collect the back rent for the government's use of the gallery. It would be nearly five years before the gallery was finished, but anticipation of the project's completion elicited considerable excitement and gratitude in the capital. The district's recorder of deeds refused to accept the standard fees for recording the official deed when the building transferred from the banker to the gallery trustees. The supervisory architect from the Department of the Treasury offered his services for free to complete the plans. Discussions between the board and General Meigs confirmed that the government would repair the damage from its occupation of the property.[67] The board hired a curator for the gallery, William MacLeod, and agreed to pay him $1,600 a year.[68] Shortly thereafter, the board appointed a committee to explore consideration of an art school in accordance with Corcoran's wishes.[69] The board likewise instructed the curator to draw up a plan for the school. By 1876 Corcoran had already purchased several lots on Seventeenth Street and, along with securities, presented the deeds to the gallery board to further the aims of the art school.[70] The gallery also put up the funds toward creating the school and temporarily suspended purchases of new art to accommodate these expenditures.[71] It was initially thought that a number of wealthy art collectors around the country, including August Belmont, would contribute paintings to the collection, but such generosity was not forthcoming.[72]

The press followed the gallery's progress with much anticipation. The *San Francisco Chronicle* in 1875 complained that no benefactors of Corcoran's stature and wealth seemed willing to provide similar largesse for that city.[73] In Boston, the *Evening Transcript* reported Corcoran planned to entertain that winter by turning the former picture gallery in his house into a grand salon.[74] Once again, the San Francisco papers anticipated the opening. In an almost real-time modern style, that city's *Evening Bulletin* reported Corcoran's paintings were being transferred from his house to the gallery.[75]

Initial trustees of the gallery included collectors James C. McGuire and William Walters, and Anthony Hyde, the banker's personal secretary.[76] Corcoran also appointed Henry Cooke, Washington's Republican governor and his sometime business associate. The final trustee was his friend and Smithsonian secretary Joseph Henry. On a buying trip to Italy, Henry convinced the Vatican to allow him to make cast molds of some of its most renowned statuary; he then provided them to the Corcoran Gallery.[77] Newspapers reported that the pope himself approved the deal in return for the Smithsonian's providing the Vatican with scientific information on certain subjects.[78] Several trustees proved instrumental in procuring art for the Corcoran Gallery while on European trips. The acquisition committee authorized Walters to spend $40,000 on art in Europe and at the Vienna International Exposition.[79] In the meantime, the trustees were busy buying paintings and sculptures for the gallery from a variety of artists and sources; soon artists, merchants, and owners were inundating the trustees with sale offers.[80]

In his original letter to the trustees, Corcoran indicated that the "wholly unpaid" rents, once received from the federal government, would flow to the trustees and that the amount would be sufficient to complete the gallery. An act of Congress in 1870 incorporated the gallery and authorized payment of the back rent. Equally important, it held that "any tax due the United States . . . be remitted and released."[81] The gallery and its benefactor were finally free and clear from government encumbrances.

Despite this progress, Corcoran was not ready to present the gallery to the city and the world until January 1874.[82] Corcoran invited nine hundred guests to a glittering bash celebrating the gallery's opening. The following day he opened the gallery to the public, and several hundred people showed up to see the banker's renowned art collection in its stylish new surroundings.[83]

The prewar design and construction of the Corcoran Gallery account for its status as the first true repository created exclusively for paintings and sculpture in the United States. Indeed, some newspapers of the day noted the Corcoran Gallery's impact on other art institutions: "It was not until [Corcoran] had announced his art benefaction that the people of New York became alarmed for fear of being eclipsed by Washington, D.C., and so went to work and founded the New York museum of art."[84] Negotiations to purchase the Douglas mansion to house the Metropolitan Museum of Art in New York were not completed until several years after Corcoran's gallery opened.[85]

The Fundraiser

In 1871, several years before the gallery was completed, Corcoran hosted a lavish fundraiser in the unfinished space to help complete the Washington Monument. Few moments in Corcoran's later life stand out as much as this gala to reflect the banker's unique ability to retain influence, build alliances, and, in a quite modern way, successfully reinvent himself. Only a few years previously, Corcoran had been linked to plots to kill President Lincoln, had fled with his money to Europe during the Civil War, and had claimed many Southerners, including Confederate generals, as close friends. In a fascinating expression of reinvention, Corcoran turned the monument party into a testament of his Northern fealty. The entire gallery was draped in white bunting. American flags and enormous paintings of General Grant and President Lincoln flanked the speakers' platform. Equally fantastic was the receiving line from which the benefactor greeted his guests. Lost on no one was that Corcoran was flanked on one side by Gen. William Tecumseh Sherman, perhaps the most reviled man in the South, and on the other side by Adm. David Porter, the secretary of the navy and the Union's principal naval hero from the Civil War.[86] If anyone could pull together such a disparate group of Americans from across ideological and literal battles lines, it was Corcoran. Through the banker's still largely undiminished ability to transcend party and faction, the capital seemed to coalesce, at least for a short time, around the fundamental purpose of the country's founders and the iconography of the first president. If the country was to heal from its deep, self-inflicted wounds, this was one of its principal inflection points.

One newspaper commented on the event's symbolism:

> One could not help thinking of the changes time has brought about, and what healing of old wounds has taken place now that it has become possible for the radical president and his wife to be the guests of a man who has been looked upon as standing at the head of the anti-Republican party, as existing among the old families of Washington. . . . This ball brought together in harmonious relations every warring element of society Washington has known in the past ten years.[87]

Said another paper more directly: "If this man was disloyal in heart to his country, certainly such charity as this may be allowed to cover a multitude of sins."[88]

Attendees included President Grant and the First Lady; Vice President Schuyler Colfax; members of the cabinet, the Supreme Court, and Congress; and many foreign dignitaries. The monument party was the first time the building was opened to the public, and both the expectations and the reviews were over the top. Periodicals of the day gushed. "The most magnificent ball ever given in Washington, or perhaps in the United States, took place last evening in the halls of the Corcoran Art Gallery," said the *Daily Patriot*. "It is safe to say that Washington has rarely witnessed a more striking assemblage. . . . We question if the stately grandeur of foreign courts, with their glitter of uniform and pride and pomp, could show such a galaxy of refinement and beauty."[89]

The Gallery in Context

With the success of his gallery, Corcoran emerged as a leading exemplar of the philanthropic elite. Connections were growing between the new urban centers of a still largely rural democracy and the emerging commercial, social, and political class that sought to put down cultural roots and to create an American sensibility in art and architecture, theater, and musical expression.[90] This upper class was eager to justify its place to the rest of society and, some argue, to create and reify cultural and social boundaries.[91] Based on Corcoran's actions surrounding the gallery, one may reasonably conclude he believed that refinements such as art could both educate people and foster social development. MacLeod's curator journals reveal Corcoran's daily interest in the gallery and the social context of his patronage. Corcoran came to the gallery almost every day, often with many guests; the gallery was typically a backdrop for the philanthropist's larger goals of networking, class projection, and rehabilitation. To be sure, Corcoran was proud of the gallery and his important art collection, and he clearly wanted to be recognized for this contribution to the city and the country. He was also serious about it. Corcoran instructed the curator to regularly update him on the state of the collection. Like many other projects, he was clearly interested in the details. "No word yet on the arrival of the statues by Ezekiel," MacLeod reported in one such instance, referring to American sculptor Moses Ezekiel.[92]

Given his personality and motives, Corcoran seemingly tried to help others while helping himself, in much the same way he did in his philanthropic and commercial pursuits. Journalists of the period probably got it right:

> We take it for granted that the twofold desire on the part of Mr. Corcoran is to gratify and inculcate taste for the beautiful and true and to encourage native talent in all the departments of art. . . . It is only by attempting to comprehend the wealth of beauty and thought [of European galleries] that we can obtain insight into the nature of Mr. Corcoran's mind in striving to do for his own country in the cause of art what has been done in Europe by the wise and good.[93]

Perplexingly, discussions about the origins of the art museum in America often fail to mention Corcoran's contributions.[94] Most historical treatments gloss over Corcoran's important decision to transform his residential art collection into a freestanding museum more than twenty years before similar institutions were completed in New York, Chicago, Boston, or Philadelphia. Many others do not mention the Corcoran Gallery at all, perhaps because its collection was not as broad or large as those of other galleries. Publications of the day seemed better able to recognize Corcoran's contributions. The *Daily Chronicle*, a Corcoran friendly paper in Washington, wrote that Corcoran's gallery was "the only one in the United States expressly designed and constructed as a great gallery. All other collections in the leading cities are preserved in buildings designed for other purposes. Senator Sumner calls it the American Louvre."[95] Whatever political disagreements they may have had, Sumner, the leading Radical Republican in the Senate and a champion of equal rights for formerly enslaved people, was an admirer of Corcoran's philanthropic endeavors and contributions to the capital.

Before the growth and expansion of universities, museums were the main site of knowledge production and diffusion. The emerging fields of natural history, technology, and archaeology encouraged museums as depositories of artifacts and expressed representation. Art museums played a similar role in education as a component of moral and social uplift, and as a marker of middle-class attainment.[96]

As urban America was transformed during the late nineteenth century, the elite in major cities united to form the flagship art institutions we recognize today: the Art Institute of Chicago, the Philadelphia Museum of Art, and the New York Metropolitan Museum of Art. Such activities continued well into the twentieth century, resulting in the collections and museums established by men from across the country, such as Andrew Mellon in Pittsburgh to Armand Hammer in Los Angeles—all of them building repositories in the Corcoran mold. Corcoran used his gallery to impart on a growing city the lessons of history, patriotism, and aesthetics that art offered viewers. Moreover, he encouraged a nationalism and patriotism expressed through portraits of famous—albeit White male—Americans. By absorbing the portraits of the nascent Smithsonian Institution, and by purchasing or commissioning portraits of other leading statesmen, Corcoran sought to develop a national collection of art to reflect his conception of the country's heroic past.[97] His role in actively trying to shape the contours of America's heritage is a recognizable precursor to the efforts of Henry Ford and the Rockefellers decades later to create a foundational, unidimensional view of American history and representation.[98] Ultimately, the Corcoran Gallery served as the capital city's principal museum of art until the creation of the Phillips Collection in 1921 and a government-sponsored national gallery was built in the 1930s, largely with the donated European collections of Andrew Mellon.[99]

Legacy of Paintings

The first paintings Corcoran donated to the new gallery from his house museum were a mix of American and European art, but American art quickly came to dominate the collection. Many were portraits, which due to the advent of photography were increasingly considered an older, dated style of artistic expression; they included works by John Singleton Copley, Raphaelle Peale, Henry Inman, and Thomas Sully. In part because portraiture declined and interest in the nation's geographic expansion rose, the artists' depictions of landscapes grew more popular. The most distinctive landscape in the gallery was Frederic Church's *Niagara*. Representing the promise of a nationalist manifest destiny, Church finished *Niagara* in 1857, just before the Civil War, and Corcoran acquired it in 1876 during the nation's centennial. At the time, Corcoran paid the most money on record for the painting.[100] Equally important, of course, was the work of Thomas Cole, whose large Hudson River School–style paintings of *The Departure* and *The Return* graced the new gallery's walls and attracted many visitors. Corcoran also bought Frederic Church's *Tamaca Palms*, an important South American work the artist exhibited at the National Academy of Design in 1855. The work held special meaning for Corcoran, as he purchased it from the estate of Abraham M. Cozzens, an influential art dealer from New York who helped shape his early collection.[101] Corcoran also became interested in South American scenes through the influence of von Humboldt, with whom the banker became friends while on a trip to Europe. The famous naturalist's book *Cosmos* is thought to have inspired Church's visit to the tropics, where he painted the lush scenery. At von Humboldt's request, the artist Eduard Hildebrandt painted *Moonrise in Madeira* for the banker.[102]

Corcoran's strong collection of American art became more valuable and appreciated over time even as his continued interest in portraiture of notable Americans reflected an idea whose time had passed. Some historic portraits were even provided to the gallery free of charge, including a painting of James Madison by Thomas Sully that Frederic Church donated in 1877.[103] Corcoran never clearly articulated his motives for creating a national portrait gallery filled with images of famous presidents, generals, and notable families, but his urge likely was rooted in trying to help unify the nation after the Civil War and to shape its patriotic memory. Corcoran attempted to foster through art a spirit of national unity and, not inconsequentially, to reestablish the place of Southern heroes in the American identity. Not surprising, the first paintings Corcoran purchased for his portrait gallery were Sully's portrait of President Andrew Jackson and a similar portrait of Robert E. Lee.[104] Many of the presidential portraits Corcoran collected for this purpose between 1874 and 1885 ended up hanging in his personal art gallery as the public gallery acquired new work.

In addition to purchasing portraits of presidents and other famous Americans, Corcoran after the war also collected leading examples of American art that were not well represented in the gallery. Sometimes Corcoran bought paintings on his own and gave them to the gallery; at other times, he made suggestions to the trustees. In 1874 Corcoran acquired Asher Durand's *Edge of the Forest*. That same year the gallery purchased William Sidney Mount's *The Long Story*, which had once belonged to Baltimore collector Robert Gilmor. The acquisition committee did not always heed the founder's advice and sometimes rejected outright Corcoran's recommendations for new purchases. His suggestions were sometimes controversial, such as the occasion he suggested the gallery buy a landscape by Albert Bierstadt called *Mount Corcoran*. The story goes that the accomplished— but duplicitous—artist was miffed that he was the only major American landscape painter without a work hanging in the Corcoran Gallery. He made repeated attempts to sell his work to the gallery but was rebuffed each time. The museum's curator, MacLeod, was not impressed with the artist or his paintings and prevented the gallery from purchasing his work. Ever resourceful, the artist approached Corcoran himself, flattering the collector by explaining that he had helped name a mountain after him and then painted it for presentation to the gallery. However, MacLeod and others at the gallery believed that Bierstadt, whether he had a hand in naming the mountain after Corcoran or not, took an existing painting of a western mountain scene that had already hung in an exhibition and renamed it *Mount Corcoran*.[105] Bierstadt loaned the painting to the museum for a while, but he obviously wanted remuneration. Corcoran took the bait and eventually purchased the painting for his home and later transferred it to the gallery, which paid $7,500 to acquire it.[106] Bierstadt was elated: "The greatest living painters would take great pride in being represented in the Corcoran Institution. . . . Mr. Corcoran and the true artists of the world are allies, friends at heart."[107]

Gallery Opening

The gallery did not formally open until January 19, 1874, although Corcoran had been giving tours of it for at least a year prior to the opening. Over the front doors was carved the phrase "dedicated to art" and the initials "WWC" for the founder.[108] Corcoran's likeness is even carved in a pediment bust. When the gallery first opened its doors, Corcoran exhibited ninety-three paintings and five sculptures, and by the end of 1874, the gallery held more than three hundred works of art, the largest collection of art in America open to the public.[109] Hundreds of invited guests crowded the main salon when the gallery first opened. European paintings were hung with those of American artists, as well as a massive portrait of Corcoran. Newspapers from around the country were impressed, if not a bit jealous. "This is all given in perpetuity to the public and three of the six days in each week it is open without money and without price to the citizens of the country who . . . rich and poor, black and white without reference to previous condition of servitude . . . may stroll at will through these galleries," wrote the *Chicago Inter-Ocean*. This munificence came not without risk, as the trustees soon found themselves discussing whether barriers were necessary to protect the paintings, which on the Continent "were paid more respect."[110] Newspapers in Philadelphia and elsewhere devoted pages of description to seemingly every painting in the gallery.[111] Thursdays through Saturdays at the gallery were free, and on other days admission was twenty-five cents.[112] Moreover, as the popularity of the gallery grew and as "the number of strangers in the city and their early movement for sight-seeing" increased, the gallery shifted its hours to earlier in the day to accommodate growing interest.[113]

Not all opinions about the gallery or Corcoran's gift were positive. After a few Republicans criticized Corcoran's gallery efforts, suggesting that philanthropic offers from suspect Southerners were not welcome, both neutral and Democratic-leaning newspapers came to his defense. "Mr. Corcoran's loyalty to this government during the term of our struggle was never open to fair imputation. He was a southern man by birth and association but never an extremist," parried the *Daily Chronicle*.[114] The *Boston Courier* and the *New York World* also came to Corcoran's defense. "The munificent gift of this well-known gentleman, for years the leading and highly respected banker of Washington, D.C., to the city does not satisfy everyone. We must say taking all things into consideration a spirit at once so generous, patriotic and Christian like his has been rarely exhibited on this earthly planet," wrote the *Courier*.[115] By comparison, the *World* impugned the character of the capital's other leading citizens: "What have the Butlers, Dows, Logans and other loyal plate passers and gatherers who enriched themselves during and by the war done in the way of contributions to Washington, D.C., or any other city?"[116]

Disdain from disgruntled Republicans simmered down after the party leadership and city fathers gathered around Corcoran and supported his gift to the capital. While a few periodicals continued to express antipathy toward Corcoran, most publications supported him and regularly recorded his good deeds and his social rehabilitation.[117] Not all the name-calling ceased, and Corcoran could not wipe away the entirety of his association with the South. Even amid the philanthropist's generosity in funding Washington's teachers, who had apparently not been paid for months due to the city's budget woes, Corcoran was still called an "incorrigible old rebel" who merited harsh punishment.[118] Yet, most political messages were undeniably positive. When Corcoran returned from Europe, Henry Cooke, a governor of the capital, held a sumptuous dinner in his honor. The event was attended by President Grant, General Sherman, and almost the entire Republican cabinet. Even Corcoran's nemesis, General Meigs, who until just weeks before had refused to relinquish Corcoran's art gallery, turned up.[119] While a few murmurings would always persist, Corcoran's rehabilitation was well underway.

Newspapers and magazines reviewed the opening and praised the new gallery. The *Evening Star*, the dominant Washington paper and not always the banker's supporter, wrote a heartfelt appreciation of the benefactor's gift to the city: "Mr. Corcoran has sent to the gallery all the artistic companions of his own mansion, and he sits tonight, very probably, in the empty hall where his Coles and Huntingtons . . . have beguiled him for 20 years consoled by the happiest of solaces, that he is doing good to others."[120]

There were a few uncharitable reviews. Curiously, the unenthusiastic evaluations mainly came a few years after the gallery had been open. The early excitement had diminished, and galleries in other major cities had finally opened. In 1882, several years after the gallery opened, the *Century* first praised it as "the most complete individual manifestation in this country of public-spirited interest in the progress of art. . . . It ranks among the best public art collections in the United States." Yet, the magazine also criticized the collection, remarking that "while containing some excellent work from well-known artists, it has also a number of inferior rank. . . . Some of the pictures are of a quality so inferior that one is surprised to find them there."[121] Moreover, in 1884 the *New York Sun* printed an editorial that suggested the gallery was an "artistic morgue." The anonymous critique insinuated that Corcoran knew little about art and allowed a variety of self-serving individuals to sway the collection to their interests. "The intrigues of designing women, of incompetent artists . . . supply the influences which control [the gallery]," the paper wrote.[122] The charge had a ring of truth to it, as Corcoran frequently relied on others, such as William Walters, Abraham Cozzens, Joseph Henry, and diplomat Thomas Green Clemson, to suggest appropriate works for the collection. When Clemson was a US diplomat during the late 1840s and early 1850s, for instance, he influenced Corcoran's purchases of Belgian art.[123] Still, the record is clear that Corcoran also made many choices on his own, even if he admitted to not being an expert in the field of painting.[124] Moreover, those of Corcoran's associates who selected art for the gallery were able and knowledgeable in the field. The gallery's records for those early years also show that the trustees and acquisition committee turned down opportunities to purchase or exhibit art much more frequently than they accepted it.[125]

To be sure, the benefactor surrounded himself with many women and artists, as the gallery's curator William MacLeod often noted in his journals. "Mr. Corcoran (came in) with a bevy of ladies," he wrote in the spring of 1876, and not long afterward, he reported seeing "Mr. Corcoran and a party of ladies" again.[126] Whether the women were designing or the artists who also accompanied Corcoran to the gallery were incompetent was clearly a matter of opinion. One journal, the *New York Express* saw it more positively:

1 | Thomas Corcoran, father of W. W. Corcoran. Painting by Charles Peale Polk. Courtesy National Gallery of Art, Washington.

2 | Hannah Corcoran, mother of W. W. Corcoran. Painting by Charles Peale Polk. Courtesy National Gallery of Art, Washington.

3 | *Mount Corcoran* painted by Albert Bierstadt. Bierstadt infamously renamed a western mountain to persuade Corcoran to purchase and display his work. Courtesy National Gallery of Art, Washington.

4 | *The Old Corcoran Gallery of Art.* Painted ca. 1880 by John H. Cocks.
Courtesy National Gallery of Art, Washington.

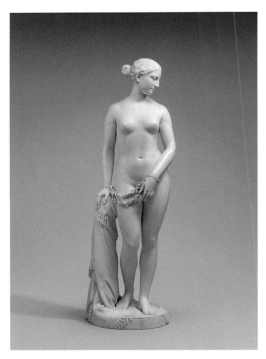

5 | *The Greek Slave*, a sculpture by Hiram Powers, caused a scandal
when Corcoran first displayed it at his Christmas parties in 1851.
Courtesy National Gallery of Art, Washington.

6 | *The Departure* and its companion piece, *The Return*, painted by Thomas Cole in 1837, highlight Corcoran's seriousness as a collector of American landscapes. Courtesy National Gallery of Art, Washington.

7 | Corcoran purchased *The Return* and its companion, *The Departure*, both painted by Thomas Cole, as part of his interest in the Hudson River School landscape artists. Courtesy National Gallery of Art, Washington.

8 | W. W. Corcoran, age seventy-nine, in gravure print of a painting by Charles Loring Elliott. Courtesy National Gallery of Art, Washington.

9 | Marble bust of Corcoran, age eighty-four, by sculptor John Quincy Adams Ward. Courtesy National Gallery of Art, Washington.

10 | Corcoran was a friend and admirer of Confederate Gen. Robert E. Lee. Corcoran purchased this painting by John Adams Elder in 1884 and gifted it to the Corcoran Gallery of Art. Courtesy National Portrait Gallery, Smithsonian Institution, Washington.

11 | Self-portrait of Louise Morris Corcoran, at age seventeen, the wife of W. W. Corcoran. Courtesy Library of Congress, Washington.

12 | Photograph of W. W. Corcoran in his seventies attributed to Mathew Brady Studio. Courtesy Library of Congress, Washington.

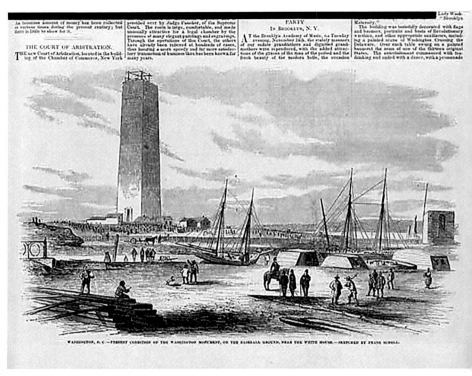

13 | Drawing of the Washington Monument under construction.
W. W. Corcoran was head of the commission in charge of completing the obelisk.
Courtesy Library of Congress, Washington.

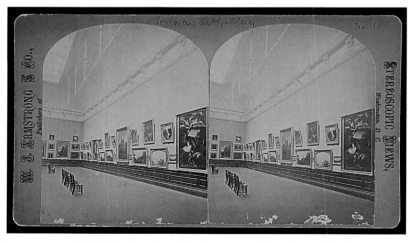

14 | Early interior view of the Corcoran Gallery of Art, undated.
Courtesy Library of Congress, Washington.

15 | W. W. Corcoran's home on H Street across from Lafayette Square. Corcoran purchased the house from Daniel Webster and made many improvements. The house was torn down in 1920. Courtesy Library of Congress, Washington.

16 | An 1882 engraving of W. W. Corcoran by H. B. Hall & Sons, New York. Courtesy National Portrait Gallery, Smithsonian Institution, Washington.

Between noon and three on any fine day you may see entering the gallery a venerable white-haired gentleman of noble presence who casts an observant glance and benignant smile upon all and everything he sees and meets. . . . Nor does he often come alone. Nothing pleases him more than to escort his lady friends through the gallery and his spirits are just of that perennial kind that makes him equally charming as an escort to damsels and dowagers.[127]

The gallery's success meant that the building was filling up rapidly with art, especially since Corcoran was planning to create his new national portrait gallery as part of it. He acquired two lots near the gallery on which he hoped to build a gallery extension as well as an art school. The land was separated from the main gallery by a plot owned by Rear Adm. Samuel P. Lee, who had a dim view of the benefactor. Corcoran wrote Lee in 1880, explaining his purpose: "I am constrained to make one more effort to purchase your lot. . . . The addition I propose to make to the gallery of art is a national portrait gallery and School of Art, and my desire to see it consummated while I live, prompts me to make you the above liberal offer: and in the event of your acceptance the building may be completed within the year 1880."[128] Corcoran tried repeatedly until his death in 1888 to convince Lee to sell, but the man never budged. This fight had its ironic twist, as Lee was a third cousin to Robert E. Lee. Like the Confederate general, Admiral Lee was a scion of the Virginia Lee dynasty and a grandson of Richard Henry Lee, but the career naval officer had refused to abandon the Union during the Civil War.[129] Admiral Lee's intransigence helped block an idea that would remain dormant until 1962, when the National Portrait Gallery was established as part of the Smithsonian Institution.

In planning for expansion, Corcoran had been persuaded by members of his board and the Washington art community that an art school was necessary for the capital. To that end, Corcoran erected a studio that served as an art school, although it was a cramped space from the start. A proper school was incorporated in the new Corcoran Gallery after the benefactor's death. Newspapers across the country in the fall of 1875 heralded that "the art benefactor of Washington is about to still further benefit the arts of that city by erecting a studio building for their accommodation."[130] From its first days, the art gallery was a strong attraction for art students, who came to study and engage in the increasingly popular task of copying significant works of art. In 1877 on an informal basis, local artist E. F. Andrews begin tutoring some of the student-copyists, after which Corcoran provided the gallery with additional funds specifically dedicated to the art school.[131] Corcoran's will also included a specific bequest for building an art school. Its construction began the year after he died, and the school opened in 1890 with forty students and two instructors.[132]

Corcoran remained involved with the gallery until his death. He advised the trustees on managing the gallery's investments and attended many of the trustees' regular meetings up until his last years.[133] The first investor in the telegraph was even present when the trustees decided in 1879 that a "telephonic connection," invented in 1876, was "inexpedient" for the gallery.[134] Meeting minutes show the trustees routinely requested Corcoran's advice, and they typically discussed the timely purchase and sale of various bonds in his presence.[135] For a period in the early 1880s, the trustees voted to suspend the Finance Committee and return the gallery's investment responsibilities to Corcoran.[136] The gallery's founder ultimately outlived quite a few of the initial and subsequent trustees, including at least three presidents of the board.[137]

By almost any measure, the gallery was a tremendous success. In the 1870s more people visited the Corcoran Gallery than visited New York's Metropolitan Museum of Art or Boston's Museum of Art, and attendance spiked to a record high the year of the nation's centennial.[138] The year after Corcoran died, his gallery recorded 109,000 visitors when the city's total population was about 177,000 people. Nearly 90 percent of the visitors entered for free.[139]

7
INTERREGNUM

THE AMERICAN CIVIL WAR FOREVER ALTERED THE NATION AND ITS capital. Margaret Leech's Pulitzer Prize–winning portrayal of wartime Washington, DC, chronicled permanent changes to the sleepy Southern town brought about by the devastating war and the subsequent peace.[1] America's most tragic conflict had immediate effects on the political, economic, and social fabric of the nation, on the capital, and on almost everyone in the city, including Corcoran. A divided nation meant less political compromise and flexibility to solve intractable problems, less financial fluidity and economic prosperity, less social cohesion and common purpose. Like many other people North and South, Corcoran found his opportunities and options constrained by the sectional crisis and the war. Nevertheless, the banker at first had a greater ability than some of his peers to retain a semblance of his normal life as the country and the city were torn apart. Corcoran's networks helped sustain him at a time when Southerners or people who sympathized with secession were leaving the capital or facing persecution.

With the election of Abraham Lincoln, Southern slave states began to leave the Union, the Confederacy was born, and the shelling of Fort Sumter in April 1861 marked the nation's descent into the Civil War. Efforts by President Buchannan and then President Lincoln to assuage Southern tempers and prevent conflict were of little avail, and opportunities for compromise and flexibility slowly but surely diminished.[2] Negotiations between stakeholders withered, positions hardened, and the backroom deals at which men such as Corcoran were so adroit could not ameliorate the unraveling situation.[3]

The economic environment created by the war proved harmful to financiers, merchants, and industrialists.[4] Commerce between the North and South waned, debts often became uncollectable, investments were suddenly worthless, and financial transactions and contracts dwindled—especially after trade between the combatants became illegal. A clandestine black market thrived, and profits in commercial pursuits (especially scarce items or war materials) were still attainable to those willing to assume the risk, particularly in border areas like the capital city. Meanwhile, Northern bankers and merchants tied to the Southern cotton trade suffered hardship as loans made on cotton as collateral and bets on cotton futures collapsed.[5] The market for Southern securities crashed as credit and loans for states' operations and infrastructure vanished in the North, sending the Confederates scurrying to Great Britain to secure credit.[6]

The social world also unraveled. The nation's capital, with its largely Southern elite, frayed in disarray. Washington, DC, was not the only city, North or South, in which the wrong side found itself increasingly unwelcome in a nation now less tolerant of dissent and fearful of spies. People with Union sympathies had to keep quiet or leave such cities as Charleston and Richmond. Southern sympathizers were less tolerated in Boston and other cities north of the Mason-Dixon Line—except for New York, which continued to condone Copperheads, Fire-eaters, and other people with Southern or even slave-holding leanings.[7] Still, the capital suffered significant changes in the dissolution of its social structure. As the *New York Express* noted when Corcoran left for Europe, "A divided nation has no charms for those who desire in old age security and repose."[8]

The world in which Corcoran thrived, both economically and socially, was overturned by the Civil War. Like other savvy financiers, the banker took steps to reduce his exposure to economic uncertainty, but his network and financial holdings took a beating. Corcoran reduced or sold his holdings of Southern securities, stopped transactions with Southern banks and investment houses—especially after the war started—and secretly turned much of his wealth into gold.[9]

On the local level, Washington, DC, became almost unrecognizable to its residents and city fathers. The city's inhabitants increased from roughly 61,000 in 1861 to nearly 250,000 in 1863, as thousands of troops poured into the region.[10] The military inundation had predictable impacts on sanitation and lawlessness: Police in 1863 made more than twenty-four thousand arrests in the capital, roughly three times the number arrested that same year in Brooklyn, a city twice its size.[11] A growing influx of Black people displaced or freed by the conflict added to the city's population and diversity. The increase occurred because of several changes, including new laws in Maryland and the capital that outlawed slavery and emancipated slaves. These actions, combined with increasing numbers of Blacks who escaped the South and made their way north, produced unparalleled population growth during this period. By some estimates, the population of Black people in the city grew by forty thousand during the war.[12] The capital was a magnet for people seeking greater opportunities; the capital's large free Black population, its emancipation policy, crossroads location, and dense urban environment proved beneficial to new arrivals.

From a commercial standpoint, the government's war needs further transformed the city. New warehouses and makeshift operations popped up all over the public spaces. The Baltimore & Ohio Railroad could barely handle the incoming freight. Cattle, horses, pigs, and mules wandered everywhere, and the Navy Yard added thousands of new workers.[13] More than five hundred new arrivals a day crowded the overwhelmed capital, and new companies formed out of thin air to obtain government contracts. Real estate prices, and the cost for just about everything, skyrocketed.[14] Most new business with the government went to big Northern firms, but even Corcoran & Riggs found itself profiting from the war, as the firm lent funds to army contractors at high interest rates. For its part, the federal government insisted that Corcoran pay hefty taxes during the war years.[15] It also seized Corcoran's investment properties on I Street, his office building (where he was donating rooms for local schools), the Harewood estate, and the gallery for wartime use.

Corcoran's long-standing connections also suffered. His perpetual access to Southern Democrats and Whigs in the White House ended as Abraham Lincoln, an Illinois Republican with few ties to the capital, became president. Corcoran retained connections with some of the Northern and Western politicians who were selected for the cabinet, such as incoming secretary of state William Seward, but his access to inside information became less reliable. Many of Corcoran's political allies left the city, and few ever returned. Virtually the entire delegation of Southern senators and representatives departed in 1861 as their states seceded from the Union. Indeed, some of them were among Corcoran's closest friends and confidants, including Senators Jesse Bright, Jefferson Davis, and John Slidell. Davis, of course, became the president of the Confederate States of America, and Slidell was named the Confederacy's envoy to France. Others, such as Washington mayor Walter Lenox—a Whig with whom Corcoran had teamed up to landscape the city's public spaces—left the capital for Richmond and enlisted in the Confederate Army. When Lenox returned to Washington in 1863 to settle a family estate, he spoke broadly of his contempt for the Union and was arrested and imprisoned by Gen. Winfield Scott.[16] Former vice president John Breckenridge, a Corcoran business associate and frequent dinner guest, became the Confederacy's secretary of war and a general.

With the departure of the Southern delegations went their wives and families, as well as the social connections, the parties, and the gentility of the nation's capital. As it did for many other people, Corcoran's group of friends and associates dwindled. That is not to say Corcoran never again shared gossip in a drawing room or passed along intrigue to powerful politicians. He retained many contacts above and below the Mason-Dixon Line. But the political and social world in which he played an elite role diminished after Lincoln's election and the war's arrival. His was a dangerous situation: His admiration for several Confederate generals became increasingly obvious, as did his sympathy for their predicament. Much of Corcoran's personal scrapbook is filled with newspaper articles chronicling the lives of Stonewall Jackson and Robert E. Lee.[17] While there is no record that Corcoran openly supported rebellion or secession, he had long been sympathetic to states' rights and adverse to federal intervention. That view by itself was sufficient to attract unwanted attention in the wartime capital.

Even Corcoran's church was affected by the struggle. When Episcopal bishop William Whittingham, a staunch Unionist, issued a prayer extolling Union military success in March 1862 to be used by all churches in the diocese, several ministers refused. One who refused was Rev. William Pinkney, a good friend and essentially Corcoran's spiritual adviser. Pinkney was pastor of the Episcopal Church of the Ascension, which still sits on Massachusetts Avenue. The congregation and its pastor were Southern in their leanings, and Corcoran had provided much of the money to build the church. Pinkney's church and several others led by equally pro-Southern ministers found their houses of worship suddenly confiscated by the government for wartime use. Reverend Pinkney was also brought up on church charges for ignoring the orders that church services include a prayer for President Lincoln. Corcoran offered the congregation temporary housing for worship in one of his H Street buildings.[18]

Wartime in the Capital

Due to its geographic location and its position as the North's capital, Washington in 1861 became simultaneously a garrison city and a hotbed of sedition.[19] The small, sleepy city was deluged by Union regiments from New York and New England that were sent hurriedly to protect the capital from falling into rebel hands and from sabotage.[20] The threats were not idle: Located below the Mason-Dixon Line and south of rebel-leaning Baltimore, the capital could be cut off from northern access, and a lightening rebel strike could capture the city.[21] The city's fortifications were weak. General Scott suggested that Fort Washington, on the Maryland side of the Potomac and apparently watched over by one elderly man, could fall to a bottle of whiskey.[22] Union troops fortified Baltimore while Southern papers such as the *Richmond Examiner* openly encouraged Maryland and Virginia rebels to capture the capital.[23] Rumors persisted that secret societies would rise up, seize the government's buildings, and take control of the city. At least one of the capital's local militias, the National Rifles, was riddled with Maryland secessionists, and a company of National Volunteers talked openly at their meetings about ways to seize the capital.[24] One anti-Union paper, the *Constitution*, advised the militias to prevent Lincoln's inauguration by force.[25]

Eight companies were initially detailed from the regular army to establish a stronger defense of the capital. After Lincoln instituted the draft, regiments from many Northern states flooded the capital.[26] Troops camped everywhere, bunking in the public buildings, including the Capitol, and taking over property as far out of the city as Corcoran's Harewood estate.[27] Ultimately, tens of thousands of soldiers clogged the city, creating disorder and mayhem, sleeping in the legislative chambers, parading through and destroying the plantings of the newly landscaped Mall, and filling the streets, brothels, and taverns of a city unprepared for the loyal invasion. The Smithsonian grounds were used indiscriminately for target practice, and reports of gunfire breaking nearby drawing room windows became commonplace.[28]

Accusations of treason occurred frequently.[29] Spies were assumed to be everywhere, and Democrats, regardless of their allegiance, were often considered suspect. Another of Washington's mayors, James Berret—a Breckenridge Democrat and a friend of Corcoran's—was widely assumed to be conspiring with secessionists. Indeed, the mayor refused to take a loyalty oath and was thrown into federal prison by Secretary of State Seward.[30] As Southerners bound for the Confederacy departed, suspicion fell on those who remained and whose families had lived peacefully in the capital since its founding. Not surprising, Corcoran became a suspect. Union officials in the increasingly paranoid capital city saw men such as Corcoran as uniquely situated to assist the South. Some thought that Southern-leaning residents and city fathers might provide the Confederacy with important intelligence and financial resources. Outside of rumor and innuendo, there is no record that Corcoran provided the Confederacy with anything more than his sympathies; if he did more, the evidence has yet to surface. In the supercharged anxious atmosphere, Corcoran was supposedly overheard placing a bounty on President Lincoln's head, sending funds to the South, aiding the Confederacy in the securities market, and putting up the money to build a rebel warship. Nothing came of the accusations. All the same, his sentiments were clear: Corcoran defended Southern socialite Margaret Bayard Smith, whom Seward banished to the South, as a "hero" in a letter to Rep. Henry May of Maryland who had been imprisoned for treason.[31] At times, Corcoran's reputation preceded him. A letter to Massachusetts governor John A. Andrew about disloyal people warned of Corcoran's Southern "proclivities."[32] Indeed, Corcoran's dinner table, affable and urbane in years past, epitomized the struggles of the country as the banker's Northern friends, such as General Scott, watched his Southern associates, including Senators Robert Toombs and Judah Benjamin, curse the president and the Union.[33]

Those seeing treason in Corcoran's behavior needed to look no further than his Lafayette Square dining room.[34] Ironically, Secretary of State Seward, a frequent guest at the banker's parties and dinner table, had authority over political arrests when the president suspended habeas corpus. Corcoran may have been arrested on suspicion of treason at least once; papers throughout the country carried the sensational news.[35] His close political connections and a lack of clear evidence probably saved him from the fate of other Washingtonians who were thrown in jail. The *Evening Star*, which just a decade later would print invective and spurious charges about Corcoran, defended him, affirming that Corcoran demonstrated little harm beyond vague Southern sympathies.

Nevertheless, suspicion about men such as Corcoran over time turned into wariness toward most old-family city residents. Congress and the city fathers rarely saw eye to eye, especially on issues of taxes and race relations, and many Northern politicians saw the capital's locals as de facto rebels.[36] Radical Republicans, especially, reasoned that since the Union cause was tied to emancipation, those who opposed it were against the Union. Requirements for loyalty oaths became increasingly common in the city during the war, and by 1864 a plurality of the Senate voted to require all citizens of the capital, which had not rebelled against the Union, to take a loyalty oath.[37] The departure of military and government officials for the South, the arrest of local Confederate spies, and the refusal of many city volunteers to serve beyond city limits increased Congress's suspicion of the native population. Rightly or wrongly, these views were shared by many Northerners who, during and after the war, looked unfavorably on the loyalty of the Washington community.[38]

Later, when debating reparations to Corcoran for the use of his art gallery during the war, some senators suggested that because Corcoran had left the country, he deserved no compensation. The joint resolution on the claim itself required that Corcoran first swear a loyalty oath before being paid by the Treasury Department; the resolution passed, thirty-four to three.[39]

Trent Affair

While Corcoran tried his best to stay out of harm's way and avoid the types of blunders or circumstances that had ruined others' lives in the Civil War capital, he was not successful. As a result, Corcoran in 1862 sold his horses and carriages, left his native city, and lived in Europe for several years to avoid further conflict and harassment.[40] The war affected the banker in direct and personal ways. Louise, Corcoran's only surviving child, in 1859 married George Eustis Jr., a New Orleans lawyer who had recently been elected to the House of Representatives. (Ironically, Eustis was close friends with a Spanish diplomat Corcoran personally had thrown out of his house, apparently kicking him in the groin, upon learning of his efforts to court Louise).[41] As did most Southern politicians, Eustis resigned his House seat when his state joined the Confederacy, and he began working to help organize and establish the South as an independent country. Eustis, already an associate of Louisiana senator and Corcoran friend John Slidell, accepted a position as Slidell's secretary when the older man left the Senate to become a Confederate diplomat.[42]

The Confederacy had originally appointed several commissioners to approach the major European powers to obtain the diplomatic recognition and the financial loans the rebels needed to buy weapons and build warships. Confederate officials anticipated that the Europeans' dependence on Southern cotton would lead to official recognition and a state of neutrality, and that England and France would then act as mediators to end the war and ensure the South's independence.[43] The North, of course, sought to prevent any European recognition of the Confederacy and, through Secretary of State Seward's timely reminder of the Monroe Doctrine's warning against hemispheric intrigue, to dissuade European intervention.

Confederate secretary of state Robert Toombs, the former senator from Georgia who was well known to Corcoran, in February 1861 dispatched a three-person diplomatic mission that included secessionist and slavery firebrand William Yancey to beseech the Europeans for aid. The commissioners met with Lord Russell, Great Britain's foreign secretary, just days after word of the attack on Fort Sumter reached England. The meeting had a positive impact, as a week later Queen Victoria issued a proclamation that recognized the state of belligerency in America and gave the South equal rights with the United States for travel on the high seas and in foreign ports.[44] The US government grew increasingly alarmed that the next step would be a British declaration of diplomatic recognition for the Confederate states. Union officials grew more agitated at this prospect when they learned that during the summer of 1861, the British had been secretly negotiating with the Confederacy about its intentions to sign the 1856 Treaty of Paris, which governed privateering and neutral shipping rights in time of war.[45] After the expansion of the Confederacy from seven states to eleven and the rebels' success at the Battle of Bull Run, the

Richmond government renewed its push for diplomatic recognition and prepared to establish diplomatic missions in London and Paris. It recalled the initial team of diplomats, appointed a second team more experienced in foreign affairs, and sent that team to Europe. The Confederacy's new envoys were John Slidell, who had been President Polk's ambassador to end the Mexican-American War, and Sen. John Murray Mason of Virginia, who served as the chairman of the Senate Foreign Relations Committee before being expelled in 1861 for supporting the Confederacy. Slidell was appointed the ambassador to Paris, and Mason, the ambassador to London.[46]

With the war underway, departing for Europe was no easy task, as the North had imposed a blockade on the Southern coast and outside important coastal cities, such as Charleston. By the first week of October, the envoys and their party—including Slidell's family, Secretary George Eustis, and his wife, Louise Corcoran Eustis—were in Charleston and preparing to depart for Europe. The original ship, a Confederate warship called the *Nashville*, was rejected as too likely to draw Union fire from a man-of-war outside the harbor. A steamer named *Theodora*, heading for Havana, took on the party and successfully evaded the blockade.[47] In Havana, the group booked passage on the RMS *Trent* bound for London.

Meanwhile, the USS *San Jacinto*, an armed Union frigate commanded by Capt. Charles Wilkes and bearing a detachment of marines, arrived in Caribbean waters in search of the Confederate raider CSS *Sumter*, which had recently captured three US merchant ships. While the *Sumter* was long gone, Wilkes discovered in St. Thomas that Mason and Slidell were shortly departing on the *Trent* from Havana. The *Trent* departed on schedule, and Wilkes was waiting for it in the narrow Bahamas Channel; the US warship fired several shots to stop the *Trent* and boarded it. Wilkes, a neighbor of both Slidell's and Corcoran's on Lafayette Square, ordered his executive officer to seize the Confederate envoys. That was achieved only by force at bayonet point. US Marines removed Mason and Slidell, as well as Eustis and Mason's secretary, and returned them to Union territory.[48] Slidell's wife and two daughters, along with Louise and Eustis's sister, stayed on the ship and arrived in London several weeks later. They eventually reached Paris, settled into a hotel on the Place Vendôme, and awaited word of the men's fate.[49]

The *Trent* Affair, as this diplomatic dustup came to be called, had international implications for the Union and almost led to war between the

United States and Great Britain.[50] Wilkes made clear that the interception of the Confederate diplomats was no chance encounter, that he had planned the confrontation, and that he had acted on his own accord and without orders from the War Department.[51] Many in the North were jubilant over the affair, and dinners were held in Wilkes's honor in Boston. Newspapers castigated the captured diplomats, and legal experts justified their removal as a legitimate exercise of American authority under international maritime law. Congress approved a resolution awarding Wilkes a gold medal.[52] Even Edward Everett, an old ally of Corcoran's and a former minister to Great Britain and secretary of state, argued that "the detention was perfectly lawful."[53] Corcoran's friend and former treasury secretary Robert Walker, assigned by the administration to keep track of Confederates in London, wrote that the government "had a perfect right under the law of nations to seize" the *Trent*.[54]

Few saw the longer historical view that the Americans' actions uncannily resembled the country's problems with British impressments that were in part responsible for the War of 1812. One of the few who did was Henry Adams. Sitting in the house he rented from Corcoran on Lafayette Square, he wrote his brother, Charles Francis Adams, the American ambassador to Great Britain. He was outraged by the government's adamant defense of the removal: "Good God, what's got into you? What in Hell do you mean by deserting now the great principles of our fathers; by returning to the vomit of that dog Great Britain? . . . You're all mad, all of you."[55]

For its part, the British government was so incensed over the armed removal of passengers from a British vessel that in addition to formal protests over the actions and demands for the release of the diplomats, it sent thousands of troops to Canada to buttress its forces in case war became necessary.[56] While some American officials blustered that the nation could show its maturity to the world by simultaneously combating the South and staving off a foreign power, Lincoln decided such a course was unwise. Just before Christmas 1861, the president ordered the Confederate diplomats' release, and a British naval vessel picked them up at Provincetown, Massachusetts. The Confederates arrived in London in early January 1862.[57]

For Corcoran, the *Trent* Affair was an emotionally trying time, given that his daughter was in Europe without her husband, who languished in a Union prison. To the best of his abilities, Corcoran did what he always did. He reached out through his friends and associates to soothe personal and political matters. Regarding matters of his family, he worked through Junius Morgan and George Peabody to help ensure Louise's safety while the *Trent* Affair took its course. Peabody had frequent contact with Slidell's wife and with Louise, and may also have had contact with Confederate agents in London.[58] More discreetly, Corcoran asked several Northern friends, including Edward Everett, to investigate the fate of George Eustis in the Fort Warren brig and to see after his son-in-law's comfort during his imprisonment. Once the Confederate officials arrived in London, Slidell and Eustis made their way to France. Corcoran finally decided to leave the city and in 1862 departed for Paris to see his daughter and to put some distance between himself and a capital where his presence seemed increasingly unwelcome.

Life for Corcoran in the Union capital had become precarious. Beyond rumors of his arrest, the banker was also accused of contributing funds to outfit the *Alabama*, a notorious Confederate gunship responsible for burning sixty-five Union merchant ships during the war, and of helping to place a Confederate loan with Slidell in the European securities market.[59] Probably Corcoran's worst crime was retaining too close relationships with Southerners who remained in Washington, DC. There was never sufficient proof that from his dining table and drawing room emerged any schemes or plots to help the Confederacy, but in those early days of the Civil War when Southern senators still dined at Corcoran's home, there was plenty of loose talk. Indeed, after the war, Congress reviewed allegations that Corcoran was overheard at dinner with the Russian ambassador and allegedly offered $1 million for someone to assassinate Lincoln, but the story was never corroborated.[60] The story was sensational enough that a House committee investigated the charge. Corcoran believed the accusation, made by a butler, was leveled at him for purposes of extortion.[61]

Gossip and speculation did not end when the banker left the city. Shortly after Corcoran departed for Europe, newspapers reported that the government had seized his property under the Confiscation Act. "Mr. Corcoran is now in Europe and is charged with engineering the Confederate loan. His property is said to be worth a million dollars. How very much obliged are the Yankees for giving them occasion to appropriate his property. No man could confer a greater obligation unless he were to put them in possession of more than a million. Between Mr. Corcoran's loyalty and his money, the Yankees prefer the latter by at least $900,999!"[62]

Corcoran in Europe

Corcoran was nearly sixty-five years old when he decided to leave the city where he had lived his entire life. From a commercial and financial perspective, the Civil War had significantly disrupted the banker's ability to manage his investments in the United States. His connections to Southern banks and the cotton empire were sundered, and Northern investment opportunities increasingly focused on manufacturing and the production of war materials. Corcoran had invested early in the Colt's Patent Fire Arms Manufacturing Company, which eventually proved to be a sensation in the armaments industry and made one of the first mass-produced items in the country. Even though he had invested early in new technology, such as the telegraph, which revolutionized communications, for the most part Corcoran's investments and interests typified the older merchant-banker class, which was not completely confident in the future of industrial capitalism. Corcoran's papers reveal little evidence of wholesale losses to his net worth, but investors with positions in Southern securities clearly suffered losses. Corcoran may have been more prescient than most. As the investment climate deteriorated during the days of the secession panic and the battle over Fort Sumter, Corcoran converted his financial holdings into gold. How much of his assets the banker successfully converted is unclear, but it was at least $34 million in twenty-first-century value.[63] The banker asked Samuel Cunard to transport his money out of the country. Cunard, along with Cornelius Vanderbilt, had vigorously opposed the banker's successful lobbying on behalf of the Collins Line subsidy in the 1850s, but as with so many people, Corcoran had converted the shipper into an ally.

Important as it was, in the early 1860s Corcoran's primary concern was not his financial situation but his personal freedom, his family, and his quality of life. A lifetime of connections built largely on Southern associations was significantly damaged. Many people in his network were rebels, and to contact them risked treason. The war transformed the lives of most Southern gentry from the capital dramatically. Hundreds of people were thrown in prison, and thousands left the city. For those not prosecuted as traitors, the conflict still affected them deeply. In a capital overwrought by rumor and gossip, Corcoran's complicity was never proven, but it may not have mattered as much as his guilt by association and his rumored arrest. The damage was done. People who wanted to see disloyalty in his allegiances and associations had little trouble finding it, whether it was true or not. Such is the nature of overheated fear and rhetoric in times of war. Perhaps Corcoran did some or all of the treasonous things of which he was accused. So far, after more than a century and a half, no records have come to light substantiating the various allegations. A decade after the war, a congressional committee investigating treasonous activities during the conflict found no credible evidence that Corcoran was anything other than simply sympathetic to the Southern cause and states' rights.[64]

Thus, in late 1862 Corcoran went to New York. From there, he boarded the RMS *Scotia* and, with most of his wealth, sailed to London. Corcoran stayed for a time in London, seeing associates such as George Peabody and Junius Morgan. He renewed acquaintances with members of the British legation who had served in Washington, DC, before the war. Corcoran may have communicated with Mason, his boyhood friend and the Confederacy's British envoy, although there is no record of it. Shortly thereafter Corcoran went to France and was reunited with his daughter and her husband. He likely spent time with his friend John Slidell, the Confederacy's French envoy. In 1863 and 1864, Corcoran traveled in Italy with George Peabody and purchased art for the gallery.

His close connections to Confederate family and friends in Europe likely did Corcoran no favors back home. Moreover, he was recognized in London as an individual who was highly influential in the right circles.[65] That makes sense given his reputation. Under the circumstances, he probably encountered both Confederate and Union intrigue. Several letters among his papers attempt to persuade Corcoran to use his connections to help arrange Confederate objectives, but there is no evidence that he acted on such suggestions. Even though Corcoran was free of the overly watchful eyes of the US capital, plenty of Northern spies in London and Paris would have reported any questionable activities to the US government.

Throughout the remainder of the war, Corcoran kept in surprisingly close contact with friends and business associates back home. Through his secretary, Anthony Hyde, Corcoran managed to collect the rents on his properties and provide instructions on buying and selling various securities. He also managed his philanthropic activities during this period, providing funds to various charities in the capital. Not all went well, however. The government's seizure of his properties resulted in lost revenue and significant damage. Throughout the duration of the war, Hyde worked unsuccessfully to reassert Corcoran's authority over his properties and to limit damage to the buildings and their grounds.[66] While some Northerners distanced themselves from Corcoran during his exile, others did not, and the banker continued to exchange correspondence with many people in his circle, including his old friend Edward Everett. No doubt the banker also gained news of importance in exile and sent private messages back home through people such as Robert Walker, who—ironically—became the Lincoln administration's representative in Great Britain to thwart Confederate ambitions. Walker frequently traveled between London and Washington, DC.

Ultimately, Corcoran settled in Paris to be closer to his daughter and did not return to Washington until after the war ended. His daughter and son-in-law eventually moved to Cannes, where Corcoran lived with them for a time. Corcoran began his return to the United States with short trips beginning in 1865 and 1866, and by 1867 the banker, and presumably his gold, were residing full time again in Washington, DC. Neither his daughter nor his son-in-law ever returned to America. Louise died of consumption in 1867 at the age of thirty.[67] Corcoran would later sail to France to retrieve his daughter's body, which was interred in Oak Hill Cemetery in 1868. Eustis himself died in France just a few years later in 1872. Corcoran then brought the couple's three children to Washington, where they lived with him in the Lafayette Square mansion for many years. Indeed, friends and admirers concerned about the banker's health and the fate of his family met the steamer *Cuba* in New York—complete with a band from the First New York Artillery—to accompany him to the capital on that occasion.[68]

Reputation

No question, Corcoran's reputation took a beating during the war. In some circles, such as with the Radical Republicans, his reputation never fully recovered. Even though the church bells in Washington tolled ninety times to signify his age and honor him at the time of his 1888 death, not everyone shared a respectful view. Corcoran was a keen follower and protector of his reputation. His personal scrapbook was filled with newspaper clippings that mentioned him almost exclusively in positive terms. Very few articles he saved criticized or defamed him, although articles with negative comments have been located through digital newspaper searches and included in the research for this book. The few negative articles in his scrapbook were always placed next to positive articles that provided what he clearly believed to be a more accurate view of his actions or legacy.[69] The same is true for the collection of letters he assembled late in life titled *A Grandfather's Legacy.* Virtually all the letters included in the volume represent positive interactions with individuals or in situations that present him as a man of virtue, patriotism, and charity. Letters criticizing him or suggesting contrary approaches to his views are scarce. The same is also true with respect to Corcoran's collected letters, which, while there are hundreds of them, rarely seem to contain a negative view.[70] If he received such letters, which he presumably did, he did not save them and did not want them seen in posterity.

The war put Corcoran in a difficult position. Many residents in Corcoran's situation who did not enthusiastically affirm support for the Union were considered suspect and saw their reputations tarnished. George Peabody is one such example, even though he lived in Europe, far away from the conflict. Peabody resided in London for decades and was aligned with the South. Despite his expatriate existence and his calculated distance from anything related to politics, Peabody was nevertheless criticized for a lack of loyalty to the Union cause and for suspicion that his British financial connections were at work helping the Confederates. These same allegations were, of course, leveled against Corcoran but did not seem stick to him as badly. While it is difficult to ascribe with certainty why Corcoran was treated with greater leniency, his still-strong networks at home, his good works, and his longevity in the capital were likely factors. Peabody's absence from Washington, DC, along with his social isolation and thin connection to his homeland, made him an easy target. Comments about his views on the Southern cause and the contention that the North could not obtain loans from a Southern-leaning England were published in the capital's newspapers.[71] Peabody also caught the ire of abolitionist William Lloyd Garrison, who both during the Civil War and after Peabody's death attacked the banker for his wartime refusal to support the Union.[72]

To be sure, Corcoran's decision to leave the country, on top of the suspicions some Republicans already held against him, hurt his prestige and stature. His actions amplified that criticism and provided justification for the government to confiscate much of his property. Still, Corcoran fared well enough. Many friends and associates in his network remained supportive of the banker, and his financial situation did not overly deteriorate. At the end of the war, Corcoran was still one of the richest men in the country. Papers noted his return to the United States positively, and groups of admirers met his carriage at the outskirts of the city to escort him home. Indeed, over time Corcoran reclaimed much of his position through an active campaign of political, social, cultural, and philanthropic rehabilitation. As a result, the damage to Corcoran's reputation from the war receded as people chose to remember his good works and not his questionable loyalties.

8

RESILIENCE AND REPAIR

CORCORAN RETURNED TO THE UNITED STATES ALMOST IMMEDI-ately after the Civil War ended, making his first trip home shortly after Appomattox. While the conflict displaced or ruined many Confederates and Southern loyalists in Washington, DC, Corcoran was luckier in his fortunes. Indeed, some of the banker's most lasting legacies for the city in the areas of culture, urban aesthetics, and philanthropy occurred in the shadow of Republican administrations in the postbellum era. Moreover, Corcoran successfully constructed a persona steeped in national reconciliation, becoming the rare person positioned adroitly between the North and the South who could help to heal and rebuild the country.

Corcoran no doubt found the capital a different place after the war. The city in which Corcoran had spent most of his life was permanently changed, and his ability to reclaim his power and prestige was challenged, to say the least. The Southern gentry no longer controlled the power structure or the social world.[1] Northerners now oversaw the national government, and their well-connected cronies, many of whom were unknown to city fathers like Corcoran, were suddenly the primary influences on the social and cultural scene. The remnants of Washington society, the local merchant and banking elite, viewed much of the city from the sidelines. A new cadre of influencers, seeking power and wealth, overshadowed the older society. Moreover, race relations also shifted, as the legislative agenda of the Radical Republicans forced African American voting and other measures of equality on a largely resistant White citizenry.[2]

While the circumstances of war impoverished some men, it made other men rich. Alexander Shepherd, a plain gas fitter's assistant at the start of the Civil War, emerged just a few years later as one of the most powerful men in Washington, DC, a principal owner of the influential *Evening Star* newspaper, and a major landholder in the city.[3] Many of the capital's significant commercial ventures were no longer controlled by Washington natives; instead, most of the banking firms and the street railways were led by Northerners from New York and Philadelphia. As wealthy men seeking new opportunities made their way to Washington, DC, many purchased valuable real estate and provided stiff competition to locals like Corcoran, who for years had achieved unrivaled commercial success and had little trouble purchasing the choicest lots of land.[4]

The physical structure of the city changed during the war and continued to change even more rapidly afterward. With tens of thousands of soldiers, newly freed Blacks, government workers, and office seekers crowding the capital, the sleepy backwater that critics and Continental sophisticates once derided now suddenly emerged as a classic boomtown. Urban development finally would turn the small, rough-hewn community into a cosmopolitan capital city along the lines that its founders had envisioned, with new buildings, parks, mansions, streets and sidewalks, lights, and broad boulevards.[5]

Suddenly, postwar Washington was finally big enough and excitedly cosmopolitan to spark enthusiasm for social and cultural refinement.[6] The capital's newspapers even dedicated reporters to cover the burgeoning cultural scene, typically gossip and the stage, as well as the vicissitudes of power and high society. Many of the newcomers, such as investment banking scion Sam Ward, gravitated to the profitable lobbying business energized by industrial capitalism and the Great Barbeque. Indeed, Ward learned the craft by mimicking Corcoran and others like him. A colorful figure who blew through several fortunes and multiple spouses, Ward ranged from Paraguay to Wall Street, from the California wilderness to the Capitol building.[7] Ward was not alone: Close confidants of President Grant's—often former Union army officers—also sought wealth, influence, or jobs in the capital, hoping the increasingly fluid and grifting city would deliver on their aspirations.[8] The Washington that observers sometimes found provincial and moribund—and unbearably humid in summer—was suddenly dynamic and exciting. A fashionable summer season even emerged, despite the weather. Newspaper reporter Mary Ames noted a "new set" of people had come to town. Rising publisher

E. L. Godkin of *The Nation* confirmed their existence as part of a new order: "Washington seems to be becoming more and more of a resort for people who want to amuse themselves in a mild climate and is greatly changed in all prospects."[9]

Even as a new elite emerged after the Civil War, Corcoran in his final years still showed a mastery of the networked connection, the backroom deal, and the reach across parties and factions. During this period, Corcoran helped finish the long-ignored Washington Monument, pursued the creation of a national portrait gallery, built refuges for people devastated by the war, completed his art gallery, helped to bring down Washington's corrupt local government, and blocked the Radical Republicans' experiment in equality, the latter of which was not a positive outcome, at least by current mores. Not bad for a man in his late seventies and early eighties in a city run by his supposed enemies. Corcoran clearly also had the favor of luck: He survived at least four serious carriage accidents and two railroad-related mishaps in his later years.[10]

The banker's accomplishments occurred when many of his peers were discredited or dead, but Corcoran retained influence to the end of his life. In his eighties, Corcoran even selected the Democratic commissioner for the three-member District of Columbia Board of Commissioners on behalf of Republican president Rutherford B. Hayes. Papers complained Corcoran had too much sway in the city's affairs.[11] Simultaneously, Corcoran burnished his network, never shying away from helping influential people gain wealth. Sen. James Beck, a Democrat elected by Kentucky in 1870, was among the many politicians whom Corcoran helped financially and politically after the war.[12] In a sign of respect to his social position, Corcoran was typically seated with members of the House of Representatives for formal events, such as the funeral of President James A. Garfield.[13]

Corcoran nurtured a new nationalist role alongside efforts to repair the ruins of the Confederacy. He routinely socialized with Robert E. Lee and a host of former Civil War generals, and he poured money into Southern institutions and individuals wrecked by the war.[14] Former Confederate general P. G. T. Beauregard, who led the attack on Fort Sumter and, thereby, started the Civil War, stayed as a guest in Corcoran's home just months after the war ended.[15] For some, these actions stymied the rehabilitation of his reputation and revealed Corcoran's true sympathies. Others shrugged it off and were more interested in his philanthropic and cultural endeavors—or in how the old man's network could benefit them. Corcoran himself freely admitted his sympathies "were with the South," but he had never acted against the Union.[16] Perhaps that is why he never hid his Confederate associations and naively assumed others would also see his connections as innocent friendships. Many disagreed. When Congress considered one of his tax claim petitions, some members of the House of Representatives broke into open laughter during the debate, as a provision of the bill required Corcoran to support the Grant administration.[17] In a similar dispute over Corcoran's postwar claims on the gallery, Sen. and former war secretary Simon Cameron accused him of being disloyal to the Union and said he never signed a letter supporting the claim even though the banker had the letter in his possession.[18] Corcoran was among many people who after the Civil War were forced to temper their views with the ascendant political and social reality.

National Reconciliation

After the Civil War, Corcoran used his wealth and resources to help create a sense of national reconciliation. One may debate whether such efforts had any lasting effect on healing the country's war wounds or on guiding its trajectory toward greater unity, but Corcoran's actions influenced both how reconciliation developed and the communication of values that such efforts represented. It may be argued whether his actions reflected a desire for personal redemption or some larger, more noble purpose. Regardless, Corcoran contributed to a society in desperate need of national healing, and his efforts seemed to make a difference.

As one of the most traumatic events in American history, the Civil War still divides national time into antebellum and postbellum periods. In the aftermath of the calamity, many Americans, including Corcoran, tried to find meaning in the conflict's horror, to play some role in binding the country's wounds, and to shape the corresponding narrative. Veterans, politicians, and publishers, among others, engaged in struggles for cultural dominance and to control the memory of the past.[19] Historians explain that the memory of major events such as the Civil War and the Reconstruction aftermath are intentionally created; individuals and groups controlling public spaces and monuments become the custodians of memory and manufacture the resultant meaning of events.[20]

True to form, Corcoran adroitly adopted the "Cause Victorious" or the "Lost Cause," depending on his circumstances and goals. He used his network of friends and associates to help further national reconciliation and polish his personal patriotic place within it. Corcoran became the president of the society dedicated to completing the Washington Monument, a marble testament to the first president. He was active in raising funds to finish the obelisk and, with architect Robert Mills and the Army Corps of Engineers, settled on a final design after false starts and impractical plans threatened to derail the project.[21] The committee held meetings at his home and made several decisions there that finalized the obelisk's design.[22] With Corcoran presiding as the chairman of the joint commission for the monument, the cornerstone was laid on Independence Day 1848 with an elaborate parade featuring military units, bands, masons, temperance groups, and various political figures in attendance, including the president.[23] It was a cold February morning in 1885 when, after the marble shaft of the monument was raised, Corcoran proudly claimed that the people had "redeemed a sacred national pledge . . . by giving to this great obelisk its culmination." After the local Masonic lodge certified the structure was plumb, square, and level, President Chester Arthur accepted the monument on behalf of the country.[24]

Corcoran's devotion to reconciliation took other forms as well. Incredibly, along with William Tecumseh Sherman, in 1883 Corcoran served on the welcoming committee for the reunion of the Army of the Potomac.[25] Corcoran helped fund the perseveration of George Washington's dilapidated Mount Vernon home and helped refurbish Thomas Jefferson's grave site at Monticello; both historic homes had been neglected for years.[26] Corcoran also offered to move the remains of Pierre Charles L'Enfant, the designer of the city, from an unmarked Maryland grave to the capital, but the Frenchman's body would not be conveyed until 1909. L'Enfant was finally honored by lying in state at the Capitol and a burial in Arlington National Cemetery. Corcoran in 1870 also gave generously to a new building for the Young Men's Christian Association, whose start became the nucleus for the Washington, DC, Public Library and the Central Union Mission. As with many other causes, the network connections in this case were clearly as important as the contributions, as virtually all the other benefactors for the project were important Republicans, including William Tecumseh Sherman, Henry Cooke, and Gen. O. O. Howard, the administrator of the Freedmen's Bureau.[27]

Corcoran spent much of his time assisting others' charitable objectives as well as his own. His time and generosity were regularly sought after for various boards of directors; they ranged from the Washington Eye and Ear Infirmary to the Washington Inebriate Asylum. He was a trustee of several colleges as well as the Smithsonian Institution and numerous other social, educational, and cultural activities. Overall, Corcoran successfully retained much of his prewar social and philanthropic influence. Except for taking the occasional trip, Corcoran mainly dedicated his time to his favorite capital and Southern causes, and to supporting his family. Watching some of his long-held plans, such as the art gallery, become reality, Corcoran enjoyed as much of the rapidly changing community as possible, tucked into his Lafayette Square mansion with three grandchildren, a niece, occasional other relatives, servants, and two Scottish terriers named Nellie and Dick.

Aiding the South

Corcoran's role in furthering national reconciliation after the war was matched by his continued sympathy for Southern causes. Others, including George Peabody, provided funds to help rebuild the South, but few of them matched the breadth of Corcoran's generosity. Corcoran supported and repaired the war-damaged South by assisting individuals ruined by the war and by building havens for indigent widows and veterans. Corcoran also spread his charity by financing universities and churches. His philanthropy supported the University of Virginia and infused funds into what would become Washington and Lee University, thus supporting the postwar endeavors of Robert E. Lee.[28] Indeed, his close connection to the Confederate general continued unabated after the war, as Corcoran frequently summered with Lee and other Confederate notables at the White Sulphur Springs Resort in West Virginia.[29] Corcoran was clearly well thought of and comfortable in this community, and he returned to it for many years after the war. Despite the notoriety of Confederate generals and other Southern sympathizers at these gatherings, Corcoran may have outshined them all.

In a letter to a local newspaper, a writer who had recently visited the resort reported, "They make way for Mr. Corcoran, whose handsome face is generally at the center of a group of ladies, for that generous gentleman is considered the greatest belle here. He certainly receives more attention than even the prettiest girls; . . . the memory of the war is never absent long from conversation here."[30] Corcoran's lifelong friend, Episcopal bishop William Pinkney, in a reflective mood after visiting the resort, described Corcoran as "the man of taste and feeling so refined that in the Aspen you behold his type in temper meek, yet inflexible of mind when bent on right unswerving steady bold."[31] Even in the last years of his life, when in declining health, Corcoran still traveled to Southern cities to attend dedication ceremonies for memorials to Robert E. Lee, John C. Calhoun, and other stalwarts in the states' rights pantheon.[32]

The capital's remaining Southern community looked to Corcoran to honor Lee in death, electing the then-elderly admirer to head the group that organized to commemorate the general's life. Indeed, Corcoran's eloquent funeral oration revealed undiminished sympathy for the South, which likely did not help his reputation in some places. At least one newspaper put Corcoran in a category of "ex-confederates."[33] The papers quoted his eulogy: "We have come together to express our deep sorrow and to mingle our tears over the loss of the good and great man, whose death affects me almost beyond utterance."[34] Not surprising, many of those elected with him to the committee commemorating Lee were part of Corcoran's network and of Southern origin or sympathy. James M. Carlisle, for example, a longtime friend and trustee for both Corcoran's gallery and his Louise Home for impoverished women, was also a principal speaker at the memorial service.

Salving War Wounds

Corcoran's concern for the human consequences of the South's defeat in the Civil War was reinforced by his overall tendency to care for society's least fortunate. He was a benefactor for many individuals and causes, and helped ease the burdens for people caught up in the Confederacy's destruction. As the devastation of the Civil War erased families, fortunes, and property, Corcoran focused in part on the destitution that the war afflicted on Southern women. A very visible Southern elite had all but vanished in the capital. The banker saw this change every time he looked out his windows; the genteel ladies no longer occupied most of the stately homes on Lafayette Square.[35] Corcoran came to recognize the impact of the war in renewing his friendships throughout the South after the war. Moreover, he interacted frequently with people who were either mere acquaintances or unknown to him. Their concerns and sad situations clearly reinforced for him the troubling plight of Southern veterans, families, and widows. Corcoran helped alleviate problems in many cities and towns, even donating funds to support the poor in such faraway Southern towns as Walterboro, South Carolina—a place he had never been.[36] In Memphis, he provided money to help transition local citizens suffering from yellow fever contagion.[37]

Corcoran was especially concerned with the plight of women who had suffered in the war. He came to the aid of destitute Southern women and helped save some of them from impoverishment. In 1868 Corcoran donated funds for a shelter for indigent women impacted by the war in Georgetown. Members of the Female Union Benevolent Society of Georgetown were seeking assistance door-to-door in the capital and called upon Corcoran, who provided the necessary funds for the project on the spot— with the condition that the interest be used as an endowment to permanently support the facility. Called the Aged Woman's Home of Georgetown, the property remains in use today for its original purpose.[38] Corcoran also purchased the Patapsco Female Institute, a failing girls' school in Ellicott City, Maryland, and gave the deed to the family of John Randolph, an old-line Virginia planter, to revive the school.[39]

He also acted from a personal impulse. Corcoran in 1869 began building a permanent refuge for indigent women that he named the Louise Home after his late wife and daughter. He indicated that its purpose was "for the support and maintenance of a limited number of gentlewomen, who have been reduced by misfortune."[40] The cause of the misfortune, of course, was the Civil War's impact on their finances and families. To build the Louise Home, Corcoran selected an entire block of land on Massachusetts Avenue and—in a departure from his usual reliance on James Renwick—employed noted architect Edmund Lind of Baltimore to build a massive mansard-roofed structure to achieve his vision.[41] Built at a cost of $200,000, the Louise Home opened in 1871.[42] Once again, Corcoran

enlisted long-trusted friends and colleagues—all of whom were also associated with the Corcoran Gallery of Art—as the initial trustees of the Louise Home: James Carlisle, George Riggs, James Hall, and Anthony Hyde.[43]
The board of female overseers included the wives of most of his trustees.
Newspapers lauded the uniqueness of Corcoran's efforts and recognized
the project's memorial to his wife. "The large-hearted benevolence of Mr.
Corcoran is widely known and his character as a princely giver abundantly
established but his latest benefaction . . . has the admiration of all good
men. The older residents of Georgetown will recall the marriage of one of
their fairest belles to Mr. Corcoran and the notice it attracted in the elegant circles in which she moved," wrote papers as far away as the *St. Louis
Post Dispatch*.[44] No one talked about the significant age difference between
the couple or the fact that her family's disapproval forced them to elope.

The Louise Home accommodated forty residents, who upon arrival
lived in admirable comfort for destitute people. The facility maintained
upstairs and downstairs maids, butlers, and cooks. Residents entered the
home through a marble-paved vestibule and entertained each other and
their guests in a high-ceilinged and chandeliered reception hall. An oc-
tagonal glass-roofed palm court and a handsome library full of art from
Corcoran's gallery, along with portraits of his wife and daughter, graced
the home.[45] "No comfort, necessity, taste, wish nor thought seems want-
ing," wrote a resident of Greenville, Alabama, to her hometown paper after a trip to Washington, DC, and a visit with an old friend residing in the
Louise Home.[46] It is no wonder women wanted to live there. At least one
story popularized about the home at the time reported that Anna Atkinson
was waiting with her trunks on the porch when the building opened, and
she remained as a resident until her death in 1907.[47]

The Louise Home was also known for some residents (or "inmates," as
Corcoran referred to them in the conveyance papers) of distinguished lineage. Among the most notable was Letitia Tyler Semple, the daughter of
President John Tyler. Semple had served as her father's hostess when he
was president, and she came to the Louise Home at Corcoran's personal
invitation. She spent most of the remainder of her life in the residence and
died there.[48] Several descendants of George Washington's also lived at the
Louise Home, including the granddaughter of the president's sister, and
a grandniece of Martha Washington's. The longest-known residency in the
home was that of Rebecca Bronough, for whom Corcoran also arranged

acceptance. Bronough's mother had boarded Corcoran when he owned the Georgetown dry goods store with his brothers and had clearly helped the banker through hard times. Bronough lived in the home for more than fifty years.[49] At one point when the Louise Home had just thirty-two residents, three of them were sisters. It appears that some of the women were old friends of Corcoran's—or something more. The obituary of Cornelia Cottinger, pasted into Corcoran's scrapbook, notes not only her long residence at the home but also her physical beauty in youth and that the philanthropist was her "frequent escort among the brilliant scenes of early society."[50] The *St. Louis Post Dispatch* noted that Corcoran evidently "has pleasure seeing many of his old friends enjoying a home of luxury and comfort of his own providing."[51]

This was no ordinary charity whose largesse was available to all women in need. White privilege and a pedigree were necessary for one's admission to the Louise Home. Other than Corcoran's personal selections, residents were determined by balloting of the home's board of twelve female directors; final approval came from Corcoran. Questions related to the management of the institution were settled in the same way, with votes by the directors and a final approval by the benefactor. Corcoran was clear in what he expected at the Louise Home: "I would impress on your minds the absolute necessity of selecting for future appointments ladies of culture and refinement, whose dignified bearing will render them a desirable acquisition to the home. Let them also be chosen from that class of individuals who have known brighter days and fairer prospects; yet who have been compelled to contend with adverse circumstances, while the sensibilities of their nature interposed an insuperable obstacle to their personal solicitation of aid."[52]

Corcoran regularly dispatched a family friend and physician to attend to the aging ladies' health concerns. The doctor, Alexander Garnett, had his own colorful legacy: He fled to Richmond at the start of the Civil War and became the personal physician to Robert E. Lee and Jefferson Davis. Garnett returned to Washington after the war and attended to the remnants of Southern society. He later became the president of the American Medical Association.[53]

Corcoran's home for indigent women was among the first such private institutions not run by a religious denomination or a town and foreshadowed the more innovative expressions of shelter and refinement that were created during the Progressive Era to protect and support women's needs. Corcoran's endowment for the Louise Home also persisted long after his death. After the original building was torn down in 1949, its funding, residents, and many furnishings were transferred to a larger home still in use today, the Lisner-Louise-Dickson-Hurt home on Connecticut Avenue in Washington, DC.[54]

The Louise Home also became a model for similar residences in Washington and elsewhere. The John Dickson Home, started by philanthropist Henry Dickson in the 1920s, was established as a refuge for indigent men and specifically modeled on the Louise Home.[55] Corcoran donated funds to establish and maintain a similar home for indigent Southern women among the ruins of Charleston after the war.[56] The banker remained interested in supporting such causes throughout the remainder of his life, and in 1885 at the age of eighty-seven, he donated funds to establish a home in Richmond, Virginia, known as the R. E. Lee Camp Soldiers' Home to support ailing and indigent Confederate veterans.[57] Just months before he died, Corcoran gave $100,000 to a Confederate home in Charleston, one of many gifts to the institution.[58] Even in the postwar Republican capital, Corcoran made no secret of his charity to the old Confederacy: The philanthropist figured prominently in a front-page notice in the Washington *Evening Star* promoting a benefit for a Confederate soldiers' home. In saluting Corcoran and other contributors, the *Richmond Dispatch* wrote: "In none of her monuments erected since the war more than in Lee Camp Soldiers Home does Virginia teach the reverence she bears those who stood by her in her hour of sorest trial. None of her monuments speak more eloquently of the cause for which so many of the flowers of the South laid down their lives."[59]

Due to its family association, the Louise Home in some ways held deeper meaning for Corcoran than even his art gallery. As Corcoran observed, "The establishment of the Louise Home had its origin in my anxiety to honor and perpetuate the memory of a beloved wife and daughter."[60] Corcoran regularly celebrated his birthday and an annual Christmas reception at the home. The old Southern elite and many others, including the president, members of Congress and the Supreme Court, and ambassadors, typically attended these fetes. Said the *Fredericksburg News* after one party: "There were more than sixty around the table in the spacious dining room, with wax candles in the gilt candelabra. Nearly all the ladies of the home and guests were present . . . representing some of the oldest and most renowned families in Virginia and Maryland."[61]

Even in his later years, Corcoran's prowess as a lobbyist and rainmaker helped the former Confederate states as they sought reunification and reconciliation after the war. As indicated, it is no coincidence that Corcoran appears in a painting depicting the Florida members' Electoral College challenge during the Compromise of 1877. He helped the delegation negotiate the disposition of the state's votes to hasten the departure of Union troops and the end of Reconstruction. Similarly, Corcoran assisted a delegation from South Carolina that sought to eliminate what it perceived as unfair tax treatment that came out of the war. Wrote the *News and Courier* of Charleston: "The South throughout her trials and sufferings has had no more staunch and steadfast friend than Corcoran and the representatives of the South Carolina taxpayers who last year vainly sought relief for their state at the hands of Congress and the President will not soon forget the warm and active sympathy they received from Mr. Corcoran in the cause of their oppressed and impoverished people."[62] Indeed, the delegation even stayed at Corcoran's Arlington Hotel, and he picked up the bill.

The Contested City

Starting with George Washington, Southerners played a leading role in the nation's capital and often held dominant positions in the White House, the congressional leadership, and the Supreme Court. Most of the earliest landholders in Washington, DC, had Southern origins, and the mercantile and political leaders in Georgetown and the nascent city frequently had Tidewater region antecedents. In addition to a significant free Black population, the capital had about three thousand African American enslaved people when the institution was abolished in the city by the Republican-controlled Congress several months prior to the Emancipation Proclamation.

Historians tend to emphasize the changes in Washington, DC, during and after the Civil War while slighting the continuity born of wealth and influence. Corcoran played a more complex role, one in which not all Southern supporters were banished from the corridors of power and elite drawing rooms. His continuing impact in the city after the Civil War, both in philanthropic and political endeavors, speaks not only to his stature and influence but also suggests that Republican control in the capital was overstated—or at least not exclusive.

Scholars also view Washington, DC, as an anomaly that adds little to the study of urban America or the Gilded Age and Progressive Era. As a result, it is rarely included in studies on the topic. That view is outdated; the capital is more analogous to the country's postbellum urban development than is typically recognized. The city's similar experiences challenge the nuances in our traditional understanding of how America developed. It is little recognized, for instance, that Washington experienced many of the same late-nineteenth-century changes that affected other cities: significant immigration that overwhelmed the physical infrastructure, corruption and political bossism that led to stricter political control, changing administrative structures and charters that altered home rule, and franchise equity that broadened—temporarily—the democratic experience.

The Gilded Age and Progressive Era witnessed massive immigration, urbanization, and industrialization that drove change and reformed political structures and governance in cities in the later part of the nineteenth century.[63] What's puzzling is that Washington, DC, had essentially the same experiences as New York, Boston, Chicago, or Philadelphia with governmental corruption and reform cycles, but the capital did not see the same immigration or industrialization patterns these major municipalities witnessed. Absent some significant factors responsible for progressive change in urban America, but still evidencing the same governance patterns, Washington tests whether the traditional forces ascribed to modernity fully account for uniformity in city development during this period.

Philadelphia was the nation's largest urban center until 1800, followed by a rapidly growing New York City. Chicago experienced rapid growth at mid-century, becoming the center of the heartland and the fulcrum of transportation and industry for a burgeoning nation. These cities experienced significant population growth from both domestic and foreign sources with the development of transportation hubs linking urban centers and industry that fostered jobs, technology, and pollution. The growth of immigration and industry, particularly in the last third of the nineteenth century, stimulated the rise of the modern city. Its diversity, congestion, economic and sociopolitical disparities, political and labor tensions, and increasing regulation culminated in many Progressive Era reforms.[64]

Washington, DC, saw little of the spike in foreign immigration and the gritty industrialization that were the typical hallmarks of the emerging urban center. Nevertheless, the capital clearly experienced similar rapid change that created many of the same conditions found elsewhere. Although the capital was a fraction of the size of New York, both cities went through profound periods of growth that made them the fastest-growing cities in the nation. To be sure, the capital did not see the extensive European immigration typical of New York and other cities, but it was equally transformed by migration of another type: A historic influx of African Americans during and after the Civil War gave the capital the largest percentage of Black people in any major American city. In the mid-nineteenth century, Washington, DC, was the fastest-growing city in the nation, largely due to the arrival of African Americans and a proliferating government sector. The burgeoning numbers of free Blacks, former enslaved people, and Northern and western transplants, plus an emerging administrative state caused considerable stress on the physical infrastructure and social fabric of the city.

The capital modernized the way other cities did—establishing major public works projects for water and sewer facilities, constructing streets and lighting, creating armories and police and fire departments, and developing public spaces such as parks and museums. Washington was no different—and often much better—than other large American cities in its modernization efforts. By the time of the Civil War, Washington's aqueduct, built by the Army Corps of Engineers, was second only to New York's Croton Reservoir project as an example to other municipalities of how to construct a safe and stable water supply. Its major public park, the National Mall, was developed years prior to similar efforts in most other big cities. Washington also boasted theaters, art museums, colleges, lyceums, and—by the 1880s—suburbs, streetcars, sidewalks, and other hallmarks of advanced urban environments.

Corruption and City Bosses

Beyond the similarities of a modern infrastructure necessitated by population growth, Washington shared other important characteristics with major cities. The capital was not immune to the rise of the city boss and the corruption involving political patronage and municipal contracts. The most notorious of such bosses, of course, was New York's William (Boss) Tweed, who after years of corrupt rule was brought down by a clique of city reformers and state legislators in 1871.[65] Connecting politics and patronage was nothing new, but cities' expensive public works programs to lay streets and sewers, and to install lights, street cars, and other conveyance systems created significant opportunities for graft and corruption involving unprecedented amounts of money. In the short period of Tweed's reign, for example, New York's debt more than tripled as contracts for public works exploded.[66] Even small cities spent tens of millions of dollars to upgrade their infrastructure, and political corruption often accompanied these programs regardless of the cities' size or location. As a result, opportunities for corruption proliferated during the Gilded Age as vast sums of tax dollars shifted hands.

This was certainly how it played out in the nation's capital. Indeed, Washington's "boss," Alexander Shepherd, was toppled at almost the same time as Boss Tweed. Shepherd, the head of public works for the city, was theoretically not as powerful as Henry Cooke, the capital's leader, but he wielded considerable influence because of his control over city contracts. He was later appointed the governor by President Grant. Similar to the circumstances that resulted in Tweed's overthrow, the capital city's old-line elite led the charge to remove Shepherd and eliminate rampant spending and perceived corruption.[67] Corcoran and his old banking partner George Riggs, among others, rebelled against the growing tax assessments they faced, the lack of consultation on city infrastructure changes made by the new political forces, and the trafficking in favors and kickbacks surrounding lucrative city public works contracts by the "Washington Ring."[68] In 1870 the citizens' group tried and failed to obtain a court injunction against perceived runaway spending. In New York and other locales, legislatures or courts intervened and put a stop to the most obvious abuses.[69] In the case of Washington, DC, a series of newspaper exposés and congressional committee investigations culminated in the end of Boss Shepherd's reign and, ultimately, of the entire city government structure.[70]

Pressure to investigate the ring came, in part, from several petitions signed by residents who objected to the reckless spending, unsavory ethics, and questionable improvement results. Corcoran was among the leaders of the group that challenged the ring and withstood the worst of the ring's enmity; ironically, at the same time, he was being lauded for the opening of his art gallery.[71] Corcoran may have caught the brunt of the ring's ire because his Southern reputation made him an easy target, but he was also among its most vigorous protesters. The *Evening Star* (partly owned by Shepherd) was the ring's principal mouthpiece, and the newspaper at first denied that Corcoran and Riggs had signed the petition. Once it became clear that these eminent city fathers were among the petitioners, the newspaper resorted to name-calling, castigating them as "notorious rebels" during the war.[72] Boss Shepherd called them "malignant liars."[73] The ring also accused the wealthy banker of tax evasion and fealty to the Confederate cause.[74]

Corcoran, in turn, defended himself in a letter published by a sympathetic paper. "My fellow citizens, the abuse which has been heaped upon me by the press of the district has been such as it has rarely fallen to the lot of even a felon to receive. . . . They have for more than a week ventilated my life . . . and questioned the motives . . . for spending my money . . . for the beauty and advantage of this district." Beyond complaining about his treatment at the hand of the ring's pet newspaper, Corcoran made specific accusations about the Commission of Public Works' infrastructure program:

> [T]he mode in which this work has been done, the absence of competition, the fact that prices were fixed by the board of public works and the work given to people of its own choosing, the large bills that have presented in all quarters . . . give rise to a very well-grounded suspicion that . . . the assessment has been excessive. This work to a great degree has been improperly done, the charge for the same often its value and the assessment in some cases amounting to more than the value of the property.

Corcoran concluded his letter with a call to other citizens: "This great irregularity certainly cannot be sustained by any principle of law and should induce a thoughtful examination by all citizens."[75]

While most local papers were too afraid of the ring to openly support Corcoran and the rebellious old elite, the *Sentinel* quickly defended him. "The honest men in the country are all not dead yet. But few of them are willing at the age and position of Mr. Corcoran to step boldly forward and stem the tide of corruption which is flooding our country. . . . He will not stop until the tyrants of Washington are ousted."[76] A retrospective compiled by the *New York Sun* concluded that "the plunder of the District began as soon as the Ring was organized."[77]

The ring was unmoved and once more took to name-calling. The *Washington Chronicle* accused the eminent citizens of nothing more than conducting a "fishing trip" against the local government. The *Evening Star* accused them of getting in the way of "young men of energy." Calling the philanthropist and his colleagues "vagabonds" and "misanthropes," the *Chronicle* wrote: "The petitioners should put on paper over their own signature precisely what is the charge against the officers of whom they complain. To tell the [congressional investigating] committee to scurry around until they can find some probable wrong to investigate is insufficient."[78] Shepherd attempted to silence his opponents by having *Washington Tribune* newspaper editor Whitelaw Reid arrested on charges of criminal libel, but Corcoran stepped in and arranged for Reid's bail. His objections against the ring continued unabated.[79] In turn, the ring accused Corcoran of having secretive ties to Boss Tweed, the very sort of man he was trying to unseat at home. Out-of-town newspapers not controlled by the ring came to Corcoran's defense. The *Baltimore Sun*, typically a Corcoran supporter, explained that the only connection, unknown to each other, was that both men owned stock in the same railroad company.[80] Other papers, however, charged that in 1870 Tweed had invested $25,000 in *the Daily Patriot*, a Corcoran-supported newspaper; Corcoran later took these securities off his hands for one-third of their value.[81] The revelation is not surprising given the breadth of Corcoran's political associations.

The *New York Tribune*'s Horace Greeley, who had helped tackle Boss Tweed, was no friend of Corcoran's. Still, the publisher was critical about the scourge of corruption in the nation's capital, reporting that early investigations found street contractors had billed twice for the materials that had been used and were reimbursed for three times their cost. Only fear of exposure had forced the ring to pay back some of the funds, the *Tribune* charged.[82] Greeley also attacked members of Congress, whom he accused of collusion with the ring.

> From one end of the United States to the other it is the common opinion
> that the district government is nothing but an organization of swindling

rings . . . in which members of the Senate and House have a pecuniary interest. The House committee discovered nothing as it was later revealed that the chairman had leaned on Ring members for funds to defray election expenses. The President then promoted Shepherd to governor. . . . Surely, they are not all smeared with asphalt or mired in the real estate pool.[83]

The *Tribune* also carried a rare verbatim interview with Corcoran regarding the ring in which the old city father criticized the financial management of the territorial government. "It is very strange, with all this revenue collected from the people, that the police force are not paid and that the schoolteachers are in even worse condition. . . . Something must be radically wrong in the financial management," Corcoran said.[84]

Ultimately, the city government was overturned, and the ring collapsed. While the end of Boss Shepherd reduced corruption at the source, it also meant the end of home rule for the nation's capital. Boss Shepherd fled to Mexico, and governance of the capital was federalized. As local control over government functions was eliminated, Congress in 1877 established a commissioner form of government to manage the city, with the commissioners appointed by the president and subject to congressional oversight.[85] This decision cast a long shadow over the capital city. The commissioner form of government lasted nearly a century and fell, only grudgingly, in the modern civil rights era when the city's mayor and council form of government were restored in 1973.[86]

Home Rule

The struggles in the late nineteenth century over home rule were generally about runaway budgets, corruption, and the expectations surrounding public management of the postbellum city.[87] The fight over municipal control and budgets, in part, determined whether cities managed their destiny or whether it was controlled for them at the state level. Sometimes it was both: Boss Tweed, through his control of the New York State legislature, succeeded in broadening New York City's home-rule charter to his advantage, giving the city—in this case, Tammany Hall—control over most administrative matters. The downfall of Boss Tweed led to the revocation of this broad grant of city power and created a backlash in the state legislature that limited home rule.[88] Additional changes reduced patronage at the city level and professionalized some functions, especially those related to contracts and infrastructure projects.[89] Of course, the same state legislature that Tweed once controlled and that had allowed him to exercise leverage over the city later needed to rectify these issues.

Other states were forced to take similar action as legislatures, citizens, and journalists fought the corrupt bosses of municipal America. By the mid-1870s, changes to city charters and state constitutions helped to end city bosses' control, to limit municipal home rule, and to reduce corruption. Many prominent cities and states shifted control from local city councils associated with corruption to mayors, strong city managers, and administrative boards and commissions.[90] These new political structures were often implemented without any productive role for the city councils as part of a purposeful weakening of their influence and, therefore, less voter representation. Independent regulatory structures also grew more prevalent in the states as they sought ways to battle corruption. Some cities and states experimented with commissions and boards, supported by a bureaucracy of experts, to manage and oversee a host of public functions, from sewers to roads, parks to schools, and hospitals to electricity.[91] The trend culminated in similar changes at the federal level as a national regulatory apparatus was constructed in the Progressive Era. Boston is generally considered to be among the forerunners of this administrative shift, and by the mid-1880s, dozens of boards and commissions were operating in multiple states.[92] Galveston, Texas, is usually recognized as the first city completely run by a commission form of government, but its creation after the 1900 hurricane that almost destroyed the city ignores the place of Washington, DC, in this important governmental transition.[93]

Profligate city spending and poor municipal management had an even greater impact when combined with the economic depression that started in 1873. Cities and towns ran up huge infrastructure, contract, and budgetary commitments that were undermined by the Panic of 1873. As a result, some cities went bankrupt, and many others curtailed or limited their infrastructure programs. States reacted by further curtailing local government action and limiting their cities' ability to tax, borrow, and spend. The result was a significant reduction in infrastructure spending in most American cities for about a decade; that tended to reduce corruption at its source. With less money to spend, many municipal governments shrank, and their more unsavory practices were, at least temporarily, less odious.[94]

Cities in the 1870s had difficulty navigating modernity without corruption. Nevertheless, this period should also be recognized for its contributions in furthering the development of effective government. Cities had many challenges in improving public functions. Corruption aside, many localities successfully improved desperately needed municipal services in this period. To the extent that cities coped with the extraordinary changes affecting them at the end of the nineteenth century—immigration, industrialization, and labor conflicts—the changes to municipal governance that helped overcome corruption and other abuses of the time were an important step in progressive reform and the emergence of modern public governance.[95]

This was certainly true in the nation's capital. Despite the corruption, it is difficult to dismiss Boss Shepherd's vision and impact. In the 1870s, Washington, DC, spent millions of dollars in a massive endeavor to modernize the city and strengthen its reputation as an international capital. Amid accusations real and imagined, the local government managed to build significant and much-needed infrastructure in the city center that had eluded previous administrations. Shepherd is remembered not only for his corrupt administration but also for establishing the structural foundations of a modern capital.[96]

It was not long before some members of Congress were convinced that management of the capital's public works program had gone awry, and—despite objections from Cooke and Shepherd—they held hearings to investigate charges of corruption. The investigations went on for several years and examined testimony from hundreds of people associated with the city's infrastructure construction program. The investigation brought to light many unsavory practices, including payments for drainage pipes, paving, and other construction materials that cost taxpayers far more than their value; malfeasance and incompetence in project management and execution that resulted in entire city blocks without sidewalks or paving that had been paid for, delivered, and reported to have been installed; sewer and water lines that were expected to connect but were ten feet apart; and dozens of mysterious payments made between contractors and influence peddlers for no obvious purpose.[97] However, as was the case in most cities, accusations of corruption and other illegal activity were very difficult to prove. In fact, corruption of the spoils and lobbying system may have been more pernicious than actual contract fraud at the time.[98] Occasionally, people did go to jail; Boss Tweed of New York was the most notable example. In Washington, DC, incredibly, no one involved in the ring went to prison, although many participants, including Boss Shepherd, left the capital or the country.

City Governance

As noted, the end of the Washington Ring meant the end of home rule in the capital. This occurred in several stages. Congress first eliminated the elected government in Washington, DC, and established a territorial government on the theory it would be more accountable and less captive to local influence.[99] When the ring's abuses were revealed, Congress moved beyond the reduction of local control, establishing federal dominance and embracing the principles of the coming Progressive Era. Congress created an insulated political structure of appointed commissioners supported by an administrative state, in this case exercised by experts and departments of the federal government, that lasted nearly a hundred years. Federal control of this American city—generations after the fall of Reconstruction—continued unabated until pressures from the cresting civil rights movement of the 1960s finally forced Congress to relinquish most of its control.[100]

It is difficult to prove but hard to ignore that this monumental change in the capital city would not have occurred without Corcoran's leadership in getting rid of the ring. At least one newspaper said as much: "That result would never have been achieved but for the energy and unflinching courage of our venerable and respected fellow citizen Mr. W.W. Corcoran. That Investigating Commission would never have been appointed but for his influence."[101]

As with actions taken by city fathers in other locales, Corcoran and his associates objected to changes that limited their influence or shifted authority from them. Many were Democrats and Southern in their leanings. In some respects, they were fighting old battles regarding deference, values, and community. They were also forced to contend with the enfranchisement of African Americans, an imposition of equality legislated by the Radical Republicans. An observant newspaper reporter even witnessed Corcoran and Riggs standing in line, waiting to vote behind a lengthy line of Black people.[102] Shepherd, Cooke, and Grant represented a Northern and Republican ascendancy that had taken over the city during Corcoran's voluntary exile. While Corcoran was successful in exposing the ring and vanquishing what he believed to be unwelcome corruption and malfeasance in the city's municipal affairs, his victory was short lived; local control was not reinstated. Corcoran and his friends may have gained a more sympathetic ear with federal control and more political access through a commission system and congressional oversight process more attentive to their influence; however, the price of their narrow victory was lost local control for nearly a century. Although not explicitly stated, perhaps Corcoran and his friends, with their customary access to Capital Hill and the levers of government, had less need for direct democracy if they could still achieve their goals the old-fashioned way through networks and favors, but that privilege was hardly bestowed on the newly enfranchised African Americans.

That much was achieved in Washington, DC, despite the corruption associated with Shepherd's ring fits well into the historical view that cities successfully weathered the corruption and influence peddling that plagued the political system. Consequent reforms went far to professionalizing the municipal administration that was crucial to city development in the Progressive Era. Some revisionists even suggest much of the Gilded Age corruption was more smoke than fire.[103] They argue that the case of Washington, DC, was greatly overblown and that the fires were fanned by a hyperventilating Democratic press intent on bringing down Republican politicians.[104] In this interpretation, corruption in city government was not a product of the Gilded Age's Great Barbeque or a consequence of wholesale changes in urban America. Rather, the corruption had been an ongoing part of city administration for decades, perhaps since the start of the republic. All that changed, according to this view, was who controlled the outcome. By the time Congress eliminated home rule in the nation's capital, dozens of boards and commissions were overseeing public programs, mostly in the regulatory area, in cities across the country. However, there is no record before this time that a commission was managing an entire city. It is hard to imagine such an important change occurring in Washington, DC, without the consummate insider playing a role in the city's new direction.[105] While it may be argued whether the commissioner form of government was appropriate for the capital (to say nothing of the consequent elimination of the franchise), the old banker helped institute a new structure of expert and bureaucratic administration that in the 1870s was still largely ahead of its time. Congress ushered in federal control over the district and ushered out the voting franchise for all men—White or Black—in the city. Corcoran and other influential city fathers thus would be forever connected to a charge of racism: They would rather disenfranchise themselves than perpetuate equal voting rights.[106]

9
LEGACY

ON FEBRUARY 25, 1888, WILLIAM WILSON CORCORAN DIED IN HIS
sleep in the mansion across Lafayette Square from the White House
where he had lived for nearly fifty years. Corcoran was eighty-nine years
old, had suffered a variety of increasingly debilitating illnesses, and finally
succumbed of their accumulation in his old age. Still, even to the end,
Corcoran retained an optimism and enthusiasm for life. "I am interested
in the present, in the everyday occurrences. I like to see my friends and to
talk with them. It seems to me that I am not an old man in that respect,"
Corcoran explained in an interview less than a year before his death.[1]

Corcoran suffered several severe illnesses in his last years that left him
near death more than once. The *New York Times* even prematurely published what amounted to a two-column obituary when he almost died in
1880.[2] He would live nearly eight more years. Few people knew of his condition in the final months, and the banker rarely ventured into society as
his health declined. He had an apparent stroke while eating dinner with
friends in June 1887 that caused partial paralysis to his right arm and leg;
after that, he needed assistance to get around although his mental acu-
ity remained strong. To the watchful, his shaky condition when receiving
communion at the altar rail of St. John's Church was a troubling manifestation of his deteriorating health. He almost collapsed receiving the sac-
rament. Friends and family bore Corcoran to his carriage and his bed. He
died of bronchitis a week after this episode.[3] Even in his last moments, he
gave to the needy: Hours before he died, Corcoran wrote out a check for
$500 to a young woman whose husband had committed suicide.

Corcoran's will provided for $3 million to be divided among his three grandchildren, with smaller amounts directed to the art gallery and the Louise Home.[4] The philanthropist had already given away many times that amount over his lifetime. "Of all my money, that which I have given away is all that is truly mine," he said.[5] Corcoran's casket was laid out in the library of his mansion, and the philanthropist was dressed in his familiar simple black suit and red rose. In addition to the First Lady, the chief justice, diplomats, and members of Congress, the attendees of Corcoran's funeral included the children of the City Orphan Asylum—one of his enduring charities.[6]

Born in Washington, DC, before the capital was even created, Corcoran endured almost to the twentieth century. Hamilton Fish, a longtime politician and secretary of state, apocryphally breathed a sigh of relief that "the old reb" was finally dead. Yet, Fish and most everyone else in Washington—even those who questioned his loyalty to the Union—recognized Corcoran's contributions to the nation's capital and to the country's commerce and culture. Corcoran lived a long and influential life that established him as a forerunner in national finance. He used his influence in the capital to vitalize art, education, politics and lobbying, philanthropy, and the built environment. Moreover, his role in expanding the reach of capital and culture in American society started a generation before the wealthy industrialists of the Gilded Age turned their attention to similar objectives.

Corcoran typically acted on his own initiative to improve the city and the society in which he lived, but he relied on a strong and like-minded network of wealthy business and political associates who shared his values. These individuals were not shy about using their money, contacts, and social status to achieve public goals as well as private objectives. While not everyone in Corcoran's financial or political circles shared his sense of duty or his vision of how best to support the community and the country, many did. Despite political or sectional differences, they coalesced around a vision of the modern American capital. The irony, of course, is that Corcoran managed to outlive just about everyone in his vaunted networks and the varied walks of his life: a generation or two of politicians, lobbyists, artists and critics, architects and landscapers, urban planners, bankers and merchants, soldiers, rebels, and philanthropists.

Corcoran's death was a big deal. It was covered on the front pages of newspapers across the country, from the major New York and Washington papers to smaller papers as far away as Texas, California, Indiana, and Iowa. Corcoran's death was news for the entire nation, and the obituaries were universally laudatory. Virtually none mentioned his self-imposed exile in Europe during the Civil War. They were silent about his Southern sympathies and the rumors of plots to kill President Lincoln or of funds for the Confederacy. Moreover, there was little mention in the obituaries about Corcoran's political and lobbying acumen. Instead, the papers and chroniclers focused on Corcoran's entrepreneurial investment skills, the founding of Corcoran & Riggs, and his wide-ranging philanthropy.

Tributes from Congress also focused on his many contributions instead of his shortcomings. Corcoran was a "munificent patron of art, science and many public and private charities, both in the national capital and the country at large, . . . [and he] has left a memory that deserves to be gratefully cherished," one summation read.[7]

Corcoran would have gracefully accepted the recognition and then probably looked for more to accomplish.

NOTES

Introduction

1. Begun in 1869, the Corcoran Gallery of Art became part of the National Gallery of Art in 2014. The associated school is now affiliated with George Washington University.
2. Bruchey, *Enterprise*, 149–52.
3. Gladwell, *Tipping Point*, chap. 2.
4. Wiebe, *Opening of American Society*, chap. 8 and epilogue.
5. "St. John's Church, Georgetown," *New York Observer*, July 7, 1870, W. W. Corcoran scrapbook, 98, Special Collections Research Center, George Washington University Archives, Estelle and Melvin Gelman Library, Washington, DC (hereafter GW Archives).

1. Beginnings

1. Corcoran, *A Grandfather's Legacy*, 3–4.
2. *Atlanta Constitution*, May 22, 1884, 4.
3. Corcoran, *A Grandfather's Legacy*, 4.
4. Corcoran, 6.
5. Bryan, "L'Enfant's Personal Affairs," 117.
6. Corcoran, *A Grandfather's Legacy*, 5.
7. "How Corcoran Made His Money," *People's Friend*, August 5, 1886, 7.
8. Corcoran, *A Grandfather's Legacy*, 5.
9. Corcoran, 6. The debt equates to roughly $1.5 million in 2023 dollars.
10. Sandage, *Born Losers*, 8. Categorical inequality with respect to race and

gender predominated throughout most of the nineteenth century, especially prior to Reconstruction, resulting in few business opportunities for women and African Americans. See Hogan, "Class, Gender and Race Inequality," 61–93. Nevertheless, African American businesses at times contravened law and custom, and often existed in separate spheres, although data is limited. See Walker and Garett-Scott, "African American Business History," 395–406.

11. Sandage, 8; and Balleisen, *Navigating Failure*, 3.
12. Johnson, "Free Blacks in Antebellum Savannah," 418–31.
13. Schweninger, "Black-Owned Businesses," 22–60.
14. Thoreau, *Walden*, 430.
15. Sandage, *Born Losers*, prologue.
16. Mann, *Republic of Debtors*, 177.
17. Mann, 38.
18. As quoted in Mann, 101.
19. Sandage, *Born Losers*, 31.
20. Balliesen, *Navigating Failure*, 3.
21. Balliesen, 12.
22. Van Ness was a mayor of the District of Columbia and a militia general in the War of 1812. He recommended that the militia retain a presence in the capital to prevent a British advance, but the secretary of war overruled him, and the British later burned the public buildings. With guidance from Corcoran, Van Ness's remains were moved to Oak Hill Cemetery in 1872.
23. Corcoran, *A Grandfather's Legacy*, 6. The Bank of Columbia was nicknamed the "White Cow" in reference to its being milked so hard by its owners that it died. Private investors and the US Treasury suffered heavy losses when the bank failed.
24. Corcoran; and *Marion (OH) Daily Star*, September 18, 1880, 2.
25. "City Property to Be Sold for Taxes," *National Intelligencer*, October 19, 1838, 4.
26. Augst, *Clerk's Tale*, 3–4.
27. Augst, 14.
28. Bruchey, *Enterprise*, 158–60.
29. Augst, *Clerk's Tale*, 14.
30. Augst, 219.
31. Carr, *32 President's Square*, 22–23, 41.
32. Cohen, *Business and Politics*, 5–7; and Carr, 22, 41–43.
33. Green, *Washington*, 3. The first bank established by African Americans in Washington, DC, was not opened until 1888. Many Blacks, especially

soldiers, used the Freedmen's Bank after the US government established it in 1865. Some banks, such as Corcoran & Riggs, accepted Black clients although many banks did not.

34. Green, 34.
35. Green, 59.
36. Green, 65.
37. Green, 75.
38. Bruchey, *Enterprise*, chap. 6.
39. Green, *Secret City*, 25–27. It bears remembering that slavery was prevalent even in the North at the beginning of the nineteenth century. Twenty percent of New York City's population was enslaved in this period.
40. Leech, *Reveille in Washington*, 60.
41. Green, *Washington*, 52.
42. Green, 54.
43. Green, 55.
44. Green, *Secret City*, 32.
45. See Rothman, *Ledger and the Chain*, for a discussion of how the slave trade reached throughout antebellum America.
46. Damani Davis, "Slavery and Emancipation in the Nation's Capital," Genealogy Notes, *Prologue Magazine* 42, no. 1 (Spring 2010), National Archives and Records Administration, Washington, DC (hereafter NARA).
47. Davis. Scholarly contributions about African Americans in the nation's capital have recently created a more nuanced picture. See, for instance, Rothman and Mendoza, *Facing Georgetown's History*; and Torrey and Green, *Between Freedom and Equality*.
48. Corcoran's father listed twenty-five people as living in his household, six of whom were slaves, on the 1800 federal census. The first census in which Corcoran is listed independently is 1840, and his entry lists one male slave and three free Black females. The 1860 census, just prior to emancipation in the capital, lists Corcoran as having no slaves. The census lists several employees, including a cook, a housekeeper, and a doorkeeper of English and Irish lineage, and one Black servant.
49. Ricks, *Escape on the* Pearl, 112.
50. Parker and Parker, *George Peabody*, part 4, 49. The notation mainly focuses on alleged connections that Peabody had with the slave trade in the 1830s. The *Salem (MA) News* in 2008 referenced research indicating that Peabody also "did business with a slave trader in the Washington, D.C., area named William Corcoran."
51. See one such example, "For Sale," *Columbian Gazette*, August 16, 1832, 3.

See also "Bank Adds to Slavery Disclosure," *Chicago Sun Times*, May 4, 2004, 12.

52. See "James Wilson Corcoran," Find a Grave Memorial, wilson-corcoran, 2021.

53. "Bank Adds to Slavery Disclosure."

54. Records of the US Circuit Court for the District of Columbia, Records of Manumission, vol. 3, Record Group 60, NARA. The District of Columbia Emancipation Act was passed in April 1862, eight months before the Emancipation Proclamation went into effect. The capital's Emancipation Act is the only instance of government-compensated emancipation in the United States. The federal government paid almost $1 million to slaveowners to free approximately thirty-one hundred enslaved people.

55. William Wilson Corcoran, "Last Will and Testament," September 6, 1887, George Washington University Archives, Washington, DC (hereafter GWU Archives). Corcoran provided a stipend of $200 to a woman named Mary Neale, "once owned by me," who is likely the same woman he freed from slavery.

56. When Roger Jones, the man to whom Corcoran sold his father's enslaved people, reneged on his promise not to sell them in the South, Corcoran sued for breach of contract but lost in court.

57. "An Exciting Slave Case," *Lackawanna Citizen*, August 16, 1850, 2.

58. Hurst, "Maryland Gentry," 1, 2.

59. Hurst, 1.

60. Hurst, 4

61. Hurst, "Business and Businessmen," 161–71.

62. Hurst.

63. Hurst.

64. Green, *Washington*, 34.

65. Green, 34–35.

66. Rotundo, *American Manhood*, 3.

67. Wood, *Radicalism*, section 2: "Republicanism."

68. Corcoran, *A Grandfather's Legacy,* 1.

69. Corcoran, 6. John Philip Sousa would later compose a military march titled the "Corcoran Cadets March" in Corcoran's memory. The piece was published in 1890, two years after Corcoran's death.

70. Carr, *32 President's Square*, 19.

71. Carr, 14. Corcoran was also influential with other famous widows, including President James Madison's wife, Dolley, whom he advised on financial and legal matters. See Wharton, *Social Life*, 302.

72. Beckert, "Merchants and Manufacturers," in Fraser and Gerstle, *Ruling America*, 98.

73. Corcoran, A *Grandfather's Legacy*, 11–16.

74. See Jacob, *Capital Elites*.

75. See Halttunen, *Confidence Men*; and Lukasik, *Discerning Characters*, for discussions of appearance, behavior, and social distinction in the antebellum era.

76. Kasson, *Rudeness and Civility*, 77.

77. Kasson, 89.

78. Hemphill, *Bowing to Necessities*, 9.

79. Hemphill, 145.

80. Corcoran, A *Grandfather's Legacy*, 11–16.

81. *Columbian Gazette*, October 14, 1833, Corcoran scrapbook, 2.

82. *The Metropolitan*, Corcoran scrapbook, unnumbered page.

83. Lystra, *Searching the Heart*, 4–7.

84. Rothman, *Hands and Hearts*, 9.

85. Rothman. Historical research has shown that African American courtships often followed the same patterns as those of upper-class Whites in their correspondence regarding gender roles and expectations. These characteristics are highlighted in the example of a Black Texas couple, Calvin Rhone and Lucia Knotts, in which the man expresses his love and impatience with the pace of the courtship and the woman seeks to slow their encounters. See Howard, "Courtship Letters," 64–80.

86. W. W. Corcoran to Louise Morris, July 23, 1835, William Wilson Corcoran papers, 1.1.19, Library of Congress, Washington, DC (hereafter LOC). My notation for the correspondence set between Corcoran and Louise in this chapter refers in sequence to the container, folder, and item number of the letter.

87. W. W. Corcoran to Louise Morris, September 14, 1835, Corcoran papers, 1.2.7, LOC.

88. Louise Morris to W. W. Corcoran, April 5, 1835, Corcoran papers, 1.1.9, LOC.

89. W. W. Corcoran to Louise Morris, July 4, 1835, Corcoran papers, 1.1.17, LOC.

90. Corcoran to Morris, July 4, 1835.

91. Louise Morris to W. W. Corcoran, April 10, 1835, Corcoran papers, 1.1.10, LOC.

92. Louise Morris to W. W. Corcoran, April 8, 1835, Corcoran papers, 1.1.10, LOC. Ironically, they instruct each other to burn their letters. Such

instructions were obviously ignored since the letters remain among Corcoran's papers today.

93. Louise Morris to W. W. Corcoran, November 10, 1835, Corcoran papers, 1.1.37, LOC.
94. Morris to Corcoran, November 10, 1835.
95. Morris to Corcoran, November 10, 1835.
96. Louise Morris to W. W. Corcoran, February 24, 1835, Corcoran papers, 1.1.14, LOC.
97. Morris to Corcoran, February 24, 1835.
98. W. W. Corcoran to Louise Morris, February 24, 1835, Corcoran papers, 1.1.5, LOC.
99. W. W. Corcoran to Louise Morris, August 30, 1835, Corcoran papers, 1.1.25, LOC.
100. Louise Morris to W. W. Corcoran, July 8, 1835, Corcoran papers, 1.1.18, LOC.
101. W. W. Corcoran to Louise Morris, June 26, 1835, Corcoran papers, 1.1.11, LOC.
102. Louise Morris to W. W. Corcoran, July 24, 1835, Corcoran papers, 1.1.20, LOC.
103. Morris to Corcoran, July 24, 1835.
104. Lystra, *Searching the Heart*, introduction.
105. Louise Morris to W. W. Corcoran, October 26, 1835, Corcoran papers, 1.1.26, LOC.
106. W. W. Corcoran to Louise Morris, October 28, 1835, Corcoran papers, 1.2.4, LOC.
107. W. W. Corcoran to Louise Morris, November 7, 1835, Corcoran papers, 1.2.10, LOC.
108. Louise Morris to W. W. Corcoran, December 4, 1835, Corcoran papers, 1.2.11, LOC.
109. Corcoran, *A Grandfather's Legacy*, 6–7.
110. Corcoran, 9–10.
111. W. W. Corcoran to Louise Corcoran, October 15, 1836, Corcoran papers, 1.3.8, LOC.
112. W. W. Corcoran to Louise Corcoran, October 17, 1836, Corcoran papers, 1.3.10, LOC.
113. Corcoran to L. Corcoran, October 15, 1836.
114. W. W. Corcoran to Louise Corcoran, October 18, 1836, Corcoran papers, 1.3.12, LOC.
115. W. W. Corcoran to Louise Corcoran, October 21, 1836, Corcoran papers, 1.3.15, LOC.

116. W. W. Corcoran to Louise Corcoran, May 26, 1837, Corcoran papers, 1.3.19, LOC.
117. W. W. Corcoran to Louise Corcoran, October 13, 1836, Corcoran papers, 1.3.3, LOC.
118. Louise Corcoran to W. W. Corcoran, August 23, 1836, Corcoran papers, 1.2.16, LOC.
119. L. Corcoran to Corcoran, August 23, 1836.
120. L. Corcoran to Corcoran, August 23, 1836.
121. Corcoran, *A Grandfather's Legacy*, 7.

2. Rise of the Political Banker

1. Gilge, "Rise of Capitalism," 163.
2. Brown Brothers & Co. would become the distinguished firm of Brown Brothers Harriman, and George Peabody's firm upon his death would be assumed by his partner, Junius Spencer Morgan, culminating in the emergence of his son J. P. Morgan as a legendary financier.
3. Wiebe sees a constricting society in *Search for Order, 1877–1920*, which covers the period after the antebellum era and situates an institutional corrective to the society he posits in his *Opening of American Society*. Similar themes are echoed in the work of Morton Keller's *Regulating a New Economy*; he sees growing uniformity in the nation's regulatory framework and political economy. Trachtenberg's *Incorporation of America* describes new hierarchies of control and order throughout society.
4. Appleby's *Capitalism and a New Social Order* and McCoy's *Elusive Republic* suggest an expanding commercial economy increasingly unencumbered by social deference. John F. Kasson, in *Civilizing the Machine*, shows the emerging shift from agriculture to industry that helped broaden the economy during the early national period.
5. Hammond, *Banks and Politics*, chaps. 12–14.
6. Perkins, *American Public Finance*, 25.
7. Bodenhorn, *History of Banking*, 45–49.
8. Amos Kendall to W. W. Corcoran, January 7, 1869, *National Intelligencer*, undated, Corcoran scrapbook, 74, GW Archives.
9. Lamoreaux, *Insider Lending*, 4–5. In later periods, however, the author contends opportunities constricted as banks were less able to discern worthy credit risks.
10. Bodenhorn, *History of Banking*, 46, 95.

11. Bodenhorn, 211–12; and Bodenhorn, *State Banking*, 4–6.

12. Bodenhorn, *History of Banking*; and Bodenhorn, *State Banking*.

13. Bodenhorn, *History of Banking*, 210–11.

14. Wright, *Origins of Commercial Banking*, conclusion.

15. Wright, 192.

16. Corcoran's bank records, held by successor bank PNC Inc., and the GW Archives, show a variety of clients.

17. See description of PNC–Riggs Bank Records, Scope and Content Note, Identifier MS 2213, Special Collections Research Center, GW Archives.

18. In an interesting parallel, Stephen Girard's Philadelphia bank operated in the building that housed the First Bank of the United States.

19. Corcoran, *A Grandfather's Legacy*, 7.

20. "Mr. Riggs' Illness," *National Republican*, August 11, 1881, 4. Corcoran also realized large real estate profits elsewhere, such as in New York City, where lots he initially purchased for $30 each sold for $4,500 each some years later. See "City Intelligence," *Daily American Organ*, November 22, 1855, 3.

21. "Mr. Riggs' Illness."

22. "Mr. Riggs' Illness."

23. Corcoran started the bank on his own but soon brought into the firm George Riggs, the son of Elisha Riggs, an important early Wall Street financier.

24. "Exchange Office," *Madisonian*, January 20, 1838, 4.

25. Carr, *32 President's Square*, 23.

26. Corcoran was very supportive of Webster's Senate speeches defending the Union against secessionist sentiments.

27. Cohen, *Business and Politics*, 20; and Carr, *32 President's Square*, 64–65. An alternate story is that Corcoran's big break came with the help of John Moulder, the chief clerk of the Treasury Department and the grand master of Corcoran's local Masonic lodge. Moulder and Corcoran were good friends, as the chief clerk of the Treasury Department would have been a helpful personage to Corcoran. See Harris, *Sesqui-centennial History*, 45.

28. Cohen, *Business and Politics*, 20; and Carr, *32 President's Square*, 64–65.

29. It is nearly impossible to determine the actual amount of Corcoran's profits, as such information is not recorded in the bank's ledgers and no tax laws would have forced the disclosure of the net proceeds. However, Carr, in *32 President's Square*, estimates the fees were around 3 percent for the initial loan. On the Mexican-American War loan of 1847, Corcoran & Riggs cornered about 80 percent themselves (and more through settlements and agreements with others). At the same rates,

this would have netted Corcoran several million dollars, as his share of the loan would have been around $108,000, Carr estimates.

30. Letters instructing the bank regarding financial matters came from various presidents and other officials, and are found in the PNC Bank records and in Corcoran, *A Grandfather's Legacy*.

31. Corcoran & Riggs would later help fund a variety of important endeavors, ranging from the telegraph to the expansion of the US Capitol, from the Mexican-American War to loaning the government $7.2 million in gold to purchase Alaska from Russia in 1867. The bank likely funded the Alaska purchase at the behest of Secretary of State William Seward, Corcoran's friend and the man for whom the then-questionable purchase of "Seward's Folly" was named.

32. Cohen, *Business and Politics*, 32. Minutes from various Smithsonian Institution Board of Regents' meetings in the early 1850s discuss instructions to Corcoran & Riggs regarding the Smithson Trust and its investment parameters. See Minutes of the Board of Regents, Smithsonian Institution Archives, Washington, DC.

33. PNC Bank records, Corcoran's letters in the Library of Congress, and his *A Grandfather's Legacy,* as well as secondary sources, contain many references to the politicians and other famous people who used the banking or brokerage services of Corcoran & Riggs.

34. Carr, *32 President's Square*, 68–69. Bankers such as Corcoran were not always considered reputable discounters and were at times accused of profiting beyond custom on notes to vulnerable people, such as pensioners. See "In the House of Representatives," *National Intelligencer*, February 19, 1848, 8.

35. Carr, *32 President's Square*, 68–69.

36. Corcoran spread his money among Democrats, Whigs, and Republicans alike and helped support the interests of several journalists, such as James Clarke Welling, who ran influential papers. Corcoran's generosity was often returned by favorable coverage. See Cohen, *Business and Politics*, 24. Cohen also concluded that Corcoran speculated with favored clients using joint accounts.

37. Such individuals included Daniel Webster, Thomas Hart Benton, Millard Fillmore, Stephen Douglas, James Buchanan, and many others, mainly politicians or influential officeholders. Cohen states that Corcoran's loans were usually repaid and rarely forgiven, but the records have little evidence of such repayments. See Cohen, 26.

38. Cohen, 36–37.

39. Cohen, 14. Few of Woodbury's papers survive, so it remains unclear

whether Corcoran was unique in obtaining inside information from the Treasury Department. Woodbury, like Forward, was a lawyer and not a financier. Appointed to the US Supreme Court by President James K. Polk, Woodbury became the first justice on the court with a law degree.

40. Merry, *Country of Vast Designs*, 376.

41. Wolff, *Capitol Builder*, 15.

42. Cohen, *Business and Politics*, 10–11.

43. Cohen, 10–13.

44. Cohen.

45. Elisha Riggs to W. W. Corcoran, December 7, 1837, unnumbered pages, in Elisha Riggs, Letterpress Book, 1832–1839, Record Group 1, Subgroup 1, Series 2, flatbox 650, PNC-Riggs Bank Records, MS2213, GW Archives.

46. George Newbold to W. W. Corcoran, December 13, 1851, in Corcoran, *A Grandfather's Legacy*, 104

47. Carr, *32 President's Square*, 59.

48. "Copartnership," *Washington Globe*, April 14, 1841, 2.

49. Indeed, the twenty-two-year-old Elisha Riggs Jr., who ultimately took over from his older half brother George, complained that he was left to the internal workings of the firm, while Corcoran was consumed with the "outdoor business" and had no time for correspondence. Riggs also complained of overwork and a lack of sherry, which he asked to be sent from New York along with recommendations for clerks. See Elisha Riggs Jr. to George Riggs, July 11, 1848, in Carr, *32 President's Square*.

50. "Life in Washington," untitled newspaper, January 1, 1857, Corcoran scrapbook, 82, GW Archives.

51. Cohen, *Business and Politics*, 9.

52. *Logansport (IN) Daily Star*, December 25, 1874, 2.

53. Nevins and Thomas, *Diary of George Templeton Strong*, 10–20.

54. Chandler and Tedlow, *Coming of Managerial Capitalism*, 115–16.

55. "Chesapeake & Ohio Canal," *Washington Globe*, January 29, 1841, 3. Corcoran also took investments in railroad companies as the canal business waned. See "Metropolitan Railroad Company," *National Intelligencer*, May 21,1853, 2. Corcoran was on the board of the Metropolitan Railroad as early as 1850.

56. See discussion of Judson v. Corcoran, *New York Daily Herald*, February 28, 1855, 4; and "United States Supreme Court," *New York Times*, April 10, 1877, 2. See decision at Supreme Court, Judson v. Corcoran, December Term, 58 U.S. 612 (1854), 615.

57. "Congressional Pets," *Southern Press*, August 4, 1852, 2.

58. Corcoran & Riggs to George Peabody, February 27, 1844, and September 10, 1845, respectively, quoted in Hidy, *George Peabody*, 266–67.

59. "Missing Links," *Western Cyclone*, March 31, 1887, 1.

60. Jesse Bright was beyond solicitous in his views of Corcoran in a letter to Sen. John Breckinridge in 1853: "God has made but few such gentlemen as Corcoran." See Jesse Bright to John Breckenridge, May 10, 1853, in Corcoran, *A Grandfather's Legacy*, 115.

61. Corcoran made some investments relatively early, even before he fully succeeded as a banker. As early as 1845, he was a one-third owner of more than forty thousand acres of land on the Indiana prairie that had been originally set aside for veterans of the War of 1812. His coinvestors were Romulus Riggs, brother of Elisha, and Robert Walker, then the head of the Democratic Party and about to be named treasury secretary. See Shenton, *Robert John Walker*, 95–97.

62. George M. Bibb to W. W. Corcoran, September 8, 1850, in Corcoran, *A Grandfather's Legacy*, 90.

63. James Buchanan to W. W. Corcoran, November 26, 1849, in Corcoran, 81.

64. "Items of News," *Baltimore Daily Commercial*, December 16, 1846, 1.

65. Chandler and Tedlow, in *Coming of Managerial Capitalism*, chaps. 7 and 8, discuss the changing nature of capitalism.

66. Cohen, *Business and Politics*, 26.

67. Cohen asserts that Corcoran resorted to outright bribery, but the evidence is not clear. More likely, Corcoran used his financial resources to make loans and purchase, and to advise on investment positions for favored people. At times they repaid him, and at other times, they did not. Given the balance between financial integrity and irregularity, Corcoran probably operated within the norms of the period prior to the Great Barbeque.

68. Daniel Webster to W. W. Corcoran, March 7, 1850, in Corcoran, *A Grandfather's Legacy*, 85. The $5,000 loan equates to more than $155,000 in 2020 dollars.

69. "News by the Mails," *New York Daily Herald*, February 28, 1851, 4.

70. Cohen, *Business and Politics*, 34–37.

71. Cohen, 32; and Green, *Washington*, 84–85.

72. Cohen, 32.

73. Cohen, 25.

74. Cohen, 28.

75. Cohen, 6–7, 14.

76. This transition was complete by the start of the Mexican-American War,

during which Corcoran & Riggs emerged as an important investment
bank, assuming significant portions of the government's debt for resale,
while the Metropolitan Bank was barely involved.

77. Cohen, *Business and Politics*, 30.

78. Cohen, 30–31.

79. Cohen, 32–33.

80. Even by 1845, just a few years after the formation of Corcoran & Riggs,
the capital's upstart bank held the second-largest amount of treasury
deposits. See "Treasurer's Statement," *National Intelligencer*, February 8,
1845, 4.

81. E. W. Clark to Corcoran & Riggs, February 15, 1845, in Sweet, "Selected
Correspondence," 31. The Clark firm eventually became Clark, Dodge &
Co., a well-known underwriter firm that survived into the 1960s.

82. Gilbert and Sons to Corcoran & Riggs, June 12, 1845, in Sweet, "Selected
Correspondence," 32. The accounts appear to show that Daniel Webster
was among the heaviest borrowers from Corcoran.

83. Robert Dale Owen to W. W. Corcoran, September 13, 1846, in Sweet, "Selected Correspondence," 42.

84. Hammond, *Banks and Politics*, 542–45.

85. Cohen, *Business and Politics*, 35.

86. Cohen, 36.

87. Cohen.

88. Cohen, 36–37.

89. Cohen, 37.

3. Selling the War

1. See Adams, *Finance and Enterprise*; and Lawson, *Patriot Fires*.

2. Carr, *32 President's Square*, 66; and Cohen, *Business and Politics*, 42–43, 75.

3. Robert C. Winthrop to W. W. Corcoran, March 24, 1847, in Corcoran,
A Grandfather's Legacy, 54.

4. George Newbold to W. W. Corcoran, August 14, 1846, in Corcoran, 51.

5. Adams, *Finance and Enterprise*, 17, 19; and Lawson, *Patriot Fires*,
introduction.

6. Carr, *32 President's Square*, 86.

7. Adams, *Finance and Enterprise*, 19–31.

8. Adams, 31.

9. Adams.

10. Scholars tend to give Girard a free pass. See Perkins, *American Public*

Finance, 331–33. On the other hand, there are some parallels with Corcoran regarding early philanthropy. Girard contributed some of his wealth to projects in education and poor relief.

11. Adams, *Finance and Enterprise*, 31–37.

12. Hammond, *Banks and Politics*, 724–25. There is little discussion in the scholarly literature of the evolution of investment banking and its role in public debt finance in the antebellum era.

13. Both Hammond's *Banks and Politics* and Redlich's *Molding of American Banking* argue that decentralized banking systems were unstable, and to prosper they needed more oversight. Bodenhorn, in *State Banking*, suggests that banks slowly took on commercial and state securities but were less involved with federal debt. All agree the transportation revolution helped expand the opportunity to resell securities in larger markets.

14. Cummings, "Financing the Mexican War," 4.

15. Corcoran, *A Grandfather's Legacy*, 8. Corcoran's joint investor for the 1848 loan was N. M. Rothschild & Sons, Europe's preeminent banking firm. Newspapers explained that the partnership meant European investors were betting again on American securities. See "Official," *National Intelligencer*, March 11, 1848, 1.

16. Benj. A. Swan et al. to W. W. Corcoran, March 16, 1849, in Corcoran, *A Grandfather's Legacy*, 72.

17. "A Washington Philanthropist," *Appleton's Journal*, January 3, 1874, unnumbered page, Corcoran scrapbook, 106.

18. "The Late Secretary of the Treasury," untitled and undated newspaper, Corcoran scrapbook, 89, GW Archives.

19. As with many onetime competitors, Corcoran turned the powerful Baring Brothers firm into business partners. Within one year of their difficult encounter over the banker's sale of the 1848 loan in Europe, the two firms were cooperating on various ventures. See Baring Brothers to Corcoran & Riggs, January 12, 1849, in Corcoran, *A Grandfather's Legacy*, 69–70. He also introduced Thomas Baring to President Fillmore at the White House. See *London Express,* October 12, 1852, 2.

20. Corcoran once again had inside information. The banker apparently had important knowledge about Baring Brothers' exposure to American debt and correctly bet the firm needed to cover the investments at higher prices.

21. Corcoran, *A Grandfather's Legacy*, 7.

22. Cohen, *Business and Politics*, 42–46, 61.

23. Cummings, "Financing the Mexican War," 85–87.

24. Curiously, Walker's biographer contends the treasury secretary had few business dealings with financiers or politicians prior to holding public office because he did not want an appearance of impropriety. He even uses Corcoran to defend his reputation. See Shenton, *Robert John Walker*, 34. Cohen, in *Business and Politics*, 26–27, asserts that Walker had numerous financial dealings with a variety of bankers and politicians prior to holding office—implying that he should have known better. Various newspapers of the time also confirm Walker's business connections with Corcoran and others.

25. Cohen, 41–42.

26. US Congress, House, "War Loans Policy," *Congressional Globe*, 29th Congress, 1st session (July 1846): 1114–15.

27. Cohen, *Business and Politics*, 40–42; and Cummings, "Financing the Mexican War," 85–86.

28. Cummings, 88–90; and Cohen, 41–43.

29. Cohen, 44.

30. Cohen, 43. Cohen notes that Walker offered members of Congress 6 percent notes at par, for which Corcoran often advanced funds.

31. Matthew Morgan & Co., with which Corcoran had numerous business dealings over the years, agreed to underwrite loans with a group of investors, but then it sold out early at reduced rates because of expectations that the loan would fall further.

32. Nevins, *Diary of Philip Hone*, 800. A wealthy investor in securities and real estate, Hone also had a significant art collection in his Manhattan home.

33. Cohen, *Business and Politics*, 45.

34. Accounts differ about the exact amount of the loan Corcoran cornered. The Treasury Report of 1847 states that of the $15.5 million in notes, Corcoran garnered about $11.7 million directly, and another $2 million was acquired by firms working on Corcoran's behalf. See Treasury Report of 1847, as cited in Shenton, *Robert John Walker*, 97. Cohen, in *Business and Politics*, states that of the $16.5 million loan, Corcoran either by himself or with others acquired $14.7 million. Cummings, in "Financing the Mexican War," uses Cohen's figures. Regardless of the exact amount, all the sources agree that Corcoran successfully cornered the 1847 loan at between 80 percent and 90 percent of the total.

35. Cohen, 47; and Shenton, 96. Cummings, 129, also cites Freeman Hunt's *Merchants' Magazine*, which questioned the secrecy of the bidding process.

36. Cohen, 45; and Shenton, 95.
37. Cohen, 47.
38. "News," *Daily National Whig*, July 29, 1847, 3.
39. "Mr. Walker's Management of the Public Treasury," *Daily National Whig*, May 29, 1847, 3.
40. *Louisville (KY) Daily Courier*, September 25, 1850, 2.
41. "Editor's Correspondence," *American Telegraph*, August 26, 1851, Corcoran scrapbook, 48, GW Archives.
42. "Washington Correspondence," unnamed newspaper, November 18, 1856, Corcoran scrapbook, 70, GW Archives.
43. Cohen, *Business and Politics*, 47–48.
44. Cohen, 49. In today's dollars, $250,000 would equate to approximately $10 million.
45. Cohen, 49–51.
46. Corcoran took at least $1 million of the loan for his personal account. Corcoran teamed up with a network of bankers and other financiers, including the Morgans, the Merchants' Bank, the Bank of Commerce, the New York Bank, and others. Cohen, *Business and Politics*, 260.
47. "Commercial Affairs," *New York Daily Herald*, October 19, 1848, 3.
48. Cohen, *Business and Politics*, 51–52; and Carr, *32 President's Square*, 85–86. Corcoran built such a reputation for risk that newspapers took to satirizing the banker, alluding to his "love for doing things on a large scale." See "Speech of Hon. Mr. Smith," *Daily National Era*, July 28, 1854, 2.
49. Cohen, 51–52.
50. Cummings, in "Financing the Mexican War," 224, states that a variety of business publications read by the financial community predicted a worsening economy that would impact credit and loan rates, further affecting the gloomy outlook.
51. "Stocks and New Loan," *Daily National Whig*, April 5, 1849, 2.
52. Cohen, *Business and Politics*, 53.
53. Cohen, 54.
54. Cohen, 55.
55. Cohen, 54–55.
56. Cohen, 54–55, 262.
57. Cohen, 57–58.
58. Cohen.
59. Perhaps emboldened by his success overseas, Corcoran bid aggressively for the Mexican war settlement that required the United States to pay for annexed territories in that country's currency and, in combination with

the Rothschilds and Baring Brothers, successfully obtained the under-lying securities. The arrangement showed Corcoran was perceived to be a strong international player.

60. Carr, *32 President's Square*, 90.
61. Corcoran, *A Grandfather's Legacy*, 7.
62. Corcoran even sold Cooke the land to situate his banking firm. See *Evening Star*, May 20, 1863, 3. Although competitors at times, Corcoran and Cooke entered real estate pools and other financial deals together. Corcoran also had multiple business ventures with Henry Cooke, Jay Cooke's brother and later the territorial governor for Washington, DC. See "From Washington," *Janesville (WI) Gazette*, July 6, 1875, 1.
63. "The New Loan," *Weekly National Intelligencer*, June 24, 1848, 3.
64. Robert Walker to Senators Houston and Rusk, September 24, 1850, in Carr, *32 President's Square*, 108–9.

4. America's Lobbyist

1. US Senate, "The Florida Case before the Election Commission," *United States Senate Catalogue*, 123.
2. Scholarly analysis of lobbying is limited. For the most part, the examination of lobbying tends to focus on narrow case studies where evidence of such activities has come to light. As early as 1929, political scientists called for greater study of the methods and results of lobbying. See Logan's "Lobbying" in 1929. More recent studies still decry the murkiness of a profession that has grown exponentially but resists effective analysis. See Gabel and Scott, "Toward a Public Policy." To the extent that the business of lobbying has changed between the nineteenth and twenty-first centuries, some suggest that outright bribery and the buying of votes have been supplanted by more sophisticated marketing and logrolling efforts. See Lane, "Some Lessons." The first known use of the term in print dates to 1817, but the term was still a rarity in the 1820s. Most early lobbying occurred at state legislatures and not the federal Congress, making Corcoran's timing and influence all the more important.
3. Nichols, *Forty Years*, 74. By the mid-1850s, unscrupulous lobbyists were already being accused of bilking innocent people out of pensions, indemnities, land warrants, Indian claims, and other securities. See "Colt's Patent, Grog and the Spoilsmen," *New York Tribune*, February 5, 1855, 4.

4. In interesting corollaries, the influence peddling went both ways. For the most part, the business community used Corcoran to influence lawmakers and the administration; however, on several occasions, cabinet secretaries and presidents used the well-connected banker to influence the business community and diplomats. On behalf of the government, Corcoran did much to persuade Wall Street to subscribe to treasury loans, and he acted as a go-between for the State Department and other countries in several treaty negotiations. Even members of Congress sought his influence with presidents, especially Polk and Buchanan.

5. "William Wilson Corcoran," *Boston Evening Transcript*, December 27, 1878, 6.

6. Jacob, *Capital Elites*, 3.

7. Jacob, 5–6.

8. Marsh, "Washington's First Art Academy," 41.

9. Catherine Sinclair to W. W. Corcoran, October 3, 1853, in Corcoran, *A Grandfather's Legacy*, 122.

10. *Boston Daily Globe*, July 4, 1889, 5.

11. Almira Lincoln Phelps, "An Article Based on Her Diary Recollections of 1854," *The Baltimorean*, June 1874, Corcoran scrapbook, 93.

12. Elisha Riggs Jr. to Elisha Riggs, February 24, 1852, in Carr, *32 President's Square*, 124.

13. *New York Times*, March 1, 1852, 4.

14. "Affairs in Washington," *New York Herald*, January 21, 1855, 1.

15. Katz, "Confidant at the Capital," 548.

16. Some of Corcoran's closest confidants included Thomas Ritchie and James Welling, both influential Washington, DC, newspaper publishers. Corcoran funded several Democratic newspapers including the *Daily Patriot* and, in the last years of his life, *The Chronicle*. Welling was a trustee and later president of the Corcoran Art Gallery's trustees at the same time he was president of Columbian College.

17. Katz, "Confidant at the Capital," 553–58.

18. Murphy, "Political Career," 101–45.

19. Newspapers of the day regularly reported when presidents sought Corcoran's advice. Presidents Grant, Hayes, Garfield, Cleveland, and Arthur, among others, always obtained his views on local matters before acting. See *Galveston Daily News*, November 22, 1885, 1.

20. Index to Letters, Corcoran, *A Grandfather's Legacy*, i–ix.

21. See Shelden, *Washington Brotherhood*.

22. Carr, *32 President's Square*, 92.

23. Some of the most powerful people in Washington consulted Corcoran

to determine what actions the government might take and persuade it toward particular activities. Even James Buchanan, as the secretary of state, asked Corcoran to use his influence to get an old journalist friend ensconced as the clerk of the House of Representatives. James Buchanan to W. W. Corcoran, November 26, 1849, in Sweet, *Selected Correspondence*, 78–79.

24. Elliot Taylor to W. W. Corcoran, March 26, 1851, in Corcoran, *A Grandfather's Legacy*, 93.

25. George M. Dallas to W. W. Corcoran, August 11, 1848, in Corcoran, *A Grandfather's Legacy*, 61–62.

26. Robert Winthrop to W. W. Corcoran, March 24, 1847, in Corcoran, *A Grandfather's Legacy*, 54.

27. Even the most powerful politicians asked Corcoran to settle claims. Daniel Webster, seeking to settle a Mexican-American War claim, offered the banker one-third of the settlement for his efforts to resolve it. Daniel Webster to Corcoran & Riggs, March 15, 1853, in Sweet, "Selected Correspondence," 103–4.

28. Cohen, *Business and Politics*, 118–19. Nearly half of a claim's value could be consumed in the effort to win it.

29. Cohen.

30. The Chickasaws' claim against the government was one of the most famous and complicated claims for damages, based on the tribe's removal from the East, and drew many interested parties. It was settled along with a variety of other claims after the Mexican-American War. In this case, Corcoran may have earned fees not due him. See "House of Representatives," *National Intelligencer*, September 21, 1850, 3.

31. Congress investigated Corcoran's role in the case of Dr. Gardiner's fraudulent claims in Mexican land, and his considerable investment was almost confiscated by the government. See "Judiciary Committee," *Washington Sentinel*, October 14, 1854, 2.

32. Cohen, *Business and Politics*, chaps. 8–12.

33. *Adams Sentinel and General Advertiser* (Gettysburg), March 13, 1854, 1.

34. Corcoran was accused of secretly cornering most of the Texas debt prior to annexation. The accusation was unmerited, as it was public knowledge that Corcoran had assumed three quarters of the debt. See "Later from Texas," *National Intelligencer*, May 29, 1852, 2. The bonds bought at five cents were redeemed at par after the federal government assumed Texas's debt, making millions in profits for the banker. Corcoran held more than $400,000 of the bond, a significant sum even before the price

more than doubled during the debates on the Compromise of 1850. See *Bloomington (IL) Daily Leader*, July 10, 1880, 3. The scheme was still notorious thirty years later, as newspapers in 1880 charged some emerging political leaders with associating with Corcoran and Bright, who were seen as the enterprise's ringleaders. See "William H. English," *The Advocate*, July 23, 1880, 1. Cohen, *Business and Politics*, has the most detailed discussion of the case.

35. Thomas Corwin to General Rusk, October 1, 1850, in Corcoran, *A Grandfather's Legacy*, 91–92.

36. Cohen, *Business and Politics*, 141; and Sweet, "Selected Correspondence," 88–89.

37. Corcoran was accused of greasing the palms of politicians to influence critical legislation, including the Texas debt bill, and was specifically named in efforts to lobby Rep. Thomas Bayly, the chairman of the powerful House Ways and Means Committee. See "Question of Privilege," *National Intelligencer*, July 22, 1854, 8.

38. See *Steam Titans: Cunard, Collins, and the Epic Battle for Commerce on the North Atlantic* (New York: Bloomsbury, 2017) by William M. Fowler for a modern discussion of the topic.

39. Carr, *32 President's Square*, 102; and Cohen, *Business and Politics*, 109–13.

40. Cohen, 109–12.

41. A Democratic Party house organ that received support from Corcoran, the *Union* published several articles on the debate about the shipping subsidy, almost all of which supported the Collins Line. The *New York Courier & Enquirer* was also a supporter of the government subsidy. That newspaper's publisher, James Watson Webb, was a friend and occasional debtor of Corcoran's. After the Civil War, Webb's paper was outspoken in its support of Corcoran's national rehabilitation.

42. Stiles, *First Tycoon*, 258.

43. Cohen, *Business and Politics*, 112–13.

44. Cohen, 260.

45. Cohen, 112.

46. This episode showed that even Corcoran's powers of persuasion and checkbook had their limits, since the banker counted both Stephen Douglas and Franklin Pierce among his friends and allies.

47. Cohen, *Business and Politics*, 112–13.

48. The Grant administration became synonymous with political corruption, although other politicians and periods were not immune. Mark Summers, in *Era of Good Stealings*, posits that although corruption

existed throughout the political system, it was probably overstated by the press and muckrakers. Given the nature of corruption, the truth will likely never be fully known.

49. McCormick, *Party Period and Public Policy*, 213; Keller, *Affairs of State*, 85–121; Campbell, *Growth of Government*, 19; and White, *Republican Era, 1869–1901*, 68–92.

50. Savvy people in Washington, DC, understood Corcoran's influence and his ability to access and persuade politicians of all parties. His friend the publisher Thomas Ritchie insisted that Corcoran immediately see the president of a different party to persuade him of specific cabinet appointments. Thomas Ritchie to W. W. Corcoran, July 1850, in Sweet, "Selected Correspondence," 82.

51. "The President and Mr. Corcoran," *Alexandria (VA) Gazette,* unnumbered page, Corcoran scrapbook, 127.

52. "President Hayes in Maryland," *The Sun*, October 12, 1877, 1.

53. Jesse D. Bright to John Breckenridge, May 10, 1853, in Corcoran, *A Grandfather's Legacy*, 115.

54. Gates, "Southern Investment," 155–85. The land deals did not always succeed, such as the bankruptcy of several choice parcels of Arkansas land Corcoran and George Riggs had purchased in trust during the 1850s. See *Little Rock Weekly Arkansas Gazette*, August 4, 1868, 4. Corcoran even invested in Illinois coal mines and railroad routes to towns not destined to see immediate growth. See *Rock Island (IL) Argus*, April 11, 1860, 3.

55. Gates, "Southern Investment," 155. Bayly was notorious as the chairman of the Ways and Means Committee for purportedly plundering the Treasury. See "Schemes to Plunder the Treasury," *Daily American Telegraph*, January 9, 1852, 2.

56. Sweet, "Selected Correspondence," 86.

57. James Shields to W. W. Corcoran, September 30, 1850, in Sweet, "Selected Correspondence," 89.

58. James Buchanan to W. W. Corcoran, November 26, 1849, in Corcoran, *A Grandfather's Legacy*, 81–82. Buchanan is one of dozens of examples of individuals who routinely asked the banker for advice or loans regarding various securities. Here Buchanan asks about the advisability of purchasing Indiana state bonds.

59. Corcoran was comfortable with early land purchases due to his own family connections. His namesake uncle, William Wilson, invested in western lands as early as the 1830s. Wilson purchased nearly four

thousand acres in Springfield, Illinois, the location destined to be the new state's capital. See Gates, "Southern Investments," 159.

60. Gates, 159.

61. Sweet, "Selected Correspondence," 34. Corcoran was involved in the lucrative claims business by the late 1830s, as indicated by correspondence between the banker and Thomas Crawford, the commissioner of Indian Affairs.

62. Gates, "Southern Investments," 165.

63. Gates, 174.

64. Gates, 181.

65. Gates, 185.

66. Gates, 166; and Sweet, "Selected Correspondence," 16.

67. "Superior City Owned by Rebels," *Dubuque Weekly Times*, October 24, 1861, 3.

68. "Items of News and Others," *New Albany Daily Ledger*, November 4, 1863, 1; and *Bloomington (IL) Pantagraph*, March 9, 1863, 4.

69. "Superior City Owned by Rebels," *Dubuque Weekly Times*, October 24, 1861, 3.

70. James K. Polk to W. W. Corcoran, May 7, 1847, in Corcoran, *A Grandfather's Legacy*, 54–55.

71. James Buchanan to W. W. Corcoran, November 26, 1849, in Corcoran, 81–82; James Buchanan to W. W. Corcoran, July 15, 1850, in Corcoran, 87–88; and Katz, "Confidant at the Capital," 552.

72. Corcoran felt so obligated to Buchanan that he arranged for the future president to have a good "negro cook" when he returned to the United States. See, for example, James Buchanan to W. W. Corcoran, August 3, 1855, in Corcoran, 139; and Katz, 554.

73. William B. Astor to W. W. Corcoran, March 16, 1849, in Corcoran, 71–72.

74. Sen. Jesse Bright led this effort on Corcoran's behalf.

75. Katz, "Confidant at the Capital," 552.

76. Katz, 553.

77. Katz, 554. There is some confusion about whether Corcoran ever fully retired. The *Evening Star* of April 1, 1854, makes such an announcement, and Corcoran indicates in his autobiography that this was the case; however, there is substantial evidence that he remained a silent partner with his old firm when George Riggs returned to manage the bank after Corcoran left. Additionally, Corcoran continued to play an active role in treasury loan-bidding arrangements. See *New York Times*, June 14, 1858, 8.

78. Katz, "Confidant at the Capital," 554.
79. Katz.
80. Katz, 555.
81. *Atlanta Daily Constitution*, November 4, 1876, 1. Tilden's loss to Rutherford B. Hayes in the Compromise of 1877 embittered Corcoran to the point that he suggested the US Constitution be amended to prevent political chicanery and electoral deadlocks. See *Fort Wayne Daily Gazette*, August 1, 1882, 4.
82. *Wellsboro (PA) Agitator*, February 24, 1874, 2.
83. Millard Fillmore to W. W. Corcoran, November 10, 1856, in Corcoran, *A Grandfather's Legacy*, 152; and Edward Everett to W. W. Corcoran, January 19, 1857, in Corcoran, 155.
84. Katz, "Confidant at the Capital," 556.
85. Katz, 555.
86. Poore, *Perley's Reminiscences*, 508–11. Grover Cleveland also stayed with Corcoran in the days prior to his inauguration.
87. Katz, "Confidant at the Capital," 556.
88. The discussion surrounding constructions of masculinity in the context of friendship and homosexuality has been thoroughly examined in recent years. As mentioned earlier, I found no evidence of any intimate or romantic relationships Corcoran had with men or women after Louise died.
89. *Sullivan (IN) Democrat*, April 26, 1860, 2.
90. Katz, "Confidant at the Capital," 558. Breckenridge bolted the Union and became a general and then the secretary of war for the Confederacy.

5. Culture and Community

1. Jacob, *Capital Elites*, 8–9.
2. Beckert, *Monied Metropolis*, 2.
3. Beckert and Rosenbaum, *American Bourgeoisie*, 1. Other works, such as Green's *Secret City*, studied the legacy of an African American elite in the capital.
4. Beckert and Rosenbaum, 1–5.
5. Jacob, *Capital Elites*, 7–9. Nash's *Urban Crucible* also examines social change and growing class consciousness in such cites as Boston and New York, seeing in large measure a balancing act between lower classes and the elite.
6. Jacob, 7–9.

7. Arnebeck, *Through A Fiery Trial*, 4; Berg, *Grand Avenues*, 7; and Bednar, *L'Enfant's Legacy*, 10.

8. Jacob, *Capital Elites*, 7–9.

9. By several accounts, Corcoran was an astute investor in real estate and made far more money investing in property than he did in banking. The *Chicago Daily Tribune* in 1874 asserted that Corcoran's real estate profits were quintuple his earnings from the government war bonds business.

10. Zunz, *Philanthropy in America*, 1–2.

11. Zunz, 4.

12. Zunz, 3–4.

13. McCarthy, *American Creed*, introduction.

14. McCarthy, 4. During the depths of the economic downturn in 1877, Corcoran foreshadowed unemployment insurance programs by distributing regular cash payments to the newly unemployed. See *Boston Daily Globe,* June 14, 1877, 5.

15. Corcoran viewed philanthropy in a broad sense. He spent his time and money on many different activities that ranged from aiding the poor to educating children, from building cemeteries and an art gallery to donating trees and other landscaping to create the National Mall.

16. Green, *Washington*, 219.

17. Green. Corcoran's approach would differ from that of his friend George Peabody, who preferred to set up an educational foundation. Peabody's approach was localized to specific institutions or cities. Corcoran had wanted more directly to oversee his art gallery personally but was forced by delays and his advancing age to establish a board of directors to manage the facility.

18. McCarthy, *American Creed*, 2.

19. Corcoran's first charitable efforts began when he was in his twenties, providing funds to churches and the Georgetown poor, as his father had done before him. He continued these efforts throughout his life and more frequently as he became wealthier.

20. McCarthy, *Noblesse Oblige*, chap. 1.

21. Rosenzweig and Blackmar, *Park and the People*, introduction.

22. Goode, *Capital Losses*, 398.

23. Arnold and Girault, *Prospectus of the Washington High School*, 16.

24. Tank, "William Wilson Corcoran," 54.

25. *Southern Churchman,* June 25, 1874, unnumbered, Corcoran scrapbook, 82, GW Archives.

26. Corcoran also gave $30,000 in property to the Church of the Ascension in Washington, DC. See Corcoran scrapbook, 36, GW Archives.

27. *Alexandria (VA) Gazette*, September 24, 1874, unnumbered, Corcoran scrapbook, 82, GW Archives.

28. Corcoran, *A Grandfather's Legacy*, contains many examples of thank you letters from a variety of individuals and institutions he supported.

29. Green, *Washington*, 219, 269.

30. Kayser, *Bricks without Straw*, 144–145; and *Daily Patriot*, October 25, 1872, in Corcoran, *A Grandfather's Legacy*, 546.

31. Robert E. Lee to W. W. Corcoran, October 2, 1869, in Corcoran, 304; and *Richmond Whig*, December 12, 1872, in Corcoran, 547–48. See also Corcoran scrapbook, 99, GW Archives, for an account of his donations to the University of Virginia.

32. *Georgetown Courier*, undated, Corcoran scrapbook, 9, GW Archives.

33. George Peabody to W. W. Corcoran, October 3, 1851, in Corcoran, *A Grandfather's Legacy*, 100–101.

34. Tank, "William Wilson Corcoran," 54.

35. George Peabody to W. W. Corcoran, October 3, 1851.

36. Constable, *Art Collecting*, 132; and *Newark Daily Advocate*, January 4, 1888, 2.

37. "Successful Swindling at Washington," *Baltimore Sun*, January 19, 1854, 2.

38. *New York Daybook*, December 31, 1850, Corcoran scrapbook, 36, GW Archives.

39. Tank, "William Wilson Corcoran," 54.

40. W. W. Corcoran notice, undated, GW Archives. A newspaper chronicler noted that she called on Corcoran one morning at 9:30 to request assistance for a charitable cause. She was already the sixth person that day to ask the philanthropist for money, which he promptly provided. See "Mr. W.W. Corcoran—His Charities in Our Capital," untitled newspaper, November 10, 1871, Corcoran scrapbook, 180, GW Archives.

41. Unknown newspaper, undated, Corcoran scrapbook, 12, GW Archives.

42. *Richmond (VA) Dispatch*, undated, Corcoran scrapbook, 12, GW Archives.

43. Corcoran's apparent selflessness also extended to acts of personal courage. Newspapers recorded several instances in which Corcoran, an excellent swimmer, saved people from likely drowning. Corcoran saved his future brother-in-law and two other people—a White man and a Black man—from the Potomac River at Georgetown, endangering his own life in the process. Shortly after he was married, Corcoran saved a boy who slipped off a gangplank at the pier where their boat was unloading in New York. The boy's father was about to jump in after him, but Corcoran pushed the man out of the way with a warning that the current was too dangerous and jumped in the water himself. See "Mr. William W.

Corcoran," *Sunday Herald,* March 3, 1878, unnumbered page, Corcoran scrapbook, 132, GW Archives.

44. *Boston Journal,* January 19, 1874, unnumbered, Corcoran scrapbook, 13, GW Archives.

45. "The President and Mr. Corcoran," *Alexandria (VA) Gazette,* unknown date, Corcoran scrapbook, 127, GW Archives.

46. "Letter from Washington," *Baltimore Sun,* May 12, 1877, 4.

47. Green, *Washington,* 59.

48. Green, 67.

49. Green, 69.

50. Green, 200.

51. Ways, "Montgomery C. Meigs," in Dickinson, Herrin, and Kennon, *Montgomery C. Meigs,* xiii, 21, 27–28.

52. Corcoran was also behind a $150,000 loan provided to support the aqueduct work.

53. Ways, "Montgomery C. Meigs," in Dickinson, Herrin, and Kennon, *Montgomery C. Meigs,* 27–28.

54. Ways. Additionally, Green, in *Washington,* 202, explains that accomplished architect Robert Mills in 1830 had prepared detailed plans for a modern water supply system after studying other municipalities, but Congress refused to fund it until after the fire. Corcoran later hired Mills to construct one of his office buildings and to complete the design for the Washington Monument. See Liscombe, *Altogether American.*

55. Therese O'Malley, "A Public Museum of Trees: Mid-Nineteenth Century Plans for the Mall," in Longstreth, *Mall in Washington,* 64.

56. Ryan, *Civic Wars.* Chapter 1 describes the initial designations of public spaces in such urban areas as New York, San Francisco, and New Orleans.

57. As with the aqueduct, Robert Mills got there first. His 1841 design for the mall was similar to what Downing later adopted. In the 1870s, Frederick Law Olmsted would become the first official landscape architect of the US Capitol and worked to advance a design for the surrounding grounds on Capitol Hill.

58. Ignatius Mudd, "Report of the Commissioner of Public Buildings," as described in O'Malley, "Public Museum of Trees," in Longstreth, *Mall in Washington,* 64.

59. *New York Evening Post,* December 4, 1851, 2.

60. Kohler and Carson, *Sixteenth Street Architecture,* 1–14.

61. O'Malley, "Public Museum of Trees," in Longstreth, *Mall in Washington,* 46–47.

62. Mudd, "Report," as described in O'Malley, 64.
63. US Department of the Interior, *Report of the Commissioner*, as also described in its *Historic American Buildings Survey*, 9.
64. "Washington in 1859," *Harper's New Monthly Magazine* 20 (December 1859) as reprinted in Oppel and Meisel, *Washington, D.C.*, 113.
65. Goode, *Capital Losses*, 76; and O'Malley, "Public Museum of Trees," in Longstreth, *Mall in Washington*, 68–73.
66. Goode.
67. *National Republican,* January 10, 1862, 3. See chapter 31, "An Act to Incorporate the United States Agricultural Society," 36th Congress, 1st session, April 19, 1860.
68. "Oak Hill Cemetery: Its Origins, History, Character, and Condition," *Daily Intelligencer*, Washington, Saturday, July 21, 1866, 1. Corcoran also donated most of the lands associated with the Catholic burial ground in Georgetown Heights.
69. "Oak Hill Cemetery"; and Brown, "Georgetown's 'Home Sweet Home,'" 21.
70. Brown, 21.
71. Kohler and Carson, *Sixteenth Street Architecture*, 23.
72. Untitled and undated newspaper, Corcoran scrapbook, 50, GW Archives.
73. "Oak Hill Cemetery," *National Intelligencer,* Corcoran scrapbook, 58, GW Archives.
74. Brown, "Georgetown's 'Home Sweet Home,'" 22.
75. Brown.
76. Newspapers reported that Corcoran's tomb cost $13,000, about four times the cost of the entire cemetery land parcel. See "Oak Hill Cemetery," *Daily Intelligencer*, 1.
77. William Wilson Corcoran, letter to the Managers of the Oak Hill Cemetery, April 24, 1871, GW Archives.
78. Corcoran. He also helped arrange for several wayward notables to be buried in Oak Hill Cemetery, including the author and evangelist Lorenzo Dow and the composer John Howard Payne.
79. Brown, "Georgetown's 'Home Sweet Home,'" 23.
80. Brown, 22–23; and Mitchell, *Chronicles of Georgetown Life*, 29–42.
81. Corcoran, letter to the Managers.
82. Mitchell, *Chronicles of Georgetown Life*, 29–42.
83. Mitchell.
84. Brown, "Georgetown's 'Home Sweet Home,'" 22; Mitchell, 29–42; and "Letter from Washington," *Baltimore Sun*, June 9, 1869, 4.
85. *Dunkirk (NY) Evening Observer*, November 10, 1883, 1; "The Improvement

of the Potomac Flats," *Evening Star*, undated and unnumbered page, Corcoran scrapbook, unnumbered page, GW Archives; "Miscellaneous," *Evening Star*, May 26, 1886, 1; and "The Commissioners Petitioned," *Evening Star*, February 7, 1889, 6.

86. Spilsbury, *Rock Creek Park*, 6.
87. Corcoran's various properties and holdings are discussed in Goode, *Capital Losses*, and in Kohler and Carson, *Sixteenth Street Architecture*. Both volumes contain multiple entries on Corcoran's real estate and property. In the mid-1880s, just a few years before his death, Corcoran was involved in lawsuits to protect some of his landholdings in Washington, DC. See "Personal," *Warren (PA) Daily Mirror*, November 6, 1886, 3; and "Washington Letter," *Rochester Republican*, February 18, 1884, 3. Corcoran also provoked some criticism as a landlord, such as the time he threw a women's political group out of their rented rooms. See "The Protest," *The Critic*, February 2, 1883, 2.
88. Corcoran leveraged talent for his architectural interests in a variety of ways. A stonecutter working on the Church of the Ascension, a project the philanthropist was supporting, was appointed as the master mechanic for the Washington Monument project. See *Harrisonburg-Rockingham (VA) Register*, December 18, 1884, 1.
89. Goode, *Capital Losses*, 64.
90. Roessle, *Historic Corner*, 1.
91. Goode, *Capital Losses*, 64.
92. Kohler and Carson, *Sixteenth Street Architecture*, 9–11.
93. Goode, *Capital Losses*, 64; and Kohler and Carson, 12.
94. Marsh, "Washington's First Art Academy," 38.
95. "Don M. Dickenson," *Appleton (WI) Crescent*, March 10, 1888, 2.
96. W. W. Corcoran to James Renwick, August 6, 1852, in Kohler and Carson, *Sixteenth Street Architecture*, 12.
97. W. W. Corcoran to James Renwick, in Kohler and Carson.
98. Anthony Hyde to James Renwick, in Kohler and Carson, 13.
99. Undated and unnumbered, *The Republic*, 1880, Corcoran scrapbook, unnumbered page, GW Archives.
100. Kohler and Carson, *Sixteenth Street Architecture*, 17.
101. *New York Daily News,* March 7, 1854, 1.
102. *New York Daily News.*
103. Goode, *Capital Losses*, 348. Corcoran eventually sold the estate and provided the proceeds to the art gallery.
104. "Letter from Washington by Mrs. M. J. Young," untitled and undated newspaper, Corcoran scrapbook, unnumbered page, GW Archives.

105. For instance, Corcoran in 1853 purchased a ninety-nine-acre tract of land that had been the Trinidad estate owned by the James Barry family since 1799. The parcel was key to future development of the capital, and he donated much of it to the small college that became George Washington University.

106. Goode, *Capital Losses*, 173.

107. Goode. Corcoran was not shy about charging high rents. Congress initially declined appropriations for the Treasury Department to transfer employees to Corcoran's new office building when it determined the rent was roughly 50 percent more than anticipated; appropriations were later approved. See "Civil Appropriations Bill," *National Intelligencer*, July 15, 1848, 8.

108. *Albany Daily Ledger*, July 6, 1853, 2.

109. Goode, *Capital Losses*, 189.

110. Klein, *Grammercy Park*, chap. 1.

111. Some twenty thousand graves remain under the park. See Burrows and Wallace, *Gotham*, 579–80.

112. Klein, *Grammercy Park*, 140.

113. Kohler and Carson, *Sixteenth Street Architecture*, 1–7.

114. Kohler and Carson; and Roessle, *Historic Corner*, unnumbered.

115. Kohler and Carson, 4.

116. *Fort Wayne Daily Gazette*, November 18, 1879, 2.

117. Kohler and Carson, *Sixteenth Street Architecture*, 1–7, cover the square's development overall, and pages 9–88 cover Corcoran's home and other properties he built on the square. Roessle, *Historic Corner*, unnumbered; and Goode, *Capital Losses*, also discuss many of the same homes, including Slidell House, 46.

118. Kohler and Carson, *Sixteenth Street Architecture*, 57–79. Corcoran seemed very solicitous of Adams and did his best to accommodate the critic. "I am so desirous to have you for my neighbor and tenant that I am willing to let the house remain vacant until you return about the first of October next," Corcoran wrote to Adams in June 1880.

119. Corcoran was on the board of Columbian College (later George Washington University) from 1869 until his death. His contributions to the college were so generous that the trustees offered to change the name of the college to Corcoran College, an honor the philanthropist declined. His reputation at the college was undiminished by accusations of treason, as glowing tributes were offered in 1866, just after the Civil War ended, for his contributions of a medical college to the institution.

120. Goode, *Capital Losses*, 46.

121. Goode. Ritchie in his will called Corcoran a noble and constant friend. President Polk brought Ritchie to the capital to edit the influential Democratic paper the *Union*, which Corcoran supported financially. Early in his career, the Richmond publisher editorialized against free Blacks and manumission, but his later views accommodated gradual emancipation. Corcoran was a pallbearer at his funeral.
122. Foreman, *World on Fire*, chap. 8.
123. Goode, *Capital Losses*, 209. Newspapers remarked on its elegance. Corcoran scrapbook, 99, GW Archives.
124. Goode, *Capital Losses*, 209.
125. *Boston Daily Globe*, March 4, 1885, 1.
126. Goode, *Capital Losses*, 209.

6. The Collector

1. Beckert and Rosenbaum, *American Bourgeoisie*, 1.
2. Luria, *Capital Speculations*, 12.
3. Lessoff, *Nation and Its City*, 6.
4. Wallach, *Exhibiting Contradiction*, 23.
5. Conn, *Museums*, 34–37.
6. Conn, 39–43.
7. Smithsonian Institution, *Annual Report*, 31.
8. Fryd, *Art and Empire*, 11–12.
9. Marsh, "Washington's First Art Academy," 10.
10. Cosentino, *Paintings of Charles Bird King*, 42.
11. Marsh, "Washington's First Art Academy," 10.
12. Marsh, 11.
13. Marsh. Most of the Smithsonian Institution's art collection was transferred to the Corcoran Gallery after the castle building caught on fire in 1865 and destroyed part of the collection. The paintings and sculptures were recalled by the Smithsonian in 1895.
14. Marsh, 12–13.
15. Fryd, *Art and Empire*, 8–9.
16. Ways, "Montgomery C. Meigs," in Dickinson, Herrin, and Kennon, *Montgomery C. Meigs*, 21. See also Wolff, *Capitol Builder*, 90.
17. Barbara A. Wolanin, "Meigs the Art Patron," in Dickinson, Herrin, and Kennon, *Montgomery C. Meigs*, 133.
18. Wolanin, 160–63.
19. Wolff, *Capitol Builder*, 251.

20. Wolff.

21. Wolff.

22. Wolanin, "Meigs the Art Patron," in Dickinson, Herrin, and Kennon, *Montgomery C. Meigs*, 163.

23. McGuire had the largest private art collection in the capital other than Corcoran's. Due to McGuire's expertise in art and his affinity for native landscapes, Corcoran named him to the gallery's board. The collections of George Riggs and Robert Chilton were more modest. All four of the collectors focused on native landscapes and American artists, and all were members of the Washington Art Association. See untitled and undated article, *New York Courier and Enquirer*, Corcoran scrapbooks, 1.

24. Marsh, "Washington's First Art Academy," 16.

25. Sarah Cash, "Encouraging American Genius: Collecting American Art at the Corcoran Gallery of Art," in Cash, Shapiro, and Strong, *Corcoran Gallery of Art*, 18.

26. Daniel Huntington to W. W. Corcoran, August 28, 1850, in Corcoran, *A Grandfather's Legacy*, 90.

27. Wallach, *Exhibiting Contradiction*, 29.

28. Untitled and undated newspaper, Corcoran scrapbooks, 1.

29. "From Washington," *Pennsylvania Inquirer*, undated, Corcoran scrapbooks, 13.

30. C. Powell Minnigerode, "The Corcoran Gallery of Art," *Records of the Columbia Historical Society of Washington, D.C.* 48 (1949): 229.

31. Marsh, in "Washington's First Art Academy," sees Corcoran as unschooled and mainly relying on others to form his collection, stating that Corcoran essentially collected art because it seemed to be the sort of thing the wealthy elite did. There is little support for this view.

32. Wallach, *Exhibiting Contradiction*, 28.

33. Cash, "Encouraging American Genius," in Cash, Shapiro, and Strong, *Corcoran Gallery of Art*, 20.

34. "Art and Artists in Washington," *National Republican*, December 5, 1870, Corcoran scrapbooks, 18.

35. Miller, *Empire of the Eye*, 2–3.

36. Troyen, "Retreat to Arcadia," 21–37.

37. Miller, *Empire of the Eye*, 2–3.

38. Miller.

39. Troyen, "Retreat to Arcadia," 19–37.

40. *The Transcript*, April 10, 1852, Corcoran scrapbooks, unnumbered page.

41. Wallach, *Exhibiting Contradiction*, 24–25.

42. Gerdts, "Daniel Huntington's *Mercy's Dream*," 171–94.

43. Marsh, "Washington's First Art Academy," 27; and Wallach, *Exhibiting Contradiction*, 28.
44. Wallach, 28.
45. The notoriety was further enhanced by the mistaken objection of famous preacher Rev. Henry Ward Beecher to the purchase of *The Greek Slave*; he did not appreciate the figure was marble and not flesh. See "Slave Case Extraordinary," undated and untitled newspaper, Corcoran scrapbooks, 9.
46. Powers's *Greek Slave* was also used as the centerpiece at the ceremony for the marriage of Corcoran's daughter Louise to George Eustis, to which nearly fifteen hundred guests were invited. See Lauren K. Lessing, "Ties That Bind: Hiram Powers' 'Greek Slave' and Nineteenth-Century Marriage," *Faculty Scholarship*, 2010, 65.
47. Green, "Hiram Powers's *Greek Slave*," 31–39.
48. Wallach, *Exhibiting Contradiction*, 28.
49. Wallach. It seemed not to matter, either, that the statue represented Greek historical events and was not directly associated with American slavery.
50. Lanham, *Catalogue of W. W. Corcoran's Gallery*, 5.
51. Lanham.
52. Marisa Bourgoin, untitled and unpublished lecture notes, 1998, possession of the author, 4.
53. Marsh, "Washington's First Art Academy," 15–16. Like the gallery, the association's goals included the advancement of the fine arts for "comprehensive national interests." See comments of the association's president, Horatio Stone, as cited in Cash, "Encouraging American Genius," in Cash, Shapiro, and Strong, *Corcoran Gallery of Art*, 22.
54. Cash, 22.
55. *Philadelphia Inquirer*, April 29, 1856, Corcoran scrapbooks, unnumbered page.
56. *Buffalo Commercial Advertiser,* undated and unnumbered page, Corcoran scrapbooks, 82. Corcoran toured Europe in the spring of 1855 with a group of former politicians, including President Millard Fillmore, a friend who believed the federal government could not forbid slavery in the South.
57. The second such building, the Metropolitan Museum of Art in New York, would not have a home until 1880.
58. Green, *Washington*, 332; and William C. Dickinson, "Montgomery C. Meigs, the New Age Manager: An Interpretive Essay," in Dickinson, Herrin, and Kennon, *Montgomery C. Meigs*, 185.

59. Corcoran's tax issues were resolved as part of the congressional charter
    he obtained for the gallery and a subsequent act of Congress the follow-
    ing year. See Kohler and Carson, *Sixteenth Street Architecture*, 35. See also
    Journal of the House of Representatives (Washington, DC: United States
    Government, January 18, 1869), 172. The Senate version of the relief bill
    for Corcoran required the banker to swear a loyalty oath to the United
    States. See *Flake's (Galveston) Daily Bulletin,* March 4, 1869, 1.
60. Corcoran scrapbooks, 26.
61. *Boston Courier,* May 16, 1869, Corcoran scrapbooks, unnumbered page.
62. Corcoran scrapbooks, unnumbered page.
63. Goode, *Capital Losses,* 65; and Kohler and Carson, *Sixteenth Street Archi-
    tecture*, 35. At least one newspaper article of the period describes succes-
    sive diplomats and other individuals occupying Corcoran's home in his
    absence and even for a time after he returned to the United States. See
    Corcoran scrapbooks, 166.
64. Green, *Washington,* 238.
65. Corcoran, *A Grandfather's Legacy*, 32–34.
66. Corcoran, Board of Managers, 2, GW Archives.
67. Art Gallery, Secretary's Record, May 15, 1869, 7–8, GW Archives.
68. Art Gallery, Secretary's Record, 49.
69. Art Gallery, Secretary's Record, 53.
70. Art Gallery, Secretary's Record, 81.
71. Art Gallery, Secretary's Record, 83. However, the trustees lifted their sus-
    pension for a time to avail the gallery of art procured from the 1876 Cen-
    tennial Exposition.
72. *Daily Chronicle* (San Francisco), May 9, 1869, unnumbered page,
    Corcoran scrapbooks, 41.
73. "The Arts," *San Francisco Chronicle,* October 9, 1875, 2.
74. *Boston Evening Transcript,* October 11, 1875, 4.
75. *San Francisco Evening Bulletin,* October 12, 1872, 1.
76. Walters was initially interested in American art and collected a fine
    group of paintings prior to the Civil War, including works by Frederic
    Church and Thomas Cole. However, Walters sold many of his American
    paintings during the war, after which he mainly collected European art.
    Corcoran used Walters's connections to Continental painters and art
    dealers to help the gallery purchase many European works of art.
77. *New York Post,* April 29, 1872, Corcoran scrapbook, 26.
78. *Appleton's Journal,* January 3, 1874, 9.
79. Walters sent back crates of paintings that newspapers reported went un-
    inspected and unassessed for customs duties. The paintings included

Death of Caesar by Gérôme, *Two Flowers* by Conder, and *Sunset* by Breton, among others, along with about seventy bronze statues. *Sunday Herald,* November 2, 1873, Corcoran scrapbooks, 43.

80. Art Gallery, Secretary's Record, 45, 52.
81. US Congress, Senate, S. 492, "A Bill to Incorporate the Trustees of the Corcoran Gallery of Art and for Other Purposes," 41st Congress, 2nd session, February 4, 1870, as reprinted as Public Charter 70, in Corcoran, *A Grandfather's Legacy*, 34.
82. The gallery remained the home of Corcoran's collection until 1897, when the Seventeenth Street gallery opened. Planning began in 1891, when the trustees purchased the land for the site. The US Court of Claims took over the old gallery, and ultimately the Smithsonian Institution assumed control of it and renamed it the Renwick Gallery after the architect who built it.
83. Green, *Washington*, 338; and Tank, "Dedicated to Art," 38.
84. Unknown newspaper, undated, Corcoran scrapbooks, 29.
85. Conn, *Museums*, 195–96.
86. "The Ball of the Season," *Daily Patriot*, February 21, 1871, Washington, DC, unnumbered, Corcoran scrapbooks, unnumbered page.
87. "On with the Dance," untitled newspaper, February 21, 1874, Corcoran scrapbooks, 172.
88. "W. W. Corcoran, the Washington City Millionaire," *Union Springs (AL) Herald*, June 30, 1869, 1.
89. "Ball of the Season." Despite depictions of Corcoran as a Southern pariah after the war, that was clearly not the case. Newspaper articles of the day, many of which are collected in Corcoran's scrapbooks, describe ongoing connections and activities with notable people in the capital and the country.
90. Harris, *Cultural Excursions*, 16. Scholars have also posited the self-conscious development of a middle class legitimated by modes of conduct and culture. This created rising expectations and an urge to participate in urban culture. See Archer and Blau, "Class Formation," 17–41.
91. Bender, *New York Intellect*; and Dimaggio, "Cultural Entrepreneurship," 33–50.
92. William MacLeod to W. W. Corcoran, July 24, 1880, Letterpress book, 1880–1882, number 65, 172, GW Archives.
93. Untitled newspaper, August 15, 1872, Corcoran scrapbook, 3.
94. Wallach, *Exhibiting Contradiction*, 24–25.
95. *Daily Chronicle*, May 19, 1869, Corcoran scrapbooks, unnumbered page.

96. See Conn, *Museums*, chap. 6, for the growing role and impact of art museums in American society during the late nineteenth century.

97. Wallach, *Exhibiting Contradiction*, 23.

98. See, generally, Kammen, *Mystic Chords of Memory*.

99. The National Gallery at first seemed almost antithetical to the Corcoran Gallery due to its very small holding of American art and initial prohibition against the acquisition of contemporary American art.

100. *Elkhart Sentinel*, June 7, 1888, 2.

101. Marsh, "Washington's First Art Academy," 39.

102. Marsh.

103. Art Gallery, Secretary's Record, 98.

104. Tank, "Dedicated to Art," 43.

105. William MacLeod, the gallery's curator, checked with the War Department regarding his suspicions about the existence of Mount Corcoran and was informed that the maps had been falsified. No such mountain existed. The Mount Corcoran story is recounted in several places, including Marisa Bourgoin's unpublished paper on Corcoran in possession of the author. See also Wallach, *Exhibiting Contradiction*, 35.

106. Art Gallery, Secretary's Record, 119.

107. Albert Bierstadt to Samuel Ward, January 18, 1878, Corcoran, *A Grandfather's Legacy*, 27.

108. Tank, "Dedicated to Art," 34.

109. At their height, not even mixed museums such as Peale's displayed as many paintings.

110. Comments attributed to William Walters, in Art Gallery, Secretary's Record, 53.

111. *Chicago Inter-Ocean*, January 26, 1874, Corcoran scrapbooks, 50; and *Philadelphia Press*, January 19, 1874, Corcoran scrapbooks, 51.

112. This arrangement was developed at the gallery's inception. See Art Gallery, Secretary's Record, 25.

113. Art Gallery, Secretary's Record, 86.

114. *Daily Chronicle*, May 19, 1869, Corcoran scrapbooks, unnumbered page. The newspaper also called for the government to compensate Corcoran for its use of Harewood as a hospital during the Civil War, a view to which some Republicans objected but others defended. Corcoran never asked the government for any compensation for Harewood.

115. *Boston Courier*, May 16, 1869, Corcoran scrapbooks, 31.

116. *New York World*, May 13, 1869, Corcoran scrapbooks, 31.

117. Debate over Corcoran's loyalties and the art gallery continued long after his death. One newspaper, incensed that the gallery contained portraits

of Confederate generals Robert E. Lee and Stonewall Jackson in full uniform—but no Union generals—wrote that Corcoran "was notorious as a Southern sympathizer." See *Athens (OH) Messenger*, August 13, 1891, 1.

118. *Cumberland (MD) Mountain City Times*, March 7, 1874, 2.

119. See *Baltimore Gazette*, May 26, 1869, and *Daily Chronicle*, May 27, 1869, Corcoran scrapbook, 36.

120. *Evening Star*, 1, undated, Corcoran scrapbooks, unnumbered page.

121. *The Century*, 1882, Corcoran scrapbooks, unnumbered page.

122. *New York Sun*, 1884, Corcoran scrapbooks, unnumbered page.

123. Thomas Green Clemson, a diplomat, confederate officer, and enslaver, founded Clemson University in South Carolina. The two men were friends, and Corcoran handled the wealthy Southerner's investments for many years, finally informing Clemson at the age of eighty-seven that the banker was too old to serve in the position.

124. Cash, "Encouraging American Genius," in Cash, Shapiro, and Strong, *Corcoran Gallery of Art*, 19.

125. See, generally, Secretary's Record and Minutes of the Results of the Board of Trustees, GW Archives.

126. William MacLeod, *Curator's Journals*, April 17, and April 19, 1876, GW Archives.

127. *New York Express*, undated, Corcoran scrapbooks, 80.

128. Corcoran Gallery of Art Letterpress Books, November 9, 1878–November 7, 1878, microfilm roll 247, frame 197, Archives of American Art, Smithsonian Institution, Washington, DC.

129. Historians often attribute to Admiral Lee the quote "When I find the word 'Virginia' in my commission, I will join the Confederacy" to illustrate how the Civil War split families apart.

130. "Art and Artists," *Boston Evening Transcript*, October 29, 1875, 6.

131. Marsh, "Washington's First Art Academy," 8. People seeking to copy the gallery's paintings were first required to submit previous work for approval. Art Gallery, Secretary's Record, 97.

132. Marsh, 87.

133. Art Gallery, Secretary's Record, 124.

134. Art Gallery, 127.

135. Art Gallery, 133. In June 1879, the trustees reported that the gallery's current account was overdrawn.

136. Minutes of the Meetings of the Board of Trustees, Vol. 1, January 17, 1881, 34, GW Archives.

137. Board presidents Carlisle, Hall, and Riggs all predeceased Corcoran,

as did other trustees, such as Dr. Henry. Corcoran was especially close with Carlisle, who shared states' rights sympathies with the benefactor. Corcoran's scrapbook contains a strident poem written by Carlisle defending Southern liberty. "1776–1861," Corcoran scrapbooks, unnumbered page.

138. "Address of Mr. MacLeod," *Evening Star*, May 25, 1878.
139. Marsh, "Washington's First Art Academy," 82.

7. Interregnum

1. Leech, *Reveille in Washington*, v–vii.
2. Potter, *Impending Crisis*, 519–20,
3. Green, *Washington*, 231–32.
4. North, *Economic Growth*, 215.
5. Leech, *Reveille*, 3, 10.
6. The Smithsonian Institution, of which Corcoran was a trustee and a manager of most of the invested funds, found itself with a smaller endowment after the devaluation of Southern securities. See McPherson, *Battle Cry of Freedom*, 441–42. Ironically, the cotton South largely escaped the Panic of 1857, while Northern securities and railroad investments were hit hard. See Foreman, *World on Fire*, chap. 7.
7. Bernstein, *New York City Draft Riots*, 11.
8. Corcoran scrapbook, unnumbered page.
9. Cohen, *Business and Politics*, 210–11.
10. Harrison, *Washington during Civil War*, 22–23; and Ellis, *Sights and Secrets*, 9.
11. Green, *Washington*, 250–51, 264.
12. Green, 277.
13. Leech, *Reveille*, 71–72.
14. Green, *Washington*, 263.
15. IRS Tax Assessment Lists, 1862–1918, Tax Year 1864, Record Group 58, Roll 2, NARA.
16. Green, *Washington*, 208, 294.
17. Some twenty pages of the scrapbook cover the deaths of Jackson and Lee. The only other deaths recorded in the scrapbook are those of Corcoran's close relatives.
18. Furgurson, *Freedom Rising*, 183.
19. Green, *Washington*, 245–46; and Leech, *Reveille*, 25.
20. Furgurson, *Freedom Rising*, 74–82.

21. Furgurson.

22. Leech, *Reveille*, 27.

23. *Richmond Examiner*, December 25, 1860, Corcoran scrapbook, unnumbered page.

24. Leech, *Reveille*, 28–29.

25. Leech, 27.

26. Furgurson, *Freedom Rising*, 74–82.

27. Soldiers protecting the Treasury Department and the White House even sheltered in the Corcoran & Riggs Bank building across Pennsylvania Avenue. Corcoran complained to the provost marshal that Union troops from New York were destroying the rare trees at Harewood, the ruin of which helped persuade him to sell the property after the war.

28. Leech, *Reveille*, 119–20.

29. Harrison, *Washington during Civil War*, 22–23, reports that some three hundred Washington residents were thrown in prison, and approximately four hundred joined the Confederate army.

30. Green, *Washington*, 234–35.

31. J. F. Lee to Henry May, July 1861, Suspected and Disloyal Persons, Official Records of the Union and Confederate Armies, 1861–1865, Microfilm Publication M262, 797, NARA.

32. George Morey to John A. Andrew, November 12, 1861, Suspected and Disloyal Persons, Official Records of the Union and Confederate Armies, 1861–1865, Microfilm Publication M262, 821, NARA.

33. Leech, *Reveille*, 25. Shelden, in *Washington Brotherhood*, 183–84, describes several private dinners in the capital in which politicians expressed their respective loyalty and opposition to the Union. Shelden's thesis in part confirms my own: Corcoran was among the Washington insiders who were adept at working across parties and factions to achieve a variety of goals. Efforts to solve the sectional crisis over dinner obviously failed.

34. Corcoran no doubt paid attention to the infamous case of Rose O'Neal Greenhow, for years a well-connected and gracious Washington hostess and Lafayette Square neighbor who frequently entertained President Buchanan, members of the cabinet, and prominent members of Congress. Greenhow was found guilty of passing secrets to the Confederates that she had gleaned from her dinner guests. Rumor also had it that Smithsonian secretary Joseph Henry, a friend of Corcoran's and reputed Southern sympathizer, used the castle's tower to signal rebels just across the river. The scientist insisted his regular presence in the tower was for meteorological and astronomical purposes.

35. I found no official records that Corcoran was arrested during the war; however, many newspapers, North and South, reported it. The *Richmond Daily Dispatch* on August 30, 1861, wrote: "It is currently reported that W.W. Corcoran has been arrested for treason by the Provost Marshal; he has supposed to be a warm friend of the Confederate cause, and to have had caucuses at his house where traitors would meet." News of his arrest circulated in the press the same day the military took possession of the art gallery. See "The Academy of Arts," *Philadelphia Inquirer*, August 27, 1861, 1.

36. Green, *Washington*, 247–48; and Harrison, *Washington during Civil War*, 21–23.

37. Green, 287–88.

38. Green, 284–86.

39. "Close of the Fortieth Congress," *New York Daily Herald*, March 4, 1869, 1. Corcoran had previously taken loyalty oaths as a condition of rents and other funds received by the government. See the *Baltimore Sun*, March 4, 1869, 4.

40. *Evening Star*, October 18, 1862, 3.

41. The wedding of Corcoran's daughter was a sumptuous affair. Newspapers and magazines across the nation covered the event. *Harper's Weekly* gushed that "everything was done that could have been done." See "Corcoran Wedding," *Harper's Weekly*, April 6, 1859, Corcoran scrapbook, unnumbered page. The Spanish diplomat was so offended by Corcoran's reaction that he challenged the banker to a duel. Corcoran, through Senators Slidell and Bright, declined the invitation, after which the diplomat threated him bodily harm if he left the United States. The entire affair was splashed across the newspapers. See *Washington Union*, July 16, 1858, 1; and "Latest News," *Daily Exchange*, July 20, 1858, 1.

42. Furgurson, *Freedom Rising*, 183.

43. See Foreman, *World on Fire*, chap. 4.

44. McPherson, *Battle Cry of Freedom*, 387–91.

45. Foreman, *World on Fire*, chap. 8.

46. Corcoran was close friends with both Mason and Slidell. He was boyhood friends with Mason, whose family owned slaves. One of Corcoran's first jobs was for Mason's father, who owned a small bank in Georgetown, where Corcoran briefly apprenticed after the dry goods business collapsed. Corcoran became friends with Slidell later in life, and the banker and senator ended up as close confidants.

47. Foreman, *World on Fire*, chap. 7.

48. McPherson, *Battle Cry of Freedom*, 389–91.

49. "Personals," untitled and undated newspaper, Corcoran scrapbook, 121.

50. Foreman, *World on Fire*, chaps. 7–8.

51. Charles Wilkes to Gideon Welles, November 18, 1861, Suspected and Disloyal Persons, US Official Records of the Union and Confederate Armies, 1861–1865, Microfilm Publication M262, 1100, NARA. US government officials such as Secretary of State William Seward were careful to not criticize Wilkes's actions but also made it clear the seizure was not a precedent for additional such actions.

52. Resolution adopted by the House of Representatives, December 2, 1861, Suspected and Disloyal Persons, US Official Records of the Union and Confederate Armies, 1861–1865, Microfilm Publication M262, 1100, NARA.

53. Adams, "Trent Affair," 548–49.

54. Robert J. Walker to William Seward, December 16, 1861, Suspected and Disloyal Persons, US Official Records of the Union and Confederate Armies, 1861–1865, Microfilm Publication M262, 1127, NARA.

55. Jones, *Union in Peril*, 89.

56. McPherson, *Battle Cry of Freedom*, 389–91.

57. McPherson.

58. See Parker and Parker, *Forgotten George Peabody*, 115.

59. "From Washington," *Chicago Tribune*, May 20, 1863, 1.

60. *Cuba (NY) True Patriot*, February 19, 1869, 1.

61. "The Corcoran Claim," *New York Herald*, undated, Corcoran scrapbook, 74; and "The Corcoran Claims Investigation," *Baltimore Sun*, February 16, 1869, 4.

62. *Richmond Daily Dispatch*, May 25, 1863, Corcoran scrapbook, unnumbered page.

63. Green, in *Washington,* states that Corcoran converted $1.25 million into gold and shipped it to England in 1862 but provides no support for the contention. Cohen, *Business and Politics*, cites $1.6 million. In today's terms, the sum would amount to roughly $34 million.

64. Treason charges were not taken lightly. William Smithson, another prominent Washington banker, had been charged twice for corresponding with the enemy and sentenced to five years in a federal penitentiary.

65. Cohen, in *Business and Politics*, 211–12, indicates that Corcoran carried messages for Southern sympathizers. This may be based on several short notes requesting his help that were found in his papers. Still, there is no evidence that he arranged financial transactions or other support for the Confederacy.

66. Corcoran outmaneuvered the government's attempts to confiscate his H Street mansion. The French ambassador to whom Corcoran leased

the home during his absence arrived just a short time before Union soldiers came to take possession. In the meantime, Corcoran had slipped away to New York to board his London-bound ship.

67. The tragedy of Louise's young death, so like her mother's death, was sadly repeated by the bride of Corcoran's young nephew. Maggie, age twenty-one, died of tuberculosis in 1870 just days after marrying James Corcoran. Wearing her wedding gown, the bride was laid out for viewing in Corcoran's mansion. See "From Washington," *Richmond Dispatch*, December 29, 1870, 3.

68. "W.W. Corcoran, His Arrival at New York," untitled and undated newspaper (his return was May 31, 1872), Corcoran scrapbook, 174.

69. See, generally, Corcoran scrapbook.

70. See, generally, Corcoran scrapbook; and Corcoran, *A Grandfather's Legacy*. Corcoran's papers, which include many letters, are archived at the Library of Congress.

71. Parker, "Legacy of George Peabody," 57.

72. Parker, 58–59.

8. Resilience and Repair

1. Leech, *Reveille*, introduction.

2. Masur, *Example for All*, 1–2.

3. Lessoff, *Nation and Its City*, 48.

4. Green, *Washington*, 289.

5. Lessoff, *Nation and Its City*, 8–10.

6. Jacob, *Capital Elites*, introduction.

7. See, generally, Jacob, *King of the Lobby*.

8. Jacob, *Capital Elites*, chap. 6.

9. Jacob, 167.

10. "Mr. Corcoran Sued," *Washington Critic*, July 12, 1886, 1; and "Thrown from Train in Station," *Evening Star*, October 19, 1870, 1. Corcoran was almost killed in an 1870 train incident when he was knocked unconscious and dragged by a moving car. See *Anglo-American Times*, November 5, 1870, 11.

11. "Telegraphic News from Washington," *Baltimore Sun*, June 5, 1877, 1.

12. *Anglo-American Times*, April 1, 1887, 17.

13. *Boston Daily Globe*, September 24, 1881, 1.

14. Greenbrier Hotel, *History of the Greenbrier*, 68–70.

15. "Washington," *New York Tribune*, October 13, 1866, 1.

16. "Letter from Washington," *Baltimore Sun*, February 18, 1869, 1.

17. "Fortieth Congress—Third Session," *Baltimore Sun*, February 16, 1869, 4.

18. "Letters from Washington," *Baltimore Sun*, February 20, 1869, 4.

19. Blight, *Race and Reunion*, prologue.

20. Brundage, *Southern Past*, introduction.

21. See Longstreth, *Mall in Washington*; Liscombe, *Altogether American*, 239–300; and Allen, *Washington Monument*, 68. Corcoran had a long-held interest in completing the monument. He began contributing $50 a year toward that goal in 1851, thirty-four years before its completion, and had even provided funds in the 1840s. He was among a group of well-known residents and leaders who warned the public that "delay was hazardous" during a fundraising campaign for the obelisk. See "Appeal to the country on behalf of the Washington national monument," H. Polkinhorn, 1856, Printed Ephemera Collection, Portfolio 202, folder 29, LOC.

22. "The Washington Monument Difficulty," *New York Daily Herald,* October 28, 1877, 11.

23. See "Proceedings on the Occasion of Laying the Cornerstone of the Washington National Monument, Order of Parade, National Park Service," *A History of the Washington Monument,* (Washington, DC: July 4, 1848), appendix C. Corcoran was singled out for his contributions and for persuading a reluctant Congress to accept the completed Washington Monument and its grounds. See *Evening Star*, February 21, 1885, 7.

24. *Dunkirk (NY) Evening Observer*, February 13, 1885, 1.

25. *Lebanon (IN) Weekly Pioneer*, May 10, 1883, 4.

26. Wallach, *Exhibiting Contradiction*, 31. Corcoran became interested in saving Mount Vernon in the early 1850s, a decade before his Civil War exile. Therefore, his efforts were not solely a manifestation of personal redemption. See *New York Daily Times,* April 26, 1852, 3. For many years, the only direct way from Washington, DC, to Mount Vernon was aboard the steamship *W. W. Corcoran*, which was destroyed by fire in 1891.

27. Tank, "Dedicated to Art," 61.

28. Corcoran provided the University of Virginia $20,000 and what newspapers called the best classical library in the commonwealth of Virginia. *Daily Patriot* (Washington), October 29, 1872, Corcoran scrapbook, 5.

29. Among Robert E. Lee's letters to Corcoran is one from 1870 in which the Confederate general admits to sympathy "with the struggles of a warlike people to drive invaders from their land." See R. E. Lee to Hon. W. W. Corcoran, August 23, 1870, Letters of General R. E. Lee, Southern Historical Society Papers, 154–55, as cited in Valley of the Shadow Memory Articles, Virginia Center for Digital History, University of Virginia.

30. "The Home Journal," undated and untitled newspaper, Corcoran scrapbook, unnumbered page. Corcoran spent more than fifty summers at White Sulphur Springs. See *Oshkosh Daily Northwestern*, June 13, 1885, 3.

31. William Pinkney, Corcoran scrapbook, unnumbered page. A portrait of Pinkney hung in Corcoran's library, and years later Corcoran commissioned a statue in his friend's memory. The commemorative statue was likely based on Pinkney's influence on Corcoran's religious faith.

32. *Newark Daily Advocate*, April 21, 1881, 1. Corcoran also organized and contributed to a campaign for erecting a major monument to Thomas Jefferson decades before the government built one on the Tidal Basin. See *Bloomington (IL) Daily Leader*, October 18, 1882, 7.

33. "The Late Gen. R.E. Lee," untitled and undated newspaper, Corcoran scrapbook, 7. Corcoran also donated much of the funds to build a mausoleum for Lee in Lexington, Virginia. "General Lee was the embodiment of my ideal conception of all that constitutes a truly good and great man," Corcoran wrote at the time. See "Mr. Corcoran's Tribute to General Lee," *Norfolk Virginian*, May 28, 1879, 2.

34. Copy of printed remarks by W. W. Corcoran upon the death of Robert E. Lee, Corcoran scrapbook, undated and unnumbered page.

35. The change in Lafayette Square residents is best seen in the biographical sketches of occupants associated with various homes in Goode, *Capital Losses*.

36. *Atlanta Daily Constitution*, May 15, 1879, 2.

37. *Atlanta Daily Constitution*, July 31, 1879. 1.

38. Press materials of the home, *Aged Woman's Home of Georgetown: Serving Women in Need for Over 140 Years*, Washington, DC, 2013, possession of the author.

39. *Titusville (PA) Morning Herald*, April 15, 1879, 1.

40. Corcoran, *A Grandfather's Legacy*, 36–37.

41. Brochure of the Lisner-Louise-Dickson Home, *Brief History*, 21.

42. Tank, "Dedicated to Art," 61.

43. Corcoran, *A Grandfather's Legacy*, 35.

44. *St. Louis Post Dispatch*, November 5, 1872, Corcoran scrapbook, 19. A report from St. Louis on April 17, 1872, showed admiration for Corcoran's approach, noting that the founder was a "pronounced Southerner and devout Episcopalian" but that such biases had no role in the selection of women for the home.

45. Lisner-Louise-Dickson-Hurt Home, *Brief History*, 21.

46. "A Washington Institution," *Greenville (AL) Advocate*, February 19, 1874, Corcoran scrapbook, 73.

47. Paul Kelsey Williams, "Scenes from the Past," *The In Towner*, April 2009, 9.
48. Lisner-Louise-Dickson-Hurt Home, *Brief History*, 22.
49. Lisner-Louise-Dickson-Hurt Home.
50. Unknown newspaper, undated, Corcoran scrapbook, 16.
51. *St. Louis Post Dispatch*, April 17, 1872, Corcoran scrapbook, 19.
52. Corcoran, *A Grandfather's Legacy*, 35–40.
53. *San Antonio Daily Express*, November 18, 1888, 3.
54. Lisner-Louise-Dickson Home, *Brief History*, 7.
55. Lisner-Louise-Dickson Home, 30.
56. Jones, *Southern Historical Society Papers*, 5:254. Corcoran also made regular generous donations to the society.
57. *Richmond Dispatch*, November 27, 1892, 2.
58. *Titusville (PA) Morning Herald*, December 28, 1887, 4.
59. *Richmond Dispatch*, November 27, 1892, 2.
60. Corcoran, *A Grandfather's Legacy*, 35.
61. *Fredericksburg News*, July 5, 1874, Corcoran scrapbook, 56.
62. *News and Courier*, Charleston, SC, April 12, 1875, unnumbered page, Corcoran scrapbook, 99.
63. Hays, *Response to Industrialism*, introduction; and Beckert, *Monied Metropolis*, introduction.
64. These issues are covered in many histories of urban America, including Wiebe, *Search for Order*; Summers, *Era of Good Stealings*; Jackson and Schultz, *Cities in American History*; and Ryan, *Civic Wars*.
65. Coincidently, one of the leaders of the reform element responsible for bringing down Boss Tweed was Andrew Green, the developer of Central Park. The situation was somewhat analogous to Corcoran's intervention in the downfall of Boss Shepherd, given his antecedent role in the National Mall's development. See Ryan, *Civic Wars*, 272–79.
66. Ryan.
67. Gillette, *Between Justice and Beauty*, 61–68. Prior to the political machine period, Corcoran on several occasions led delegations of the city's eminent citizens to raise the president's awareness of problems affecting the capital's infrastructure and social conditions. See "Washington News and Gossip," *Evening Star*, January 22, 1870, 1.
68. Per the *Evening Star*, corruption affected appropriations that left the city nearly bankrupt, as teachers and police officers went without pay, interest on the district's debt went unpaid, and the city was "systematically plundered." Petitions by Corcoran and others convinced Congress to create a committee to investigate corruption, a story avidly followed

around the country. See also *Fort Wayne Daily Sentinel*, February 3, 1874, 2.

69. Ryan, *Civic Wars*, 272–79, also gives credit to the *New York Times*.

70. Green, *Washington*, chap. 14.

71. Lessoff, *Nation and Its City*, 57–71. Lessoff correctly describes the struggle as, in part, a battle over city control between the new regime and the old city fathers. Even Boss Shepherd toured the art gallery on opening day.

72. "The District Ring," *Chicago Daily Tribune*, January 28, 1874, 1.

73. "The Last Great Fraud," *Baltimore Sun*, September 11, 1872, 1.

74. The charge was true, of course, as Corcoran had not paid taxes on his property during his European exile. However, these issues were settled when the government agreed to pay the rent for its Civil War use of the gallery and Congress approved the gallery's charter in 1869. Corcoran also defended his payment of taxes during the period in which the ring was operating. See *Washington Sentinel*, March 4, 1872, Corcoran scrapbook, 72. One newspaper castigated Corcoran, saying that if the banker had paid his taxes, teachers who had not been paid for many months could have received paychecks. Anthony Hyde, Corcoran's private secretary, reminded the paper's readers that the banker not only paid his taxes but also had been paying the teachers' salaries during the financial crisis. Another commentator said Corcoran had the "reputation of always being a chronic grumbler about his taxes." See "Mr. Corcoran's Defense," *Evening Star*, February 10, 1874, 2.

75. William Wilson Corcoran, letter to *Washington Sentinel*, February 7, 1874, Corcoran scrapbook, 61.

76. Corcoran letter to *Washington Sentinel*. The paper was bankrolled by Corcoran and edited by Louis Frederick Schade, a colorful Democratic stalwart who used the newspaper to help drive Alexander Shepherd from office.

77. "The Scandals of Grantism," *New York Sun*, February 13, 1880, 4.

78. "Mr. Corcoran and the District Government," *Evening Star*, February 6, 1874, 2; and *Washington Chronicle*, February 10, 1874, Corcoran scrapbook, 63.

79. "From Washington," *Madison State Journal*, January 19, 1875, 1.

80. *Baltimore Sun*, February 17, 1874, Corcoran scrapbook, 63.

81. "Economics of Tweed," *Eau Claire Daily Free Press*, December 21, 1875, 1; and "Boss Tweed in Journalism," *New York Times*, February 19, 1872, 5. Corcoran also had business ties with Alexander Shepherd, includ-

ing as coinvestors in an investment pool tied to the firm of Jay Cooke. See "More of Estate of Jay Cooke and Co.," *Journal of Commerce*, July 7, 1875, 1.

82. *New York Tribune,* January 28, 1874, Corcoran scrapbook 63.

83. *New York Tribune.*

84. "Ring Rule at Washington," *New York Tribune*, April 19, 1873, 4.

85. Green, *Washington*, 360–62. Perhaps not coincidentally, the imposition of federal control in the nation's capital in conjunction with the elimination of suffrage came at the same time Reconstruction ended in the South, largely eliminating minority suffrage in regions where Radical Republicans had mandated it.

86. Gillette, *Between Justice and Beauty*, 190–91.

87. Teaford, *Unheralded Triumph*, chap. 1.

88. Teaford, in *Unheralded Triumph*, notes the twin efforts to reduce local control and to expand the role of professionals succeeded in improving cities in the last third of the nineteenth century.

89. Summers, *Era of Good Stealings*, 146–47; and Teaford, chap. 6.

90. Teaford.

91. Teaford.

92. Lessoff, *Nation and Its City*, 268.

93. The establishment of an unelected commissioner form of government in the nation's capital in 1874 predates Galveston's commission structure by twenty-five years.

94. Summers, *Era of Good Stealings*, 147.

95. Teaford, *Unheralded Triumph*, chap. 1.

96. Lessoff, *Nation and Its City*, 8–10.

97. Summers, *Era of Good Stealings*, 143–46.

98. Summers, 296–97.

99. Green, *Washington*, 339; and Lessoff, *Nation and Its City*, 52–53.

100. Even in the modern home-rule era, Congress still retains review authority over legislation passed by the DC Council, and the city's citizens have no voting representation in the national legislature.

101. "Mr. W. W. Corcoran," *The Sentinel*, June 27, 1874, Corcoran scrapbook, 94. Corcoran's role in capital-related politics was well known. After the demise of home rule, few appointments to the board of commissioners or other posts were made without Corcoran's advice or approval. See "Washington," *Star Tribune*, January 16, 1881, 1.

102. "Letter from Washington," *Baltimore Sun*, May 24, 1869, 4.

103. Summers, *Era of Good Stealings*, 300–304.

104. Lessoff, *Nation and Its City*, 75.
105. "Government and the District," *New Era*, February 10, 1870, 2.
106. See for example, *Bismarck Daily Tribune*, January 6, 1911, 6.

9. Legacy

1. *Boston Daily Globe*, December 28, 1887, 4.
2. "W.W. Corcoran's Illness," *New York Times*, July 13, 1880, 2.
3. "A Life Well Spent," *Iowa Courier*, March 7, 1888, 1; and *Hagerstown Herald and Torchlight*, June 9, 1887, 3. Corcoran had previously survived several illnesses, including partial blindness and strokes. Illness several years prior to his death gave his doctors "no hope for his recovery." See *Bloomington (IL) Daily Leader*, June 7, 1882, 1.
4. *Fort Wayne Sentinel*, February 29, 1888, 1.
5. *Logansport (IN) Journal*, May 30, 1884, 7.
6. "Funeral of W.W. Corcoran," *Evening Star*, February 27, 1888, 5.
7. *Decatur (IL) Daily Republican*, February 28, 1888, 2.

SELECTED BIBLIOGRAPHY

Archival Sources

Archives of American Art. Smithsonian Institution, Washington, DC.
Corcoran, William Wilson. Papers. Library of Congress, Washington, DC (LOC).
Girard, Stephen. Papers. American Philosophical Association, Philadelphia.
Morgan, J. S. Papers. Morgan Library, New York.
National Archives and Records Administration, Washington, DC.
Special Collections Research Center. George Washington University Archives.
  Estelle and Melvin Gelman Library. Washington, DC (GW Archives).
Virginia Center for Digital History. University of Virginia, Charlottesville.

Books

Adams, Donald R., Jr. *Finance and Enterprise in Early America: A Study of Stephen Girard's Bank, 1812–1831.* Philadelphia: University of Pennsylvania Press, 1978.

Adrian, Charles R. *A History of American City Government: The Formation of Traditions.* New York: University Press of America, 1987.

The Aged Woman's Home of Georgetown. *The Aged Woman's Home of Georgetown: Serving Women in Need for over 140 Years.* 2013.

Allen, Thomas B. *The Washington Monument: It Stands for All.* New York: Discovery Books, 2000.

Appleby, Joyce. *Capitalism and the New Social Order: The Republican Vision of the 1790s.* New York: New York University Press, 1984.

Arnebeck, Bob. *Through a Fiery Trial: Building Washington, 1790–1800.* Baltimore: Madison Books, 1997.

Arnold, Edwin, and Arsene N. Girault. *Prospectus of the Washington High School for Young Gentlemen.* Washington, DC: J & G. S. Gideon, 1843.

Augst, Thomas. *The Clerk's Tale: Young Men and Moral Life in Nineteenth-Century America.* Chicago: University of Chicago Press, 2003.

Balleisen, Edward J. *Navigating Failure: Bankruptcy and Commercial Society in Antebellum America.* Chapel Hill: University of North Carolina Press, 2001.

Barrell, John. *The Political Theory of Painting from Reynolds to Hazlitt: The Body of the Politic.* New Haven, CT: Yale University Press, 1986.

Beckert, Sven. "Merchants and Manufacturers in the Antebellum North." In Fraser and Gerstle, *Ruling America*, chap. 3.

———. *The Monied Metropolis: New York City and the Consolidation of the American Bourgeoisie.* Cambridge: Cambridge University Press, 2003.

Beckert, Sven, and Julia B. Rosenbaum. *The American Bourgeoisie: Distinction and Identity in the Nineteenth Century.* New York: Palgrave Macmillan, 2010.

Bednar, Michael. *L'Enfant's Legacy: Public Open Spaces in Washington, D.C.* Baltimore: Johns Hopkins University Press, 2006.

Bender, Thomas. *New York Intellect: A History of Intellectual Life in New York City from 1750 to the Beginnings of Our Own Time.* Baltimore: Johns Hopkins University Press, 1988.

———. *Toward an Urban Vision: Ideas and Institutions in Nineteenth Century America.* Baltimore: Johns Hopkins University Press, 1975.

Berg, Scott, W. *Grand Avenues: The Story of the French Visionary Who Designed Washington, D.C.* New York: Pantheon Books, 2007.

Bernstein, Iver. *The New York City Draft Riots: Their Significance for American Society and Politics in the Age of the Civil War.* New York: Oxford University Press, 1990.

Black, David. *The King of Fifth Avenue: The Fortunes of August Belmont.* New York: Dial Press, 1981.

Blight, David W. *Race and Reunion: The Civil War in American Memory.* Cambridge, MA: Harvard University Press, 2002.

Bodenhorn, Howard. *A History of Banking in Antebellum America: Financial Markets and Economic Development in an Era of Nation Building.* New York: Cambridge University Press, 2000.

———. *State Banking in Early America: A New Economic History.* New York: Oxford University Press, 2003.

Bouligny, M. E. P. *A Tribute to W. W. Corcoran, of Washington City.* Philadelphia: Porter & Coates, 1874.

Bruchey, Stuart. *Enterprise: The Dynamic Economy of a Free People.* Cambridge, MA: Harvard University Press, 1990.

Brundage, W. Fitzhugh. *The Southern Past: A Clash of Race and Memory.* Cambridge, MA: Harvard University Press, 2008.

Burrows, Edwin G., and Mike Wallace. *Gotham: A History of New York City to 1898.* New York: Oxford University Press, 1999.

Bushman, Richard L. *The Refinement of America: Persons, Houses, Cities.* New York: Alfred A. Knopf, 1992.

Campbell, Ballard C. *The Growth of Government: Governance from the Cleveland Era to the Present.* Bloomington: Indiana University Press, 1995.

Cannadine, David. *Mellon: An American Life.* New York: Alfred Knopf, 2006.

Carr, Roland T. *32 President's Square: Part I of a Two-Part Narrative of the Riggs Bank and Its Founders.* Washington, DC: Acropolis Publishing Co., 1980.

Cash, Sarah, Emily Dana Shapiro, and Lisa Strong, eds. *Corcoran Gallery of Art: American Paintings to 1945.* Washington, DC: Corcoran Gallery of Art, 2012.

Cashman, Sean Dennis. *America in the Gilded Age: From the Death of Lincoln to the Rise of Theodore Roosevelt.* New York: New York University Press, 1993.

Cawelti, John G. *Apostles of the Self-Made Man.* Chicago: University of Chicago Press, 1965.

Chandler, Alfred. *Scale and Scope: The Dynamics of Industrial Capitalism.* Cambridge, MA: Harvard University Press, 1994.

———. *The Visible Hand: The Managerial Revolution in American Business.* Cambridge, MA: Harvard University Press, 1977.

Chandler, Alfred, and Richard S. Tedlow. *The Coming of Managerial Capitalism: A Casebook of the History of American Economic Institutions.* Princeton, NJ: Irwin, 1985.

Cohen, Henry. *Business and Politics in America from the Age of Jackson to the Civil War: The Career Biography of W. W. Corcoran.* Westport, CT: Praeger, 1971.

Conn, Steven. *Museums and American Intellectual Life, 1876–1926.* Chicago: University of Chicago Press, 1998.

Constable, W. G. *Art Collecting in the United States: An Outline of a History.* New York: Thomas Nelson & Sons, 1965.

Corcoran, William Wilson. *Deed and Charter of the Corcoran Gallery of Art, 1869.* GW Archives.

———. *A Grandfather's Legacy.* Washington, DC: Henry Polkinhorn, 1879.

———. Letterpress Books of William Wilson Corcoran. 67 vols. LOC.

———. Letters to William Wilson Corcoran. 27 vols. LOC.

———. Scrapbook of William Wilson Corcoran. GW Archives.

Cosentino, Andrew J. *The Paintings of Charles Bird King (1785–1862).* Washington, DC: Smithsonian Institution, 1977.

Cummings, James Wilson. "Financing the Mexican War." PhD diss., Oklahoma State University, 2003.

Dickinson, William C., Dean A. Herrin, and Donald R. Kennon, eds. *Montgomery C. Meigs and the Building of the Nation's Capital.* Athens: Ohio University Press, 1991.

Dunn, Gano. *Peter Cooper: A Mechanic of New York.* New York: Newcomer Society of North America, 1949.

Elias, Stephen N. *Alexander T. Stewart: The Forgotten Merchant Prince.* Westport, CT: Praeger, 1992.

Ellis, John B. *The Sights and Secrets of the National Capital.* New York: United States Publishing, 1869.

Farrell, Betty G. *Elite Families: Class and Power in Nineteenth-Century Boston.* Albany: State University of New York Press, 1993.

Foreman, Amanda. *A World on Fire: Britain's Crucial Role in the American Civil War.* New York: Random House, 2010.

Fraser, Steve, and Gary Gerstle, eds. *The Ruling Class: A History of Wealth and Power in a Democracy.* Cambridge, MA: Harvard University Press, 2005.

Fryd, Vivien Green. *Art and Empire: The Politics of Ethnicity in the U.S. Capitol.* New Haven: Yale University Press, 1992.

Furgurson, Earnest B. *Freedom Rising: Washington in the Civil War.* New York: Knopf, 2004.

Gillette, Howard, Jr. *Between Justice and Beauty: Race, Planning, and the Failure of Urban Policy in Washington, D.C.* Baltimore: Johns Hopkins University Press, 1995.

Gladwell, Malcolm. *The Tipping Point: How Little Things Can Make a Big Difference.* Boston: Little, Brown, 2000.

Goode, James M. *Capital Losses: A Cultural History of Washington's Destroyed Buildings.* Washington, DC: Smithsonian Institution, 2003.

Green, Constance McLaughlin. *The Secret City: A History of Race Relations in the Nation's Capital.* Princeton, NJ: Princeton University Press, 1969.

———. *Washington: Village and Capital, 1800–1878.* Princeton, NJ: Princeton University Press, 1962.

Greenbrier Hotel. *The History of the Greenbrier: America's Resort.* Charleston: Greenbrier Pictorial Histories Publishing, 1989.

Griffin, Clifford. *Their Brothers' Keepers: Moral Stewardship in the United States, 1815–1865.* New Brunswick: Rutgers University Press, 1960.

Gutheim, Frederick, and Antoinette J. Lee. *Worthy of the Nation: Washington, DC, from L'Enfant to the National Capital Planning Commission.* Baltimore: Johns Hopkins University Press, 2006.

Gutheim, Frederick, and Wilcomb Washburn. *The Federal City: Plans and Realities*. Washington, DC: Smithsonian Institution, 1976.

Guttman, Herbert. "The Reality of the Rags to Riches 'Myth': The Case of the Paterson, New Jersey, Locomotive, Iron, and Machinery Manufacturers, 1780–1880." In *Nineteenth-Century Cities: Essays in the New Urban History*, ed. Stephan Thernstrom and Richard Sennett, 98–124. New Haven, CT: Yale University Press, 1969.

Hall, Peter Dobkin. *The Organization of American Culture, 1700–1900: Private Institutions, Elites, and the Origins of American Nationality*. New York: New York University Press, 1982.

Halttunen, Karen. *Confidence Men and Painted Women: A Study of Middle-Class Culture in America, 1830–1870*. New Haven, CT: Yale University Press, 1982.

Hammond, Bray. *Banks and Politics in America from the Revolution to the Civil War*. Princeton, NJ: Princeton University Press, 1957.

Harris, Neil. *The Artist in American Society: The Formative Years, 1790–1860*. Chicago: University of Chicago Press, 1982.

———. *Cultural Excursions: Marketing Appetites and Cultural Tastes in Modern America*. Chicago: University of Chicago Press, 1990.

Harris, Ray Baker. *Sesqui-centennial History of the Grand Lodge, Free and Accepted Masons, District of Columbia, 1811-1961*. Washington, DC: Grand Lodge F.A.A.M., 1962.

Harrison, Robert. *Washington during Civil War and Reconstruction: Race and Radicalism*. Cambridge: Cambridge University Press, 2011.

Hays, Samuel P. *The Response to Industrialism, 1885–1914*. Chicago: University of Chicago Press, 1957.

Hemphill, C. Dallett. *Bowing to Necessities: A History of Manners in America, 1620–1860*. New York: Oxford University Press, 1999.

Hidy, Muriel E. *George Peabody, Merchant and Financier, 1829–1854*. New York: Arno Press, 1978.

Hidy, Ralph W. *The House of Baring in American Trade and Finance*. Cambridge: Cambridge University Press, 1949.

Hilkey, Judy. *Character Is Capital: Success Manuals and Manhood in Gilded Age America*. Chapel Hill: University of North Carolina Press, 1997.

Howe, Daniel Walker. *Making the American Self: Jonathan Edwards to Abraham Lincoln*. New York: Oxford University Press, 2009.

Ingham, John N. *The Iron Barons: A Social Analysis of an American Urban Elite*. Westport, CT: Greenwood Press, 1978.

Jackson, Kenneth T., and Stanley K. Schultz, eds. *Cities in American History*. New York: Alfred Knopf, 1972.

Jacob, Kathryn Allamong. *Capital Elites: High Society in Washington, D.C., after the Civil War.* Washington, DC: Smithsonian Institution, 1995.

———. *King of the Lobby: The Life and Times of Sam Ward, Man-about-Washington in the Gilded Age.* Baltimore: Johns Hopkins University Press, 2010.

Johnston, William R. *William and Henry Walters, the Reticent Collectors.* Baltimore: Johns Hopkins University Press, 1991.

Jones, Howard. *The Union in Peril: The Crisis over British Intervention in the Civil War.* Omaha: University of Nebraska Press, 1997.

Jones, J. William, ed. *Southern Historical Society Papers.* Vol. 5. Reprint edition. Charleston: Nabu Press, 2012.

Josephson, Matthew. *The Robber Barons: The Great American Capitalists, 1861–1901.* New York: Mariner Books, 1966.

Kammen, Michael. *Mystic Chords of Memory: The Transformation of Tradition in American Culture.* New York: Vintage Books, 1991.

Kasson, John F. *Civilizing the Machine: Technology and Republican Values in America.* Boston: Hill and Wang, 1976.

———. *Rudeness and Civility: Manners in Nineteenth-Century Urban America.* New York: HarperCollins, 1990.

Kayser, Elmer Louis. *Bricks without Straw: The Evolution of George Washington University.* New York: Appleton-Century-Crofts, 1970.

Keller, Morton. *Affairs of State: Public Life in Late Nineteenth Century America.* New York: Cambridge University Press, 1977.

———. *Regulating a New Economy: Public Policy and Economic Change in America, 1900–1933.* Cambridge, MA: Harvard University Press, 1990.

Kirkland, Edward Chase. *Dream and Thought in the Business Community, 1860–1900.* Chicago: Ivan R. Dee, 1990.

Klein, Carole. *Gramercy Park: An American Bloomsbury.* Baltimore: Johns Hopkins University Press, 1987.

Kohler, Sue A. *The Commission of Fine Arts: A Brief History.* Washington, DC: Commission of Fine Arts, 1990.

Kohler, Sue A., and Jeffrey R. Carson. *Sixteenth Street Architecture.* 2 vols. Washington, DC: Commission of Fine Arts, 1978.

Laird, Pamela Walker. *Pull: Networking and Success since Benjamin Franklin.* Cambridge, MA: Harvard University Press, 2006.

Lamoreaux, Naomi. *Insider Lending: Banks, Personal Connections, and Economic Development in Industrial New England.* New York: Cambridge University Press, 1996.

Lanham, Charles. *Catalogue of W. W. Corcoran's Gallery.* Washington, DC: Henry Polkinhorn, 1857.

Lawson, Melinda. *Patriot Fires: Forging a New American Nationalism in the Civil War North.* Lawrence: University of Kansas, 2002.

Leech, Margaret. *Reveille in Washington, 1860–1865.* New York: Simon Publications, 1941.

Lessoff, Alan. *The Nation and Its City: Politics, "Corruption," and Progress in Washington, D.C., 1861–1902.* Baltimore: Johns Hopkins University Press, 1994.

Liscombe, Rhodri Windsor. *Altogether American: Robert Mills, Architect and Engineer.* New York: Oxford University Press, 1994.

Lisner-Louise-Dickson-Hurt Home. *A Brief History.* Washington, DC: undated brochure.

Longstreth, Richard. *The Mall in Washington, 1791–1991.* Washington, DC: National Gallery of Art, 2003.

Lubin, David. *Picturing a Nation: Art and Social Change in Nineteenth-Century America.* New Haven: Yale University Press, 1994.

Lukasik, Christopher J. *Discerning Characters: The Culture of Appearance in Early America.* Philadelphia: University of Pennsylvania Press, 2010.

Luria, Sarah. *Capital Speculations: Writing and Building Washington, D.C.* Lebanon: University of New Hampshire Press, 2006.

Lystra, Karen. *Searching the Heart: Women, Men, and Romantic Love in Nineteenth-Century America.* New York: Oxford University Press, 1989.

MacLeod, William. *Curator's Journals: Corcoran Gallery of Art.* Washington, DC: 1876. GW Archives.

Madsen, Axel. *John Jacob Astor: America's First Multimillionaire.* New York: Wiley Publishing, 2001.

Mann, Bruce H. *Republic of Debtors: Bankruptcy in the Age of American Independence.* Cambridge, MA: Harvard University Press, 2002.

Marsh, Allan Thomas. "Washington's First Art Academy, the Corcoran School of Art." Ph.D. diss., University of Maryland at College Park, 1983.

Masur, Kate. *An Example for All the Land: Emancipation and the Struggle over Equality in Washington, D.C.* Chapel Hill: University of North Carolina Press, 2010.

McCarthy, Kathleen D. *American Creed: Philanthropy and the Rise of Civil Society, 1700–1865.* Chicago: University of Chicago Press, 2003.

———. *Noblesse Oblige: Charity and Cultural Philanthropy in Chicago, 1849–1929.* Chicago: University of Chicago Press, 1982.

———. *Women's Culture: American Philanthropy and Art, 1830–1930.* Chicago: University of Chicago Press, 1993.

McCormick, Richard L. *The Party Period and Public Policy: American Politics from the Age of Jackson to the Progressive Era*. New York: Oxford University Press, 1986.

McCoy, Drew. *The Elusive Republic: Political Economy in Jeffersonian America.* Chapel Hill: University of North Carolina Press, 1996.

McPherson, James M. *Battle Cry of Freedom: The Civil War Era.* New York: Oxford University Press, 1988.

Merry, Robert. *A Country of Vast Designs: James K. Polk, the Mexican War, and the Conquest of the American Continent.* New York: Simon & Schuster, 2009.

Miller, Angela. *Empire of the Eye: Landscape Representation and American Cultural Politics, 1825–1875.* New York: Cornell University Press, 1993.

Mitchell, Mary. *Chronicles of Georgetown Life, 1865–1900.* Cabin John, MD: Seven Lakes Press, 1986.

Morris, Charles R. *The Tycoons: How Andrew Carnegie, John D. Rockefeller, Jay Gould, and J. P. Morgan Invented the American Supereconomy.* New York: Holt, 2006.

Nash, Gary. *The Urban Crucible: The Northern Seaports and the Origins of the American Revolution.* Cambridge, MA: Harvard University Press, 1986.

Nevins, Allan, ed. *The Diary of Philip Hone, 1828–1851.* New York: Dodd Mead, 1970.

Nevins, Allan, and Milton Halsey Thomas, eds. *The Diary of George Templeton Strong.* Vol. 2, *The Turbulent Fifties, 1850–1859.* Seattle: Macmillan, 1952.

Nichols, Thomas Low. *Forty Years of American Life.* London: John Maxwell, 1864.

North, Douglass C. *The Economic Growth of the United States, 1790–1860.* New York: W. W. Norton, 1966.

Oak Hill Cemetery Company. *Annual Report of the Board of Managers, 1869–1896.* Vol. 1. Washington, DC: Henry Polkinhorn, n.d. GW Archives.

Oppel, Frank, and Tony Meisel, eds. *Washington, D.C.: A Turn-of-the-Century Treasury.* Secaucus, NJ: Castle Books, 1987.

Parker, Franklin. *George Peabody: A Biography.* Nashville: Vanderbilt University Press, 1971.

Parker, Franklin, and Betty Parker. *The Forgotten George Peabody: A to Z Handbook.* Privately published, n.d.

———. *George Peabody: A–Z Handbook of the Massachusetts-Born Merchant in the South.* Part 4 of 7. Privately published, n.d.

Perkins, Edwin J. *American Public Finance and Financial Services, 1700–1815.* Columbus: Ohio State University, 1994.

Pessen, Edward. *Riches, Class, and Power before the Civil War.* Lexington, KY: Transaction Publishers, 1973.

Poore, Benjamin Perley. *Perley's Reminiscences of Sixty Years in the National Metropolis.* Reprint. Charleston, NC: Nabu Press, 2010.

Potter, David M. *The Impending Crisis, 1848–1861.* New York: Harper Perennial, 1976.

Redlich, Fritz. *The Molding of American Banking: Men and Ideas.* New York: Martino Fine Books, 2012.

Ricks, Mary Kay. *Escape on the Pearl: The Heroic Bid for Freedom on the Underground Railroad.* Washington, DC: William Morrow, 2007.

Roessle, Theophilus. *A Historic Corner in a Historic City.* New York: Engraving and Printing, 1890.

Rosenberg, Chaim. *The Life and Times of Francis Cabot Lowell, 1775–1817.* Boston: Lexington Books, 2011.

Rosenzweig, Roy, and Elizabeth Blackmar. *The Park and the People: A History of Central Park.* New York: Cornell University Press, 1992.

Rothman, Adam, and Elsa Barraza Mendoza. *Facing Georgetown's History: A Reader on Slavery, Memory, and Reconciliation.* Washington, DC: Georgetown University Press, 2021.

Rothman, Ellen K. *Hands and Hearts: A History of Courtship in America.* Cambridge, MA: Harvard University Press, 1987.

Rothman, Joshua D. *The Ledger and the Chain: How Domestic Slave Traders Shaped America.* New York: Basic Books, 2021.

Rotundo, E. Anthony. *American Manhood: Transformations in Masculinity from the Revolution to the Modern Era.* New York: Basic Books, 1993.

Ryan, Mary P. *Civic Wars: Democracy in Public Life in the American City during the Nineteenth Century.* Los Angeles: University of Southern California Press, 1997.

Sandage, Scott A. *Born Losers: A History of Failure in America.* Cambridge, MA: Harvard University Press, 2005.

Savage, Kirk. *Standing Soldiers, Kneeling Slaves: Race, War, and Monument in Nineteenth-Century America.* Princeton, NJ: Princeton University Press, 1997.

Schultz, Stanley K. *Constructing Urban Culture: American Cities and City Planning, 1800–1920.* Philadelphia: Temple University Press, 1989.

Shelden, Rachel A. *Washington Brotherhood: Politics, Social Life, and the Coming of the Civil War.* Chapel Hill: University of North Carolina Press, 2013.

Shenton, James P. *Robert John Walker: Politician from Jackson to Lincoln.* New York: Columbia University Press, 1961.

Smithsonian Institution. *Annual Report.* Washington, DC: Smithsonian Institution, 1856.

Spilsbury Gail. *Rock Creek Park.* Baltimore: Johns Hopkins University Press, 2003.

Stiles, T. J. *The First Tycoon: The Epic Life of Cornelius Vanderbilt.* New York: Vintage, 2010.

Strouse, Jean. *Morgan: American Financier.* New York: Random House, 1999.

Summers, Mark. *The Era of Good Stealings.* New York: Oxford University Press, 1993.

Sweet, Robert Thomas. "Selected Correspondence of the Banking Firm of Corcoran & Riggs, 1844–1858, Showing the Emergence of Washington as a Financial Center." Ph.D. diss., Catholic University of America, 1982.

Teaford, Jon. *The Unheralded Triumph: City Government in America.* Baltimore: Johns Hopkins University Press, 1984.

Thoreau, Henry David. *Walden or Life in the Woods.* New York: Thomas Y. Crowell, 1910.

Tocqueville, Alexis de. *Democracy in America.* New York: Vintage Books, 1945.

Torrey, Barbara Boyle, and Clara Myrick Green. *Between Freedom and Equality: The History of an African American Family in Washington, DC.* Washington, DC: Georgetown University Press, 2021.

Trachtenberg, Alan. *Incorporation of America: Culture and Society in the Gilded Age.* New York: Hill and Wang, 2007.

US Congress. House. *Congressional Globe.* 29th Congress, 1st session, July 1846.

——. *Congressional Globe.* 30th Congress, 1st session, 1846.

——. *Report of the United States Art Commission.* Ex. Doc. No. 43. 35th Congress, 1st session, 1858.

US Department of the Interior. *Historic American Buildings Survey: The National Mall & Monument Grounds, Washington, District of Columbia, DC.* Washington, DC: US Department of the Interior, compiled after 1933 (HABS No. DC-678).

US Department of the Interior. Census Office. *Report of the Commissioner of Public Buildings.* Washington, DC: October 15, 1857.

——. *Report on the Population of the United States, Eleventh Census: 1890.* Washington, DC: 1890.

US Senate. *United States Senate Catalogue of Fine Art.* Senate Doc. 107-11. Washington, DC: Government Printing Office, 2002.

Wallach, Allan. "Long Term Visions, Short Term Failures." In *Exhibiting Contradiction: Essays on the Art Museum in the United States.* Cambridge: University of Massachusetts Press, 1988.

Warren, Kenneth. *Triumphant Capitalism: Henry Clay Frick and the Industrial Transformation of America.* Pittsburgh: University of Pittsburgh Press, 1996.

Ways, Harry C. "Montgomery C. Meigs and the Washington Aqueduct." In

Montgomery C. Meigs and the Building of the Nation's Capital, ed. William C. Dickinson, Dean A. Herrin, and Donald R. Kennon, 27–28. Pittsburgh: Ohio University Press, 2001.

Wharton, Anne Hollingsworth. *Social Life in the Early Republic*. Philadelphia: J. B. Lippincott, 1902.

White, Leonard D. *The Republican Era, 1869–1901: A Study in Administrative History*. New York: Free Press, 1958.

Wiebe, Robert H. *The Opening of American Society: From the Adoption of the Constitution to the Era of Disunion*. New York: Alfred A. Knopf, 1984.

———. *The Search for Order, 1877–1920*. New York: Hill and Wang, 1967.

Wilson, William H. *The City Beautiful Movement*. Baltimore: Johns Hopkins University Press, 1989.

Wolff, Wendy, ed. *Capitol Builder: The Shorthand Journal of Montgomery Meigs, 1853–1859, 1861*. Washington, DC: Government Printing Office, 2001.

Wood, Gordon S. *The Radicalism of the American Revolution: How a Revolution Transformed a Monarchical Society into a Democratic One Unlike Any That Had Ever Existed*. New York: Vintage Press, 1992.

Wright, Robert E. *Origins of Commercial Banking in America, 1750–1800*. New York: Rowman & Littlefield, 2001.

Zunz, Olivier. *Philanthropy in America: A History*. Princeton, NJ: Princeton University Press, 2012.

Periodicals

Adams, Charles Francis, Jr. "The Trent Affair." *The American Historical Review* 17, no. 3 (April 1912): 548–49.

Archer, Melanie, and Judith R. Blau. "Class Formation in Nineteenth-Century America: The Case of the Middle Class." *Annual Review of Sociology* 19 (1993): 17–41.

Brown, Kathy Ann. "Georgetown's 'Home Sweet Home.'" *American Cemetery: The Magazine of Cemetery Management* 21 (May 1998).

Brown, Letitia W. "Residence Patterns of Negroes in the District of Columbia, 1800–1869." *Records of the Columbia Historical Society* 47 (1971).

Bryan, W. B. "L'Enfant's Personal Affairs." *Records of the Columbia Historical Society*, no. 2 (1899).

Curti, Merle. "American Philanthropy and the National Character." *American Quarterly* 10, no. 4 (Winter 1958): 420–37.

Dimaggio, Paul. "Cultural Entrepreneurship in Nineteenth-Century Boston." *Media, Culture and Society* 4, no. 1 (1982): 33–50.

Farr, James. "Social Capital: A Conceptual Theory." *Political Theory* 32 (February 2004).

Gabel, Terrance G., and Clifford D. Scott, "Toward a Public Policy and Marketing Understanding of Lobbying and Its Role in the Development of Public Policy in the United States." *Journal of Public Policy and Marketing* 30, no. 1 (Spring 2011).

Gates, Paul Wallace. "Southern Investment in Northern Lands before the Civil War." *Journal of Southern History* 5, no. 2 (May 1939): 155–85.

Gerdts, William H. "Daniel Huntington's *Mercy Dream*: A Pilgrimage through Bunyanesque Imagery." *Winterthur Portfolio* 14, no. 2 (Summer 1979).

Gilge, Paul A. "The Rise of Capitalism in the Early Republic." *Journal of the Early Republic* 16, no. 2 (Summer 1996): 163.

Green, Vivien M. "Hiram Powers's *Greek Slave*: Emblem of Freedom." *American Art Journal* 14 (Autumn 1982): 31–39.

Harmeling, Susan S., Saras D. Sarasvathy, and R. Edward Freeman. "Related Debates in Ethics and Entrepreneurship: Values, Opportunities, and Contingency." *Journal of Business Ethics* 84, no. 3 (2009): 341–65.

Hogan, Richard. "Class, Gender and Race Inequality." *Race, Gender & Class* 8, no. 2 (2001): 61–93.

Howard, Vicki. "The Courtship Letters of an African American Couple: Race, Gender, Class and the Cult of True Womanhood." *Southwestern Historical Quarterly* 100, no. 1 (July 1996): 64–80.

Hurst, Harold W. "Business and Businessmen in Pre–Civil War Georgetown." *Records of the Columbia Historical Society* 50 (1980): 161–71.

———. "The Maryland Gentry in Old Georgetown, 1783–1861." *Maryland Historical Magazine* 73 (Spring 1978): 1–12.

Johnson, Whittington B. "Free Blacks in Antebellum Savannah: An Economic Profile." *Georgia Historical Quarterly* 64, no. 4 (Winter 1980): 418–31.

Katz, Irving. "Confidant at the Capital: William W. Corcoran's Role in Nineteenth-Century American Politics." *The Historian* 29 (August 1967).

Lane, Edgar. "Some Lessons from Past Congressional Investigations of Lobbying." *Public Opinion Quarterly* 14, no. 1 (Spring 1950): 14–32.

Logan, Edward P. "Lobbying." *Annals of the American Academy of Political and Social Science* 144 (July 1929).

McLoughlin, William G. "Pietism and the American Character." *American Quarterly* 17, no. 2 (Summer 1965): 163–86.

Miller, Angela. "Everywhere and Nowhere: The Making of the National Landscape." *American Literary History* 4, no. 2 (June 1991): 207–29.

Murphy, Charles. "The Political Career of Jesse Bright." *Indiana Historical Society Publications* 10, no. 3 (1931): 101–45.

Parker, Franklin. "The Legacy of George Peabody: Special Bicentennial Issue." *Peabody Journal of Education* 70, no. 1 (Fall 1994).

Schultz, Stanley K., and Clay McShane. "To Engineer the Metropolis: Sewers, Sanitation and City Planning in Late-Nineteenth-Century America." *Journal of American History* 65, no. 2 (September 1978): 389–411.

Schweninger, Loren. "Black-Owned Businesses in the South, 1790–1880." *Business History Review* 63, no. 1 (Spring 1989): 22–60.

Shapely, Peter. "Charity, Status and Leadership: Charitable Image and the Manchester Man." *Journal of Social History* 32, no. 1 (Fall 1998): 157–77.

Szreter, Simon. "The State of Social Capital: Bringing Back in Power, Politics, and History." *Theory and Society* 31, no. 5 (October 2002): 573–621.

Tank, Holly. "Dedicated to Art: William Corcoran and the Founding of His Gallery," *Washington History* 17 (Fall/Winter 2005): 26–51.

———. "William Wilson Corcoran: Washington Philanthropist." *Washington History* 17 (Fall/Winter 2005): 52–65.

Troyen, Carol. "Retreat to Arcadia: American Landscape and the American Art-Union." *The American Art Journal* 23, no. 1 (1991): 20–37.

Walker, Juliet E. K., and Shenette Garett-Scott. "Introduction: African American Business History: Studies in Race, Capitalism and Power." *Journal of African American History* 101, no. 4 (Fall 2016): 395–406.

Newspapers

Adams Sentinel and General Advertiser (Gettysburg, PA)

The Advocate (Tipton, IN)

Albany Daily Ledger

Alexandria (VA) Gazette

Alton (IL) Daily Telegraph

American Telegraph (Washington, DC)

Anglo-American Times (London)

Appleton (WI) Crescent

Athens (OH) Messenger

Atlanta Constitution

The Baltimorean

Baltimore Daily Commercial

Baltimore Sun

Bismarck Daily Tribune

Bloomington (IL) Daily Leader

Bloomington (IL) Pantagraph

Boston Daily Globe
Boston Evening Transcript
Chicago Daily Tribune
Chicago Sun Times
Columbian Gazette (Washington, DC)
The Critic (Pittsburgh)
Cuba (NY) True Patriot
Cumberland (MD) Mountain City Times
Daily American Organ (Washington, DC)
Daily American Telegraph (Washington, DC)
Daily Chronicle (San Francisco)
Daily Constitution
Daily Exchange (Baltimore)
Daily National Era (Washington, DC)
Daily National Whig (Washington, DC)
Daily Patriot (Washington, DC)
Decatur (IL) Daily Republican
Dubuque Weekly Times
Dunkirk (NY) Evening Observer
Eau Claire Daily Free Press
Elkhart Sentinel
Evening Star (Washington, DC)
Flake's Daily Bulletin (Galveston, TX)
Fort Wayne Daily Gazette
Fort Wayne Daily Sentinel
Galveston Daily News
Hagerstown Herald and Torchlight
Harrisonburg-Rockingham (VA) Register
Iowa Courier
Janesville (WI) Gazette
Journal of Commerce (New York)
Lackawanna Citizen
Lebanon (IN) Weekly Pioneer
Little Rock Weekly Arkansas Gazette
Logansport (IN) Daily Star
London Express
Louisville (KY) Daily Courier
Madison State Journal
The Madisonian (Washington, DC)

Marion (OH) Daily Star
The Metropolitan (Washington, DC)
National Intelligencer (Washington, DC)
National Republican (Washington, DC)
New Albany Daily Ledger
Newark Daily Advocate
New Era (Washington, DC)
New York Daily Herald
New York Evening Post
New York Herald
New York Post
New York Sun
New York Times
Norfolk Virginian
Oshkosh Daily Northwestern
People's Friend (Salem, KS)
Philadelphia Inquirer
Richmond (VA) Daily Dispatch
Rochester Republican
Rock Island (IL) Argus
Salem (MA) News
San Antonio Daily Express
San Francisco Chronicle
San Francisco Evening Bulletin
Southern Press (Washington, DC)
Star Tribune
Sullivan (IN) Democrat
The Sun (Baltimore)
Titusville (PA) Morning Herald
Union Springs (AL) Herald
Warren (PA) Daily Mirror
Washington Critic
Washington Globe
Washington Post
Washington Sentinel
Washington Union
Wellsboro (PA) Agitator
Western Cyclone (Nicodemus, KS)

INDEX

ABOUT THE AUTHOR

Mark L. Goldstein is an author, educator, and retired member of the federal Senior Executive Service. Mark served as a director at the US Government Accountability Office (GAO), the investigative agency of the US Congress. He also held other public service positions, including as the deputy director and chief of staff to the presidentially appointed District of Columbia Financial Control Board, responsible for bringing the capital city out of bankruptcy; a legislative adviser to the commissioner of the Internal Revenue Service; and a senior staff member of the US Senate Committee on Governmental Affairs under Sen. John Glenn. Prior to government service, Mark was a journalist for newspapers and magazines.

This is Mark's second book. His first book, *America's Hollow Government: How Washington Has Failed the People* (Business One Irwin), received several awards and was a text in college government courses. Mark has earned honors from the American Library Association, the Associated Press, the Society of American Business Press Editors, the American Society for Public Administration, and the GAO.

Mark holds a BS in journalism from Syracuse University, an MPA from George Washington University, an MA from the University of Maryland at College Park, and a PhD from the University of Maryland at College Park. Mark is an elected fellow of the National Academy of Public Administration and has been awarded professional and research fellowships at the John F. Kennedy School of Government at Harvard University and at Wolfson College, Cambridge University. He has been an adjunct faculty in undergraduate and graduate-level courses in US history, government, and politics, and in public administration at colleges in the Washington, DC, area and in South Florida. A frequent public speaker, Mark has testified before committees of the US Congress more than seventy-five times and appeared in major media outlets, including CNN, C-SPAN, the *Washington Post*, the *New York Times*, National Public Radio, and ABC Evening News.